The Chemeketa Handbook
WRITING &
RESEARCH
for College

Beta 1 Edition

Edited by Daniel Couch

with additional contributions from
Bethany Gabbert, Alissa Hattman, Traci Hodgson, Roy K. Humble,
Adam Karnes, Brian Mosher, Mary Ellen Scofield, Steve Slemenda,
Sam Snoek-Brown, Michael Ward, and Travis Willmore.

CHEMEKETA **PRESS**

The Chemeketa Handbook

Writing and Research for College

ISBN: 978-1-943536-16-0

Beta Edition 1.0

Chemeketa Press

Chemeketa Press is a nonprofit publishing endeavor at Chemeketa Community College. Working together with faculty, staff, and students, we develop and publish affordable and effective alternatives to commercial textbooks.

A portion of the proceeds from the sale of this book will help support the important work of the Chemeketa Writing Center. The rest of the proceeds will be used to develop new textbooks.

Publisher: Tim Rogers

Managing Editor: Steve Richardson

Production Editor: Brian Mosher

Editorial Support: Travis Willmore, Steve Slemenda

Design Manager: Kristen MacDonald

Cover Design: Yu Ra Kim, Candace Johnson

Interior Design: Candace Johnson, Micaleigh Daniels, Amanda Pruett

Additional contributions to the design and publication of this textbook come from the students and faculty in the Chemeketa Visual Communications program.

Additional funding for this project comes from the Chemeketa Liberal Arts and Social Sciences Department (Don Brase, dean).

Printed in the United States of America.

Table of Contents

Part 1:
WRITING BASICS

Part 2:
RESEARCH BASICS

About Beta Editions

Chemeketa Press publishes textbooks using a software development model. Once a book is essentially ready, we send it to the classroom even though it's still in the final stages of development. We do this so that students start saving money as soon as possible and, more importantly, so that students and faculty will help us finish the book.

In exchange for a reduced price, we ask you to help us track down "bugs" in the book — typos, omissions, and other errors. We also ask you to let us know how well the book does its job and where it could do better. Whenever you have something to share, please share it. You can talk with your professor, who will talk with us, or you can email the Press directly at **collegepress@chemeketa.edu.**

Thank you for participating in this exciting project that helps make college more affordable by reducing the price of textbooks.

Preface

This book exists because the English and Writing Center faculty of Chemeketa Community College want a better writing handbook for their students.

Like most college textbooks, the available writing handbooks are more expensive than they should be. That's a problem. A larger problem is that most of those handbooks are written not to students but to the instructors who order those books. They use the language of scholars, of people who don't need a writing handbook, and that makes learning harder than it has to be for the people who do need a handbook, who are just beginning their journey toward scholarship.

The Chemeketa Handbook delivers the same information as those other handbooks, but we present the ideas with accessible language, practical instructions, and useful examples. We must occasionally use technical terms to describe the inner workings of writing and research. When that happens, though, we take a moment to explain the term and then illustrate it with examples. But aside from that, we present these ideas in such a way that you don't need a second handbook to figure out what this handbook is saying.

We also recognize that most students will use this book as a reference guide. There's no need to read the book from the first page to the last. We know you already understand much of what this book covers, but for the areas where you have lingering questions, we have answers. A detailed table of contents at the end of the book will guide you to the specific content you're looking for.

You'll notice the book is divided into two main sections — writing and research. The first four chapters cover writing basics. We start with paragraphs in Chapter 1 and then narrow our focus to sentences in Chapter 2 and punctuation and mechanics in Chapter 3. By Chapter 4, word choice, we're talking about the selection of individual words, asking you to choose them like you might choose just the right apple at the grocery store.

In the second half of the book, we examine the basics of college research, explaining how to find useful information, assess its reliability, and integrate it into your own writing. In the final three chapters of the book, we map out the three most popular documentation systems so that you can accurately give credit to your sources of information as you write papers in any of your classes.

Although we do our best to answer your questions about writing and research at college, remember that you have many other resources. First of all, you didn't assign that paper to yourself. You have a professor nearby, and you'll find that most professors are at their best when you ask them questions. As a college writer, you also have direct access to college librarians. They know almost everything, and they know how to find anything they don't know. Ask them for help, too. And finally, there's a good chance that you also have access to a college writing center. The people who work at a writing center love to talk about this stuff — some so much they worked on this book. Make an appointment. Then make another.

We want you to write with confidence. *The Chemeketa Handbook* is an affordable and friendly book that will answer many of your questions. For the rest, just raise your hand and ask.

— Daniel Couch

PART ONE
Writing Basics

Paragraphs

A paragraph is a set of sentences that work together to present one main idea about something.

In the body of a formal paper, body paragraphs present supporting ideas for the main idea of your paper. These might be examples or reasons or facts or definitions. They all help to explain and defend the main idea of your paper. Each paragraph has its own supporting idea to make, too, but that idea is a smaller part of the paper's main idea.

The opening and closing paragraphs also present one main idea. The opening presents the purpose of the paper — your topic, what you're focusing on, and your main idea or thesis. The closing paragraph or paragraphs send the readers off with the importance of your main idea — why it matters or what they should do about it.

To show readers where paragraphs begin and end, you have two choices. In most college papers, the conventional option is to indent the first line of a paragraph by a half-inch. This and most of the paragraphs in this book use indentation. The indentation is a visual cue for readers that a new supporting idea is about to begin.

In some formal writing — such as business letters or reports — you have the option of adding a blank line between paragraphs to show where they begin and end. That's called block paragraphing, and when you do that, you don't indent. The next two paragraphs use block paragraphing to show where each begins and ends.

See how a block paragraph works? Now remember to *not* use a block paragraph for almost all of your college writing.

In this chapter, we'll look at how to write effective body, opening, and closing paragraphs. We'll end by looking at some common problems with paragraphing and how to fix them.

1. Body Paragraphs

In the body of a paper, the paragraphs explain ideas in two ways. First, topic sentences state the main idea directly. Second, supporting sentences explain that idea in more detail. Transitional words and phrases also help to guide readers through the paragraph so that the idea is clear.

A. Topic Sentences

The topic sentence provides two main pieces of information — the topic of the paragraph and the author's main idea about that topic. This sentence is often the first or last sentence of the paragraph.

1. **Rabid Bats front man Tommy Botulism's stage outfits alone are worth the price of a concert ticket.** For example, Botulism once took the stage wearing nothing more than a loincloth made of bat wings. Another time, he wrapped himself so tightly in dense silk netting that he looked like a human larva propped in front of the microphone for the two-hour set. However, the crowd favorite is his pink leather jumpsuit covered in sequins that fire laser beams into the audience. "It's all about the look, man," says Botulism. "They don't care what you sound like so long as you got the look." Consequently, the lead singer has become more known for his creative costuming than for his trademark nasal screech.

In this **topic sentence,** the topic is seeing the Rabid Bats in concert. The main idea about this topic is that seeing Tommy Botulism's wild clothing is a reason to go.

2. **The first annual National Pickle Ball Day (August 13) was a big success and not just for Pickle Ball players.** Acme Greeting Cards reported that consumers across the country exchanged some 30 million cards wishing each other a Happy Pickle Ball Day. Apparently, a large number of those sentiments were shared by people who don't actually know anything about Pickle Ball.

One example is Bob Meriwether, who sent cards to all his neighbors and friends without ever having heard of the sport. "I just didn't want to get a Happy Pickle Ball Day card from someone and look like a schmuck because I didn't know about it," said Meriwether. In a press release following Pickle Ball Day, Acme praised the nation for honoring this sport so enthusiastically and reminded consumers that it's the card that counts, not what it means.

> In this **topic sentence**, the topic is National Pickle Ball Day. The main idea about this topic is that it was a big success.

B. Supporting Sentences

The supporting sentences in a paragraph explain the topic sentence in more detail. They do so with additional information — examples, quotations, facts, and so on — and explanations of why that information is important.

1. Rabid Bats front man Tommy Botulism's stage outfits alone are worth the price of a concert ticket.

   > This is the **topic sentence**. The idea stated here helps to present the main idea of the paragraph as a whole. This is also the idea that the supporting sentences will present in more detail.

2. For example, Botulism once took the stage wearing nothing more than a loin cloth made of bat wings.

   > In this **supporting sentence**, an example helps readers to understand what sort of outfits Botulism wears on stage.

3. Another time, he wrapped himself so tightly in dense silk netting that he looked like a human larva propped in front of the microphone for the two hour set.

   > This **supporting sentence** is another example of the same point.

4. However, the crowd favorite is his pink leather jump suit covered in sequins that fire laser beams into the audience.

   > This is a third example of the singer's outfits. Taken as a whole, the three examples provide a sample of what to expect from Botulism on stage.

5. "It's all about the look, man," says Botulism. "They don't care what you sound like so long as you got the look."

   > In these two **supporting sentences**, a quotation provides new evidence to support the point that Botulism wears interesting outfits by showing the singer's own understanding of the gimmick.

6. Consequently, the lead singer has become more known for his creative costuming than for his trademark nasal screech.

   > This fact ends the paragraph by concluding that the singer's popularity comes from his outfits more than his music.

Here's the same breakdown of supporting sentences from the second example paragraph.

1. The first annual National Pickle Ball Day (August 13) was a big success and not just for Pickle Ball players.

   This is the **topic sentence**. It presents an idea that will help to illustrate the paragraph's main idea about unnecessary greeting card holidays. It also slips in a fact that tells us when National Pickle Ball Day happens. Mark your calendars.

2. Acme Greeting Cards reported that consumers across the country exchanged some 30 million cards wishing each other a Happy Pickle Ball Day.

   This **supporting sentence** presents a fact about the number of cards exchanged that helps readers understand what "big success" means.

3. Apparently, a large number of those sentiments were shared by people who don't actually know anything about Pickle Ball.

   This **supporting sentence** is not an example, fact, or quote. Here, the author provides an explanation for the huge number of cards exchanged that sets up the upcoming quote.

4. One example is Bob Meriwether, who sent cards to all his neighbors and friends without ever having heard of the sport.

   This **supporting sentence** introduces an example of the sort of person mentioned in the previous supporting sentence.

5. "I just didn't want to get a Happy Pickle Ball Day card from someone and look like a schmuck because I didn't know about it," said Meriwether.

   This **supporting sentence** offers a quotation from Meriwether to illustrate why people would send cards for a holiday they don't understand.

6. In a press release following Pickle Ball Day, Acme praised the nation for honoring this sport so enthusiastically and reminded consumers that it's the card that counts, not what it means.

   In the final **supporting sentence**, this fact shows that this invented holiday was a big success for Acme most of all.

C. Transitional Words and Phrases

Transitional words and phrases help your readers see how the different supporting sentences are organized or how different ideas are related to each other.

1. Rabid Bats front man Tommy Botulism's stage outfits alone are worth the price of a concert ticket. **For example**, Botulism once took the stage wearing nothing more than a loin cloth made of bat wings. **Another time**, he wrapped himself so tightly in dense silk netting that he looked like a human

larva propped in front of the microphone for the two hour set. **However**, the crowd favorite is his pink leather jump suit covered in sequins that fire laser beams into the audience. "It's all about the look, man," says Botulism. "They don't care what you sound like so long as you got the look." **Consequently**, the lead singer has become more known for his creative costuming than for his trademark nasal screech.

These **transitional words** demonstrate how different ideas relate to each other. "For example" introduces an example of the idea just mentioned. "Another time" shows readers that another example is coming. "However" introduces a contrasting idea. In this case, the contrast is one of how the outfits rank. The pink jumpsuit that fires laser beams contrasts favorably with all the other outfits, named and unnamed. "Consequently" shows readers that all of the evidence in the supporting sentences leads up to the conclusion in the final sentence.

You have many transitions to choose from. Here are just a few of your options:

To Show Relationships	To Show Organization
Addition: and, in addition to, also, too, moreover, additionally, furthermore, as well as	**By Time:** before, later, after, then, next, in 1998, later that year, since November
Contrast: but, however, not, unlike, albeit, otherwise, regardless, on the other hand	**By Ranking:** the most important, also important, of less importance
Example: for example, one example of, one illustration is, namely, such as, in fact	**By Location:** in Salem, near, next to, a little farther, beyond, among
Cause: because, it follows that, since, for	
Qualification: except for, although, unless, despite	
Agreement: similarly, likewise, as, like	

D. Paragraph Groups

In the body of a paper, paragraph groups are sets of paragraphs that work together to present a more complex supporting idea. Each paragraph in the group still presents one idea of its own, but these ideas then work together to present the more complex paragraph group idea.

For example, if your essay's main idea is that the Rabid Bats are likely destined for the same kind of stellar fame enjoyed by the Rolling Stones, the body of your essay may be divided into several supporting paragraph groups — a group that focuses on the music, a group that focuses on the performance, a group the focuses on marketing, and so on. Within the music group, you would then have paragraphs that look at different aspects of that supporting idea.

Paragraph Group Ideas	Supporting Paragraph Ideas
The Music: The Rabid Bats' music is beautiful.	1. The lyrics are poetic. 2. The melodies tug at your soul. 3. The songs are a perfect balance of guitar, bass, drums, and accordion.
The Performance: The Rabid Bats are live rock and roll at its best.	1. The costumes alone are worth the price of the ticket. 2. The light show is dazzling and hypnotic. 3. The fires they set on stage are real and thus dangerous.
The Marketing: The Rabid Bats' marketing approach is creative.	1. The albums feature unique packaging. 2. The band's cross-merchandising efforts bring their music to unexpected audiences. 3. Their promotional events are unpredictable.

2. Opening and Closing Paragraphs

In addition to body paragraphs, formal papers use opening and closing paragraphs to introduce readers to the paper as a whole or show readers how the paper as a whole has just presented a pretty good main idea.

A. Opening Paragraphs

The primary job for the opening paragraph is to tell readers what to expect from the paper. The opening does this with three pieces of information:

- **Topic:** the subject of the paper as a whole

- **Focus:** the narrowed area of the topic that the paper will examine

- **Thesis:** the main idea that the paper explains, which is a reasonable idea that the author has about the focus

A secondary job for the opening is to engage the readers' interest so they will want to keep reading. In formal writing, this is less important because your readers (professors, scholarship committees, etc.) usually *have* to read what you have written whether you engage their interest or not. However, even with formal audiences, an engaging opening will still make the paper more enjoyable to read and thus more effective.

You have many options for how to accomplish the work of the opening paragraph. What follows are just three of the most common approaches.

MOVING FROM GENERAL TO SPECIFIC

Moving from the general to the specific means starting with a broad topic and then narrowing down to the actual and much narrower focus of your paper. This shows readers the general context for your paper — where your topic fits on the time line of history or within some larger category.

1. The Strawberry Alarm Clock, the Electric Prunes, the Buggles, and Shocking Blue were one-hit-wonder groups that made a big but brief splash on the rock charts and then faded from the scene. This is the fate of most rock bands. Only a few bands become enduring legends. The Beatles, the Who, and the Rolling Stones are among the elite and relatively small number of groups whose fame is enduring and secure for decades to come. Those who achieve such iconic status in a business rife with fickle fame do so through an exceptional combination of talent, versatility, and showmanship. Because they display all these qualities, the **Rabid Bats**, currently on tour with their new album *Stinky Wishes*, <u>may be headed for a place at the top with the Big Names of Rock and Roll.</u>

> The paragraph begins broadly with a larger discussion of rock-and-roll bands who made a splash. Then it narrows to the relative small group of bands who make a splash and endure. Then it narrows still more to the actual **topic** of the paper, the Rabid Bats, and its focus, the question of how long they will endure. It closes with the paper's <u>thesis</u>, the idea that the Rabid Bats have what it takes to become enduring legends of rock and roll.

AN ATTENTION GRABBER

An attention grabber is a statement that's designed to surprise, amuse, or possibly shock readers. This is found more commonly in informal writing — as seen in tabloid headlines or Internet clickbait, for example — but attention-grabbing will work in a formal paper if it's not too over-the-top and if you follow the attention grabber with a clear presentation of the topic, focus, and thesis of the paper.

2.   Anything can happen at a **Rabid Bats** concert. Take their recent performance at the Hollywood Bowl, for example, in which lead singer Tommy Botulism flung a bucketful of live snakes into the front-row. This is just one example of the sort of dangerous showmanship that — along with great music and skillful marketing — suggests that the Rabid Bats are no mere flash in the pan. In fact, <u>they may be headed for a place at the top with the enduring Big Names of Rock and Roll.</u>

> The image and shock value of live snakes assaulting the audience is compelling — who's not going to want to read further? It also introduces the **topic** of the paper, the Rabid Bats. This attention grabber by itself, however, is not enough. So the opening then moves on to introduce the focus of the paper — the question of whether they are a flash in the pan or not. It ends with its <u>thesis</u>, that showmanship, great music, and great marketing suggest that the Rabid Bats have what it takes to become legends of rock and roll.

AN ENGAGING ANECDOTE

An anecdote is a short story — real or hypothetical — that illustrates a part of the topic and engages readers by inviting them to imagine what's happening. Again, you must then follow this up with a more direct introduction of the topic, focus, and thesis.

3.   It was just another Tuesday afternoon. I was sifting through the handful of mail that included the usual bills, catalogs, and junk. Then a yellow envelope addressed in familiar handwriting caught my eye. I slit the envelope and pulled out a greeting card. The front said, "**Happy National Pickle Ball Day**" in flowery print. Inside, scrawled in green ink, were the words, "Thinking warmly of you, son." It was signed by my mother. I shook my head, tossed the card aside, and said, "National Pickle Ball Day? Really?"

    The answer is yes. National Pickle Ball Day is a real thing. The Acme Card Company declared the 13th of August, which is the month with the lowest greeting card sales, as National Pickle Ball Day and promoted it heavily. <u>The result was another crass gimmick for the greeting card industry to use to peddle its products.</u>

> The anecdote in the first paragraph provides the readers with a story that is easy to visualize and that thus engages their imaginations. It also indirectly introduces the **topic** of this paper — National Pickle Ball Day. By itself, this paragraph is a good start for an opening, but formal writing requires more direct introduction of what to expect from the paper. That's where the second opening paragraph comes in.

> In the second paragraph, we get down to business. The paragraph presents the topic directly and then presents the paper's focus — the origin of this holiday. It ends with the <u>thesis</u>, that the holiday originated as another crass gimmick the greeting card industry to peddle its products.

B. Closing Paragraphs

The closing paragraph (or two) concludes the paper by doing two things. First, it shows readers how the body of the paper explains and defends the thesis of the paper. Second, it points toward the future implications of that thesis being true. Once readers finish the paper, they will hopefully continue to think about the ideas the paper presented and perhaps do something because of those ideas. Just as with opening paragraphs, there are many strategies for getting the job done in closing paragraphs.

DOING SOMETHING ABOUT IT

One option for the closing is to begin by presenting how your paper has defended its thesis and then give readers some ideas about what they can do on their own.

1.   The greeting card industry will continue to play on our emotions and pick our pocketbooks as long as we lamely play into their strategy of manufactured recognition days like National Pickle Ball Day. It's all about selling the goods through ad campaigns of sugary sentiment and guilt-tripping — but we don't have to buy it. If these invented holidays are largely ignored by the public, they won't be around the following year to plague us again. Greeting cards have their place, but use of them should be determined by consumers, not by market manipulation. We can keep Mother's Day and Father's Day. We can send cards marking the birthdays of our loved ones. **Beyond that, however, we should save the postage and keep our wallets closed.**

    > The closing begins by summarizing the <u>thesis</u> of the essay, that the greeting card industry is using gimmicky recognition days to sell its products. The author then assumes that because the paper has made a good case for this idea, readers will be open to a **call to action** — don't buy what they're selling.

THE DANGER OF DOING NOTHING

A similar option is to present the potential cost of ignoring further action. Instead of showing readers what they can do with your idea, you warn them about what will happen if they do nothing.

2.   Consumers have the ultimate power in determining what stays on the shelves and what does not. However, if we mindlessly buy into inane promotions like National Pickle Ball Day, we relinquish that power. <u>The greeting card industry will continue to play on our emotions and pick our pocketbooks as long as we lamely play into their strategy of invented holidays.</u> It won't end with National Pickle Ball Day. **Until we say no, we will be spending more time in the greeting card aisle and more money on cards to people we barely know.**

> This closing begins with the idea that the readers can do something about this problem and then reminds them about the topic and its <u>thesis</u> that the greeting card industry is using manufactured recognition days like National Pickle Ball Day to trick us into buying more product. The paragraph then ends with the consequences of not exercising our power as consumers.

A NOD TO THE FUTURE

Once the body of the paper has established the validity of the thesis, another way to close is by considering the future implications of that idea.

3. <u>The Rabid Bats are well on their way to the highest levels of rock status.</u> Their musical virtuosity, phenomenal concert performances, and savvy marketing ensure as much. But the Bats will break even newer ground if rumors pan out about innovative social media gadgetry that may hit the scene within a year — a combination of holographic visuals, smell-o-rama, and a virtual reality interaction that allows fans to be on stage with the group in real time. The groundbreaking technology, called "Bats in Your Brain," promises to take the experience of rock music to a new level of intensity. Other bands will be sure to follow, but the Rabid Bats will be leading the way.

> This closing quickly wraps up the essay by stating the <u>thesis</u> of the paper in the first sentence and summarizing the main supporting ideas in the next sentence. The closing then looks at the future possibilities for the Rabid Bats, and rock in general, inviting readers to keep thinking about the topic.

A RETURN TO THE OPENING

If you began the paper with an anecdote or question, one way to end the paper is by following up on the anecdote or answering the question.

4. I returned the National Pickle Ball Day card to my mother with a note enclosed saying how wonderful it was to hear from her and asking if she would buy me tickets to see the Pickle Ball Championships in Dill, Tennessee, for next year. I never got another National Pickle Ball Day card from her again.

That's how it can be with the greeting card industry, too. If you're tired of promotions like National Pickle Ball Day, stop buying into those promotions. If we as consumers ignore the promotion, it won't be around next year. We can keep Mothers Day and Fathers Day. We can send cards marking the birthdays of our loved ones. Beyond that, we should save the postage and keep our wallets closed.

> This paragraph brings the essay full circle — wrapping it up with a closing that in some way completes the opening paragraph. This sort of closing can be satisfying to the reader. However, you still need to attend to the task of reminding readers of your main idea and why it makes sense. In this case, that happens in the second paragraph of the closing.

3. Common Problems

A. Unfocused Paragraphs

A paragraph is unfocused when it lacks a clear main idea. It may be that no topic sentence identifies a main idea, so readers aren't sure what the supporting sentences support. A more likely problem is that a supporting sentence strays from its job of supporting the topic sentence. In some cases, supporting sentences might support more than one idea, dividing the focus of the paragraph into at least two directions. It may be that all of the supporting sentences are writing about the topic but not about the topic sentence idea.

Whatever causes the lack of focus, the problem is the same — readers become confused. They expect each paragraph to make a point, so when it doesn't do that, readers aren't sure what to think. This distracts them and makes them unsure about the meaning of the rest of the paper. If it happens in more than one paragraph, the readers may stop reading.

HOW TO FIX UNFOCUSED PARAGRAPHS

The first thing to do is make sure *you* know what point the paragraph should make. You do that by identifying — or writing — the topic sentence for that paragraph and placing it prominently at the beginning or end of the paragraph. If a missing topic sentence is what made the paragraph hard to follow, then your job is done. Nice work.

However, if the problem is found in the supporting sentences, consider one of the following options.

OPTION 1: REMOVE OR EDIT UNRELATED SUPPORTING SENTENCES
Take a good, hard look at the topic sentence. Then go through the supporting sentences and make sure that each sentence and clause helps to explain that idea.

1. **Problem:**

Creative marketing has always been a big part of the Rabid Bats success, and the group's new album *Stinky Wishes* is a great example. **The songs are totally danceable and well-written.** It's also the first scratch and sniff rock CD — the disc actually smells like guano. In addition, each CD comes with a small vial of an oily poop cologne called "Batfumes." Furthermore, the CD is being promoted as an alternative air freshener when played in the car, **the best place to listen to these songs.** As a result, sales of *Stinky Wishes* have gone through the roof — and the belfry.

The **unrelated sentences and clauses** don't contribute meaning to the topic sentence about the creative marketing of *Stinky Wishes*. <u>Another sentence</u> sounds unrelated but could be edited to more clearly explain how it is that smelling like bat poop is a good thing.

Solution:

Creative marketing has always been a big part of the Rabid Bats success, and the group's new album *Stinky Wishes* is a great example. With this first scratch and sniff rock CD, the disc actually smells like guano, and the fans are loving it. In addition, each CD comes with a small vial of an oily poop cologne called "Batfumes." Furthermore, the CD is being promoted as an alternative air freshener when played in the car. As a result, sales of *Stinky Wishes* have gone through the roof — and the belfry.

Now all the sentences are focused on the band's marketing. The <u>potentially unrelated sentence</u> now connects the marketing to the band's success.

OPTION 2: SEPARATE IDEAS AND EXPAND

You may find that part of the paragraph helps to support the topic sentence and the rest presents a second idea. If that's the problem, the solution is to divide that paragraph into two — one for each idea. Make sure each paragraph has a clear topic sentence. If necessary, you can then expand each paragraph with additional supporting sentences its topic sentence idea.

2. **Problem:**

To see the Rabid Bats in concert is to experience live rock and roll at its best — a loud, raucous, high-energy show of great music combined with visual wizardry that never disappoints. The Bats bring to the stage not only their exceptional musicianship but each performance also showcases state-of-the-art pyrotechnics with the best light show in the business. This group has evolved from its late '70s raw punk limitations into one of the most sophisticated and fascinating progressive rock voices in the business. Their just released CD, *Stinky Wishes,* has already been critically acclaimed for its provocative lyrics and intricate, compelling arrangements. It just doesn't get better than the Rabid Bats.

The paragraph begins with a topic sentence — "To see the Rabid Bats in concert is to experience live rock and roll at its best." The two sentences that follow provide some detailed supporting information for that idea. However, then the paragraph shifts direction to introduce another topic sentence that is worthy of further explanation — "The group has evolved from its late 70s raw punk limitations." The result splits the focus and fails to fully explain either idea.

Solution, Part 1:

    To see the Rabid Bats in concert is to experience live rock and roll at its best — a loud, raucous, high-energy show of great music combined with visual wizardry that never disappoints. Once they fly onto the stage in their leather wingsuits, they do not stop for the next three hours. The first song leaps out at over 160 decibels and a pace that makes punk rock sound like a gentle Sunday School tune. And it only gets louder and faster from there . . ..

> The first step to solving this problem is giving the first main idea its own paragraph. We won't get into *all* the supporting sentences, but even with this start you can see that this idea is clearer when it's allowed to have its own paragraph.

Solution, Part 2:

    The Rabid Bats have evolved from their late '70s raw punk limitations into one of the most sophisticated and fascinating progressive rock voices in the business. Their newly released CD, *Stinky Wishes*, has already been critically acclaimed for its provocative lyrics and intricate, compelling arrangements. The title cut, for example, begins with a riff on Dylan Thomas and ends with a haunting reinvention of the Mr. Rogers classic "Won't you, please?! Won't you PLEASE?! Please won't you BE! MY! NEIGHBOR!"

> That's a great song, and now that this idea has its own paragraph, we can get into details like that in the supporting sentences.

OPTION 3: START OVER

If a paragraph is really just a collection of different ideas about the topic, set it aside and start over with a new topic sentence for a new paragraph. Then make sure all the supporting sentences help to explain that idea. Or if you have a topic sentence but the supporting sentences are all over the place, then dump the supporting sentences and start over with a new set of supporting sentences to that topic sentence. Make sure that each sentence helps to explain that idea.

3. **Problem:**

    The Rabid Bats live at the Paramount Theater last Saturday was everything a Bats fan could hope for. **The Bats have been playing together since 1978.** The group played several of their standard tunes as well as some new songs from their highly anticipated CD, *Stinky Wishes*. The energy is always high at a Bats concert. <u>The lead singer, Tommy Botulism, played accordion on some of the songs, but not often.</u> The Paramount is a fun place for a concert, and the Bats seemed to enjoy themselves thoroughly. **The music scene in Portland is great.**

This paragraph is a series of statements that are facts about the Rabid Bats (mostly), but they don't add up to one main idea. There's a sentence about a Bats concert, a sentence about when the Bats started, a sentence about the tunes they played, a sentence about the energy in the concert, and so on. These don't add up to one main idea about the concert, so it's no surprise that there's no topic sentence for these other sentences to support. This paragraph, unfortunately, is beyond repair. It's time to take one of these sentences and start over.

Solution:

The Rabid Bats live at the Paramount Theater last Saturday was everything a Bats fan could hope for — a high-energy performance that showcased the group's musical versatility and crowd-pleasing theatrics. Lead singer Tommy Botulism ignited the stage in his neon orange leather jumpsuit, whirling like a dervish throughout the 90-minute set. He also literally ignited his accordion (à la Jimi Hendrix) at the end of the group's theme song, "Bite Me Back," fanning the flames with his trademark derby hat. The crowd was worked into a lather of screaming enthusiasm that never waned as the group served up several old favorites as well as new tracks from their just-released CD, *Stinky Wishes.*

Now that we focus on just one idea, the main idea is clear — the Bats gave a captivating performance at the Paramount. The topic sentence states the paragraph's idea, and the supporting sentences provide information that illustrates this idea about how theatrical the performance was — Tommy Botulism's jumpsuit and whirling, setting the accordion on fire, fanning the flames, and working the fans up into a screaming horde. All of the supporting sentences now help to illustrate the main idea.

B. Disorganized Paragraphs

Disorganized paragraphs do not arrange their supporting sentences according to a clear pattern of organization. In some cases, the supporting sentences are arranged according to a pattern or organization, but readers are unable to recognize that pattern because of a lack of transitions to point it out.

When readers don't see how the sentences of a paragraph work together, they struggle to figure out what point the paragraph is trying to make. This also makes it harder for them to move from paragraph to paragraph and make sense of the paper as a whole.

HOW TO FIX DISORGANIZED PARAGRAPHS

Readers more easily see how the supporting sentences work together when those sentences are organized in a pattern — a chronological pattern, for example, or a ranking pattern of most to least. You can do two things to make sure that your sentences are organized and that the organization is easy to see.

STEP 1: ORGANIZE A DISORGANIZED PARAGRAPH

If no organizational pattern is present in a paragraph, the solution is to add one and then use it to organize the sentences.

1. **Problem:**

Success for most rock bands means a year or two of fame before fading into obscurity. The Beatles, the Who, and the Rolling Stones have achieved iconic status. The music business is rife with fickle fans. The Rabid Bats are currently on tour with their newest album, *Stinky Wishes*. **The Bats may be headed for a place at the top with the Big Names of Rock and Roll.** The Strawberry Alarm Clock, the Electric Prunes, the Buggles, Shocking Blue — all were one-hit-wonder groups that made a big but brief splash on the rock charts. Those who achieve longstanding fame do so through an exceptional combination of talent, versatility, and showmanship. Many groups are just a forgettable blip on the radar of rock history.

This paragraph has **a topic sentence**, but it's buried in the middle of the supporting sentences. In addition, the supporting sentences all help to explain the topic sentence's idea, but because they are presented in random order, the reader has to mentally rearrange them to see the whole idea — kind of like solving a puzzle, only not any fun.

Solution:

The Rabid Bats may be headed for a place at the top with the Big Names of Rock and Roll. Since the beginning of rock and roll, success for most rock bands has usually meant a year or two of fame before fading into obscurity. In recent decades, groups such as the Strawberry Alarm Clock, the Electric Prunes, and Shocking Blue — all one-hit wonders — are now forgettable blips on the radar of rock and roll history. At the same time, the Beatles, the Who, and the Rolling Stones are among the few who have achieved iconic status and longstanding fame. The Rabid Bats are now establishing themselves as a band of exceptional talent, versatility, and showmanship. They have earned their right to claim a place in the elite club of timeless rockers.

With the **topic sentence** at the start of the paragraph, readers have an easier time seeing the main point right away. Just as importantly, the supporting sentences are now organized in a generally chronological pattern: 1) the beginning of rock and roll, 2) in recent decades, 3) at the same time (recent decades), and 4) now. You might also notice that the main point is restated in the final sentence. That's a nice way to reinforce the main idea.

STEP 2: ADD TRANSITIONS TO POINT OUT ORGANIZATION

Sometimes a paragraph is organized, but readers don't really notice the organization. The result is the same as if it were disorganized — they get confused. In that case, fix the problem with transitions that make the organization obvious.

2. The Rabid Bats may be headed for a place at the top with the Big Names of Rock and Roll. **Since the beginning of rock and roll**, success for most rock bands has usually meant a year or two of fame before fading into obscurity. **In recent decades**, groups such as the Strawberry Alarm Clock, the Electric Prunes, and Shocking Blue — all one-hit wonders — are now forgettable blips on the radar of rock history. **At the same time**, the Beatles, the Who, and the Rolling Stones are among the few who have achieved iconic status and longstanding fame. The Rabid Bats are **now** establishing themselves as a band of exceptional talent, versatility, and showmanship. They have earned their right to claim a place in the elite club of timeless rockers.

Because this paragraph uses chronological order, each of these **transitional words and phrases** shows readers where each sentence fits on a time line. This helps readers to see how the supporting sentences are organized.

C. Clichéd Opening Paragraphs

A cliché is an initially colorful phrase like "at the end of the day" or "walk the talk" that has been used so many times that it has now become dull and boring.

A clichéd opening employs a strategy that has been used so many times it too has become boring and ineffective. Here are just a few opening strategies that no longer engage readers:

- **Dictionary definitions:** "According to Merriam-Webster's dictionary, 'music' is defined as . . ."

- **Excessively general openings:** "Since the beginning of time, music has been..."

- **Boring questions:** "Have you ever wondered why music ...?"

- **Announcing your intention:** "In this paper, I will attempt to explain why music . . ."

HOW TO FIX CLICHÉD OPENING PARAGRAPHS

There's no way to fix a clichéd opening. Don't even try.

The only thing you can do is to remove it from your paper, look upon it with disgust if not shame, and then replace it with one of the effective openings discussed earlier in this chapter.

Sentences

A sentence states an idea with two main ingredients — a noun and a verb:

Noun	Verb
Marjorie	smiled.
Rain	fell.
She	frowned.

The noun names or describes the subject of the idea, so this half of the sentence is called the **subject**. The verb describes the subject or tells us what the subject does. This half of the sentence is called the **predicate**, and it's usually longer than a single verb because our ideas tend to be more complex than that:

Subject	Predicate
My dear Aunt Marjorie	smiled happily to herself.
The afternoon rain	fell like tears from Heaven.
The gentle woman	stopped while she admired her colorful way with words.

At an early age, you learned how to combine subjects and predicates without learning any of the terms or the rules that apply to them. You just started talking and kept talking (and talking) until now you can create sentences intuitively. That's all you need for conversation and informal writing such as texts, emails, and notes of complaint on the refrigerator.

However, formal writing — school papers, job applications, legal papers, business plans, and so on — expects you to explain yourself precisely and carefully. In other words, it expects you to use sentences that consistently follow the formal rules of grammar, not just the informal rules that apply to conversation. If you ignore that demand, two things will happen. First, your writing won't be as effective as it should be. Second, and perhaps worse, your ideas won't be taken as seriously as they deserve.

To show you how sentences work in formal writing, this chapter will look at the three main ingredients in sentences:

- **Clauses:** These are groups of words that contain a subject and predicate. The examples above are all clauses, and so is "while she admired her colorful way with words," which also contains a subject ("she") and predicate ("admired her colorful way with words").

- **Phrases:** These are groups of words that together add up to a single unit. "My dear Aunt Marjorie," for example, is a noun phrase because all four words help to describe a single thing — or person, actually, in this case.

- **Parts of Speech:** These are the eight main types of words — noun and verb are two of them. Each part of speech has to be used in certain ways in order for your ideas to make sense.

We'll end the chapter with a look at some of the common problems that college writers run into and how to solve them.

1. Clauses

Clauses present ideas within sentences. Every clause consists of two main ingredients — a subject and a predicate. The subject is a noun phrase that presents the topic of the idea. The predicate is a verb phrase that states your idea about that topic.

If a clause makes sense all by itself, it's a main clause (also known as a sentence). If it doesn't make sense all by itself, it's a dependent clause that presents a supporting idea within a sentence.

A. The Main Clause

The **main clause** states the main idea of a sentence. It's also known as an **independent clause** because it is a complete idea all by itself — just like you are independent when you no longer depend on others to pay for your food and electricity and shoes.

1. **She** <u>lied</u>.

   Sometimes the **subject noun phrase** and <u>predicate verb phrase</u> are single words.

2. **The tall woman** <u>lied about her height</u>.

   Usually, though, other words and phrases describe the **subject** and <u>predicate</u> more precisely.

3. **The tall woman from Albany** <u>lied when I asked her about her height</u>.

   Here's another **subject noun phrase** and <u>predicate verb phrase</u>.

4. **I** <u>was shocked at her lie because I could see with my own eyes that she was at least as tall as my uncle, who is six foot seven</u>.

   Here's one more **subject noun phrase** and <u>predicate verb phrase</u>.

In English, the subject of a clause usually comes first and is followed by the predicate. However, we can also introduce a clause by shifting part of the predicate to the beginning:

5. <u>When I asked her about her height</u>, **the tall woman from Albany** <u>lied</u>.

   If you do move part of the <u>predicate</u> to the beginning of a clause like this, separate it from the **subject** with a comma.

6. However, **she** <u>was polite about it</u>.

   If you put a transitional word like "however" before a clause, separate it from the **subject** with a comma, too.

B. Dependent Clauses

Dependent clauses present supporting ideas that help to describe the subject or the predicate of a main clause. They still have a subject and a predicate, but for one reason or another, they depend on a main clause to make sense.

Example 3 above has a dependent clause in the predicate:

> when **I** <u>asked her about her height</u>.

This clause doesn't make sense on its own, even though it has a subject ("I") and predicate ("asked her about her height"). It only makes sense when it's helping the main clause by explaining when the woman lied. Example 4 above has several dependent clauses in it:

> because **I** could see with my own eyes that she was at least as tall as my uncle, who is six foot seven

> ▌ This clause explains why I was shocked at her lie.

> that **she** was at least as tall as my uncle, who is six foot seven

> ▌ This clause explains what I could see with my own eyes.

> **who** is six foot seven

> ▌ This clause explains how tall my uncle is. He's *really* tall, but he's starting to stoop a little.

As you can see, none of these dependent clauses makes sense on its own. Each only makes sense when it helps to explain some other verb or noun. Each depends on that main clause to make sense.

C. Types of Dependent Clauses

Dependent clauses can help to explain main clauses in many different ways, and they fall into several categories that are each punctuated differently.

SUBORDINATE CLAUSES

Subordinate clauses consist of the usual subject and predicate and then a subordinating conjunction that joins this dependent clause to the main clause of a sentence by noting how exactly the subordinate clause helps to explain the main clause.

1. I like ice cream *if* **it** is just a little bit soft.

   > ▌ This subordinate clause begins with the *subordinating conjunction* and then adds the supporting idea with its supporting **subject** and predicate. The main clause is "I like ice cream."

2. I like ice cream *when* **the temperature outside** is hot.

   > ▌ This subordinate clause explains when I like ice cream.

3. I like ice cream *even though* **it** is so bad for me.

   > ▌ Sometimes a *subordinating conjunction* consists of two words working together.

4. I like ice cream *because* **ice cream** is part of my self-image.

   > ▌ You'll notice that there's no comma before the *subordinating conjunction*. Even if you hear a pause, don't use a comma to separate a subordinate clause from the main clause.

5. *Although* **you** may be surprised at this, I like ice cream.

> If the sentence begins with a subordinate clause, however, you *do* separate it from the subject of the main clause with a comma.

RELATIVE CLAUSES

Relative clauses also have a subject and predicate. They usually support the main clause by providing more information about a noun. A relative pronoun — "that," "who," "which," or "whose" — connects the relative clause to that other noun. Consider this main clause:

The road is full of potholes.

We can add more information to the main clause with relative clauses that help to explain the two nouns, "road" and "potholes."

1. The road **that** runs past my house is full of potholes.

> This relative clause describes the subject noun, "road." The **relative pronoun** is the subject of the relative clause.

2. The road is full of potholes **that** are killing my car.

> This relative clause describes the noun "potholes." The **relative pronoun** is the subject of the relative clause.

If you think that the information from the relative clause is essential to the meaning of your sentence, then you use a **restrictive relative clause**, and you don't separate it from the main clause with any commas. Whenever you use "that" to start a relative clause, you are automatically deciding that the information is essential.

If the information in the relative clause is not essential to the meaning of the sentence, then you can use a **nonrestrictive relative clause**:

3. The road, **which** runs past my house, is full of potholes.

> Nonrestrictive relative clauses are considered interruptions or asides within the main clause, so you separate them from the main clause with commas.

Using restrictive or nonrestrictive relative clauses changes the meaning of the sentence slightly.

4. The road **that** runs past my house is full of potholes.

> I'm talking about the road that runs past my house — not any other roads.

5. The road, **which** runs past my house, is full of potholes.

> You already know which road we're talking about. By the way, it also runs past my house.

6. The road is full of potholes **that** <u>are killing my car</u>.

   ▌ These are really bad potholes.

7. The road is full of potholes, **which** <u>are killing my car</u>.

   ▌ You already understand how bad the potholes are. By the way, they are killing my car.

If the noun phrase you want to describe is a person, use the relative pronoun "who":

8. I'm cooking this hamburger for the professor **who** <u>gave me a D</u>.

   ▌ Omitting the comma makes this a <u>restrictive relative</u> clause and shows that I have many professors. This *E. coli* burger is for the only one who gave me a D.

9. I'm cooking this hamburger for the professor**,** **who** <u>gave me a D</u>.

   ▌ Using a **comma** makes this <u>a nonrestrictive relative clause</u> and shows that there is only one professor, and in spite of the fact that I feed him, he gave me a D.

NOUN CLAUSES

Noun clauses operate as noun phrases within a main clause, but they also contain their own subject and predicate. They begin with a word like "that," "how," "whatever," or "whether" — or a phrase like "whether or not."

1. **Whatever you want to order** <u>is fine with me</u>.

   ▌ This **noun clause** is the subject of the main clause. It is the thing that the <u>predicate verb phrase</u> describes.

2. **Whether or not you order French fries** <u>makes no difference to me</u>.

   ▌ Here's a similar example. This **noun clause** is the thing that makes no difference to me.

3. I **know** <u>that the French fries will give you a heart attack</u>.

   ▌ This <u>noun clause</u> is an object noun clause for the **verb** from the main clause. It is the thing that I know.

4. However, I **support** <u>whatever you decide to do</u>.

   ▌ This <u>noun clause</u> is also an object noun clause for the **main verb**. It is the thing that I support.

Even though you sometimes hear a pause before or after a noun clause, it's an essential part of the main clause, so *don't* use a comma to separate it from the rest of the main clause.

2. Phrases

Phrases are groups of words that operate as a unit to present one part of an idea. There are three main types of phrases in English sentences — noun phrases, verb phrases, and prepositional phrases.

A. Noun Phrases

The words of a noun phrase work together to name or describe a person, place, thing, or idea. They consist of a proper noun (such as "Bobby"), a common noun (such as "bartender"), or a pronoun (such as "she") — along with any other words that describe that noun. The order in which these elements are arranged is remarkably consistent, as you can see in this table:

Adjectives	Noun or Pronoun	Prepositional Phrases	Relative Clauses
	Bobby		
	Bobby	from Klamath Falls	
the	accountant		
the old, mean	accountant	at my office	who looks like a cat
one hundred	bottles	of beer	
my	cat		
the pretty	cat		that Mom stole for me
	she		
	she	who watches	

When we want to write about actions as things — like cheating at solitaire, for example, as a thing that you do — we use special noun phrases called **gerunds** and **infinitives**. Both of these phrases transform verbs into noun phrases so that you can talk about doing those actions in the same way you talk about physical objects and places and ideas.

GERUND PHRASES

To create a gerund, you take the base form of any verb and add "–ing." "Complain," for example, becomes "complaining." Gerund phrases are structured more like verb phrases, which are described later in this chapter, but you can also use adjectives to describe the gerund.

Adjectives	Gerund	Object Noun Phrases	Other Stuff
	babysitting		
	babysitting	your hamster	
	babysitting	your hamster	last week
	babysitting	your hamster	while you were in Sun River
my recent	babysitting		of your hamster

Use gerund noun phrases wherever you would use other noun phrases.

1. **Babysitting your hamster** made me realize the importance of friendship.

   This **gerund phrase** is the **subject** of the sentence. It's the thing that made you realize the importance of friendship.

2. I truly <u>loved</u> **babysitting your hamster**.

   This time, the **gerund phrase** is the **object** of the <u>main verb</u> in this sentence, the thing that you truly loved.

3. I even wrote a poem <u>about</u> **babysitting your hamster**.

   The gerund is the **object** of a <u>preposition</u>.

INFINITIVE PHRASES

An infinitive is the preposition "to" and the base form of any verb — "to be," for example, or "to go" or "to complain" or "to babysit." An infinitive phrase consists of an infinitive like these and then any other optional words that help to describe it.

Infinitive	Object Noun Phrases	Other Stuff
to count		
to count	my toes	
to count		on my sister
to count	sheep	when I need to fall asleep

Use infinitive phrases wherever you would use any other noun phrase in a sentence.

1. **To count sheep when I need to fall asleep** <u>is a waste of time</u>.

   This **infinitive phrase** is the **subject** of this sentence. It is the thing that the <u>predicate verb phrase</u> describes.

2. My mother always <u>said</u> **to count sheep when I need to fall asleep**.

> This time the **infinitive phrase** is the **object** of the <u>main verb</u> in this sentence, the thing that your mother always said.

3. My mother always said to count sheep when I need **to fall asleep**.

> There's also an **infinitive phrase** *inside* the dependent clause that begins with "when." It's the **object** of the <u>verb</u> in that clause, the thing that I need.

B. Noun Phrases in Sentences

Within a sentence, noun phrases have four different jobs to do. They can be **subjects**, **objects**, **complements**, or **appositives**.

SUBJECTS

The subject is the star of the sentence. The predicate either tells us what the subject does, or it describes the subject. Either way, it's the subject's show.

1. **My uncle** lost his phone.

> The **subject** of this sentence did something.

2. **His phone** <u>was a brand new iPhone</u>.

> The <u>predicate verb phrase</u> describes the **subject** of this sentence.

3. **The poor man** <u>put</u> it on top of his car.

> In English, the **subject** usually comes first in a sentence and is followed by the <u>verb</u>.

4. <u>Then</u> **he** drove out of the parking lot.

> However, sometimes an introductory <u>adverb</u> comes before the **subject**.

5. <u>As you might have guessed</u>, **the phone** slid off and smashed against the pavement.

> If the sentence begins with a transitional word or introductory phrase or clause, put a comma between the <u>introduction</u> and the **subject**.

6. **Losing this phone** made my uncle reflective about how we are slaves to our possessions.

   <u>To lose this phone</u> made my uncle reflective about the nature of possessions.

> **Gerund phrases** sound more natural as subjects than <u>infinitive phrases</u>.

Objects are noun phrases that are affected by verbs or that prepositions connect to the rest of the sentence. One type of object noun phrase is the **direct object**. This is the thing that the verb directly affects. If you kick a window, for example, the window is the object of your kick.

1. My uncle lost **his phone** again.

   The **direct object** is the thing that my uncle lost. This time he left it on a table at a restaurant.

2. He asked **me** to call my aunt.

   I am the **direct object** being asked — again.

3. I shook **my head**.

   I shook **my fist**.

   I don't enjoy **making my aunt mad**.

   Gerund and infinitive phrases can also be **direct objects**. However, some verbs (like "enjoy") *require* gerunds as **direct objects**.

4. I don't want **to make my aunt mad**.

   Other verbs (like "want") require infinitive phrases as **direct objects**.

5. I don't like **making my aunt mad**.

   I don't like **to make my aunt mad**.

   And other verbs (like "like") can use either infinitive or gerund phrases as **direct objects**. So take your pick with verbs like that.

Another type of object is the **indirect object**. This is a noun phrase that the verb affects — but not directly. When you throw a can of beets, the can is the direct object of the throw. If you throw a can of beets at your brother, your brother is the indirect object. You don't throw him, but what you do throw hits him on the side of the head.

6. My uncle paid <u>me</u> **twenty dollars** to call my aunt and tell her about the phone.

   He paid **twenty dollars** to <u>me</u> to call her and tell her about the phone.

   The **direct object** isn't necessarily the noun phrase immediately after the verb. It all depends on how you phrase the sentence. An <u>indirect object</u> might come first, or it might come later.

7. She asked <u>me</u> **a question**.

   She asked **a question** of <u>me</u>.

8. I told <u>her</u> **the truth**.

   I told **the truth** to <u>her</u>.

   The truth was "twenty dollars."

9. She just laughed.

> Some verbs (like "laugh") don't usually take any object, direct or indirect. They just happen.

A third type of object is the **object of a preposition**. This is any noun phrase that's connected by a preposition to another noun, verb, or adjective.

10. My aunt's laughter sounded *good* <u>to</u> **me**.

> I am the **object** of the <u>preposition</u>. This phrase describes an *adjective*.

11. I *laughed* <u>with</u> **my aunt**.

> This <u>preposition</u> connects the **object noun phrase** to a *verb*.

12. Then it was *quiet* <u>for</u> **a minute**.

> This <u>preposition</u> connects the **object noun phrase** to an *adjective*.

13. <u>After</u> **another minute**, she told me that my uncle and I were both <u>in</u> **big trouble**.

> You get the idea.

COMPLEMENTS

A complement noun phrase completes the meaning of a sentence by providing necessary information about either the subject or object of the sentence.

1. <u>My heart</u> *is* **an ocean of emotion**.
2. <u>Listening to my heart</u> *is* **a thing that I do**.
3. <u>You</u> *might be* **my closest friend**.

> When a **complement** noun phrase describes the <u>subject</u> of a sentence, a *linking verb* connects the two noun phrases.

4. However, you just called <u>me</u> **a fool**.

> A **complement** noun phrase can also rename or describe a <u>direct object</u>.

5. That makes <u>my heart</u> **a raging sea**.

> **Complement** noun phrases always follow the <u>direct object</u>.

APPOSITIVES

An appositive noun phrase is an interruption of a sentence that renames or describes the noun phrase right before it.

1. <u>Potatoes</u>, **my vegetable of choice**, are so starchy that I get fat just looking at them.

> The **appositive** must follow immediately after <u>the noun phrase that it renames or describes</u>.

27

2. <u>My second favorite vegetable</u>, **the tomato**, is more of an unpleasant fruit than a vegetable.

> Because **an appositive** is an interruption of the main sentence, you separate it from the main sentence with commas.

3. I refuse to eat <u>Brussels sprouts</u>, **the so-called king of vegetables**.

> If the **appositive** comes at the end of the sentence, you only need to separate it from <u>the noun phrase it describes</u> with a single comma.

C. Verb Phrases

The words in a verb phrase describe an action or — when the verb is a linking verb — the subject of the sentence. Verb phrases can consist of a single verb, but they usually consist of a verb and other words or phrases that help to describe that verb more precisely. Although the verb phrase usually begins with the verb, the structure isn't as regular as you find with noun phrases.

WITH ACTION VERBS

Let's suppose that the subject of our sentence is "the cell phone." Here are different ways to create verb phrases for that subject using the word "ring."

Verb(s)	Other Stuff	Notes
rings **rang** <u>is</u> **ringing** <u>has been</u> **ringing** <u>will</u> **ring**		A verb phrase can consist of a single **main verb** or a set of <u>helping verbs</u> and a main verb that explains what the subject does. Different forms of the verb show when the action happens.
rings	loudly in the morning for two minutes	Usually, though, adverbs and prepositional phrases provide more information about the **main verb**.
is ringing	even though I told my boyfriend I'd be home in ten minutes	Subordinate clauses provide supporting ideas about the **main verb**.
ruined	my peaceful state of mind	Often verbs do things to an object noun phrase.
<u>never</u> **rings**		You can change the meaning of the **verb** to mean the opposite with a <u>negative adverb</u>.
did <u>not</u> **ring** is <u>not</u> **ringing**		<u>Negative adverbs</u> need to come before the **main verb**.

WITH LINKING VERBS

Linking verbs link the subject to additional information about the subject. Let's say that the subject is "my sister-in-law." Here are different ways to use linking verbs to describe her:

Linking Verb	Other Stuff	Notes
seems	friendly to most people polite before you get to know her	The **linking verb** can connect an adjective to describe the subject noun phrase.
is	from L.A. between jobs because of attitude issues in the bathroom again	You can also link prepositional phrases back to the subject.
has been	a dedicated Cleveland Browns fan my nemesis for the past three years	With complement noun phrases, the **linking verb** shows that the subject has been one of these things.
is not **was** never will never **be**	funny on time a gentle soul	Negative adverbs with a linking verb tell readers that the following descriptions do not apply to the subject.

D. Prepositional Phrases

Prepositional phrases consist of a single preposition — such as "on" or "to" or "from" — and a noun phrase. Within a sentence, they describe verbs and nouns, often explaining where something is or when it is happening.

AS ADJECTIVES

With noun phrases, prepositional phrases always follow the noun they describe, and they are never separated from that noun with commas.

1. The tattoo <u>parlor</u> **on the corner** seems pretty sketchy.

   The **prepositional phrase** explains where the <u>noun</u> is located.

2. The <u>customers</u> **in the window** appear to be dangerously angry.

   This **prepositional phrase** identifies which <u>nouns</u> look angry.

3. <u>Anyone</u> **in their right mind** would check out the reviews first.

   Sometimes **a prepositional phrase** helps to define the boundaries of a <u>noun</u>. Anyone who is *not* inside this boundary will walk on in.

4. However, a <u>friend</u> **of mine** just walked right in.

   A **prepositional phrase** can also show that a <u>noun</u> belongs to another noun.

5. He wanted a <u>tattoo</u> **of Justin Bieber on his forehead**.

   You can use more than one **prepositional phrase** to describe a <u>noun</u>. "Of Justin Bieber" is one phrase and "on his forehead" is the other. You still don't add any commas in there.

6. He wanted a <u>tattoo</u> **in green ink of Justin Bieber on his forehead**.

   However, more than two **prepositional phrases** after the <u>noun</u> are hard to follow.

AS ADVERBS

In verb phrases, prepositional phrases always follow the main verb they describe, and once again, they are not separated from that verb with commas because they are considered essential information about that verb.

1. I <u>was playing</u> **in the street.**

   This **prepositional phrase** explains where the <u>verb</u> takes place.

2. I <u>was hit</u> **by a car**.

   This **prepositional phrase** explains how the <u>verb</u> happened.

3. Fortunately, I <u>was</u> **inside a bigger car.**

  > With linking verbs, the **prepositional phrase** describes the subject noun phrase, but it still follows the <u>verb</u>.

4. My mom's car is where I <u>play</u> **with my toys.**

  > This **prepositional phrase** is inside a dependent clause, but it still follows the <u>verb</u> there, too.

5. She always <u>parks</u> **in the street** *because it's easier than parking at the curb.*

  > **Prepositional phrases** follow the <u>verb</u> and always come before any *dependent clauses.*

6. Maybe she will <u>try</u> *harder* **after this.**

  > Only *adverbs* can slip in between the <u>verb</u> and a **prepositional phrase.** *Adverbs* go wherever they want, basically. There's no stopping them.

AS INTRODUCTIONS AND TRANSITIONS

Although you often hear pauses before and after prepositional phrases when you are speaking, they are almost always considered essential parts of a noun phrase or verb phrase, so don't separate them from the rest of the clause with commas. Resist the temptation.

However, there are two exceptions — when prepositional phrases are used as introductions to a sentence or as transitional phrases within a sentence.

1. **In the morning,** <u>my cat</u> eats Cheerios.

  > Because this **prepositional phrase** comes before the <u>subject</u> of the sentence, we separate it from the subject of the sentence with a comma.

2. <u>Cats,</u> **in my opinion,** <u>should not be limited to the "cat food" imposed on them by corporations.</u>

  > This **prepositional phrase** is a transition that interrupts the <u>main clause</u> of the sentence, so we separate it from the main clause with a comma on either side.

3. **In my opinion,** <u>people</u> should not be limited to eating corporation-defined "people food," either.

  > If a transitional **prepositional phrase** introduces a sentence, we separate it from the <u>subject</u> of the sentence with a comma. See the comma rule on "Introductory Words or Phrases" in the commas section of Chapter 3 for more.

3. Parts of Speech

The words in any language belong to different categories — also known as **parts of speech** — and each category has a different function. **Noun**, for example, is one familiar category, and as you probably know by now, nouns have a specific job to do. They name a person, place, thing, or idea. In English, a **noun** is one of seven main parts of speech, and each one has at least one job to do:

- **Nouns** (like "Salem" or "broccoli") name places, people, things, or ideas.

- **Adjectives** (like "crowded" or "green") describe nouns.

- **Pronouns** (like "she" or "we") refer to nouns so that we don't have to repeat the noun several times in a row.

- **Verbs** (like "stares" or "go") name different things that nouns can do.

- **Adverbs** (like "very" or "smoothly") describe verbs.

- **Prepositions** (like "to" or "with") show relationships between nouns and other parts of a sentence.

- **Conjunctions** (like "and" or "because") connect words or phrases together.

As a speaker of a language, you've learned through practice how to use these different parts of speech correctly. It's automatic and unconscious. As a writer, however, you have to understand what you're doing more consciously in order to correctly structure and punctuate your sentences.

To talk about that, we rely on technical terms like these for the parts of speech, so here's a closer look at what the parts of speech are in English and the jobs they perform in our sentences.

A. Nouns

Nouns name a person, place, thing, or idea. **Common nouns** are nouns that could apply to any of several people, places, or things. **Proper nouns** are the official names for specific people, places, or things. Because they're so proper, we capitalize them.

1. A **director** makes **movies**.

> These are **common nouns** because they apply to any director or movie.

2. <u>Errol Morris</u> is a **director**.

> This <u>proper noun</u> is the official name for one particular director. "Director" is a **common noun** for the job he does.

3. <u>Errol Morris</u> sometimes gets on my **nerves**.

> These are specifically my nerves, but this is still a **common noun** because I don't have pet names for each of my individual nerves.

4. His **films** show in lots of **theaters**.

> These are **common nouns** that name groups of things. No specific names are used.

5. However, his **films** seldom come to <u>Salem Cinema</u>.

> This <u>proper noun</u> is the name of one particular theater.

Most nouns can name either a single thing or many things. If a noun names a single thing, it's called a **singular noun**. If it names many things, it's a **plural noun**. In most cases, you turn a singular noun into a plural noun by adding the letter "s" to the end of the word.

6. If you like <u>cats</u>, you'll like my **cat**.

> To turn this **singular noun** into a <u>plural noun</u>, you just add an "s."

7. If you like <u>flies</u>, you'll like my **fly**.

> **Singular nouns** that end with a "y" often need to replace "y" with "ies" when they become <u>plural nouns</u>.

8. I'll trade you one big **toy** for three little <u>toys</u>.

> However, if there's another vowel before the "y," like with this **singular noun**, you just add an "s" to make it a <u>plural noun</u>.

9. The **glass** on the **couch** distinctly reminds me of other <u>glasses</u> on other <u>couches</u>.

> With **singular nouns** that end in an "s" or similar sound, add "es" to create a <u>plural noun</u>.

10. The **tooth** on that **goose** is just like the <u>teeth</u> on those <u>geese</u>.

> Yikes. With some older **singular nouns**, the old-fashioned <u>plural noun</u> spellings persist. You'll have to memorize these exceptions. A dictionary will help you out.

11. Your one **child** is chasing my three <u>children</u>.

> Here's another old-fashioned <u>plural noun</u>.

A few nouns can't be turned into plural nouns because they name things that can't be divided into separate units and counted — nouns like "salt" or "happiness" or "advice." These are called **mass nouns**.

B. Adjectives

Adjectives are words that describe nouns and pronouns. They can describe their nouns and pronouns with many characteristics — quantity ("three," "many"), characteristics ("angry," "ugly," "soft"), ownership ("my," "her"), and more.

DESCRIPTIVE ADJECTIVES

The most common type of adjective is the one that describes a noun's characteristics.

1. The **thirteenth** floor does not exist in my building.

    I This **descriptive adjective** tells us the position of the nonexistent noun.

2. Wasps *are* always **angry**.

    The **adjective** describes the emotional state of the noun, "wasps." Notice that this adjective is connected to the noun by the *linking verb*. Not all adjectives can do that, but descriptive ones can.

3. Wasps are probably angry about all the **rotten**, **stinking** food they eat.

    If I were a wasp, *I* would also be **angry**, **aggressive**, and **relentless**.

    You can also list **descriptive adjectives** together before or after a noun or *pronoun*.

4. I have a **wasp** mindset.

    Not to confuse things, but nouns can sometimes be used as **descriptive pronouns** to describe other nouns. "Wasp" was our noun in the two sentences above and now here it is as an adjective that describes "mindset."

QUANTITY ADJECTIVES

Quantity adjectives describe the number of a noun. Numbers tell us exactly how many of the noun there are. **Indefinite adjectives** give a sense of how many there are, but they don't provide a specific number.

1. I would like **three** cheeseburgers.

    I The **number** tells us exactly how many of the noun you would like to eat.

2. I would like **some** cheeseburgers.

    This **indefinite adjective** tells us that you would like more than one but not necessarily a lot of the noun.

3. I would like **many** cheeseburgers.

    This **indefinite adjective** tells us that you would like a lot of the noun, but it doesn't tell us exactly how many.

4. I would like **no** <u>cheeseburgers</u>.

> This **indefinite adjective** tells us that you've finally come to your senses. Cheeseburgers are not very good for you.

DETERMINERS

Determiners show which noun we mean. When they show up in a noun phrase, they're always the first words used. **Articles** are a type of determiner that show whether we mean one particular noun or one among several possible nouns.

1. **The** thirteenth <u>floor</u> does not exist in my building.

> The **article** shows that we mean one particular <u>noun</u>.

2. This is **a** hard <u>concept</u> for my guests to understand.

> This **article** shows that we mean one of several possible <u>nouns</u> that the guests could struggle with.

3. I need to get **an** <u>apartment</u> in another building.

> If the word immediately following the **article** "a" starts with a vowel sound — as this <u>noun</u> does — use "an" instead of "a."

Demonstrative adjectives also show which noun we mean by showing whether the noun is associated with us or not.

4. **This** <u>pimple</u> is distracting me.

> The **demonstrative adjective** "this" suggests that a singular <u>noun</u> is close at hand — that it's my pimple.

5. **These** <u>pimples</u> are distracting me.

> The **demonstrative adjective** "these" suggests that a plural <u>noun</u> is close at hand.

6. **That** <u>pimple</u> is driving me crazy.

> The **demonstrative adjective** "that" suggests that a singular <u>noun</u> is not close at hand — that it's someone else's pimple.

7. **Those** <u>pimples</u> are distracting me.

> The **demonstrative adjective** "those" suggests that a plural <u>noun</u> is not close at hand.

Possessive adjectives are versions of pronouns or noun phrases that show that a noun belongs to some other noun.

8. **My** <u>uncle</u> owns a gas station.

> The **possessive adjective** is a pronoun that shows the <u>noun</u> belongs to me.

9. **My** *three unfortunate* <u>cousins</u> work at **his** *gas* <u>station</u>.

   If you use a **possessive adjective**, it must come before the <u>noun</u> and any *quantity* or *descriptive adjectives*.

10. **Their** *entire* <u>salary</u> consists of candy bars and chili dogs.

    That's really not fair to them.

11. **My uncle's** <u>children</u> deserve better than this.

    You can create a **possessive adjective** with many noun phrases by adding an apostrophe and "s" to the end of it.

12. They can't stand the **chili dogs'** bitter <u>flavor</u>.

    If the noun is plural and has an "s" at the end already, you just add an apostrophe to create a **possessive adjective**. You can read more about this in the Apostrophe section of Chapter 3.

ADJECTIVE ORDER

English has developed some patterns for organizing a set of adjectives around a common noun. These patterns are usually intuitive and thus invisible for many who grow up speaking English, but if you try rearranging this order in a noun phrase, you'll see that it's been quietly guiding your noun phrases all this time.

	Example 1	Example 2	Example 3	Example 4
Determiner	the	my	a	
Quantity	three			some
Descriptive Adjectives				
Judgment		beautiful	clever	hip
Size	little			
Age		old	five-year-old	young
Shape				
Color	brown		golden	
Material		bronze		
Proper				Salem
Purpose		magnifying		graphic
Noun	bears	glass	retriever	designers

C. Pronouns

Pronouns stand in for a noun that's been used in a previous sentence or part of a sentence. They come in many varieties — personal, relative, interrogative, demonstrative, indefinite, possessive, and reflexive.

PERSONAL PRONOUNS

Personal pronouns usually refer to actual people, but they can also refer to things. The noun the pronoun refers to is called the **antecedent** of the pronoun. There are three categories of personal pronouns in English:

- **First person:** "I" and "we"

- **Second person:** "you" (either a single person or several)

- **Third person:** "he," "she," "it," and "they"

These examples show you what the pronouns look like when they are used as the subject of a sentence. The wording usually changes when they are used as an object noun phrase:

- **First person:** "me" and "us"

- **Second person:** "you"

- **Third person:** "him," "her," "it," and "them"

1. The toaster is broken. **It** won't toast my bread.

   "It" is a third-person singular **pronoun**. The antecedent is in the previous sentence.

2. My sister and I went to a toaster store. **We** couldn't believe the cost to repair **it**.

   "We" is a first-person plural **pronoun** and the subject of this sentence. The antecedent is in the prior sentence. "It" is still a third-person singular **pronoun** that refers to the toaster.

3. **They** wanted to *charge* **us** $100.

   "They" is a third-person plural **pronoun**. The antecedent is the people at the toaster store. "Us" still refers to my sister and me, but now this first-person plural **pronoun** is an **object** noun phrase for the *verb*.

4. **You** wouldn't *pay* **them** $100, would **you**?

   "You" is a second-person **pronoun** that might be singular (if there is one of you reading this) or plural (if you are reading this together with friends). "Them" refers to the jerks at the toaster store, but because they are now the object of the *verb*, the wording changes for this third-person plural **pronoun**.

POSSESSIVE PRONOUNS

Possessive pronouns come in two flavors. The first is the **possessive adjective** that is presented in the adjectives section. Because it is a type of personal pronoun, it comes in the same three categories:

- **First person:** "my" and "our"

- **Second person:** "your"

- **Third person:** "his," "her," "its," and "their"

The second type of personal pronoun stands on its own and means "the thing that belongs to me" — or you or him or her:

- **First person:** "mine" and "ours"

- **Second person:** "yours"

- **Third person:** "his," "hers," and "theirs"

1. **Your** books are used, but **his** books are new.

   "Your" and "his" are both examples of the possessive-adjective type of **pronoun** that tells us who owns the noun.

2. **Yours** didn't cost as much as **his**.

   "Yours" and "his" are now personal **pronouns** that stand on their own as noun phrases. They refer to "your books" and "his books." You were the smart shopper.

3. **My** car is valuable, but **yours** is just expensive.

   "My" refers to me, the author of this sentence. It is a possessive-adjective type of **pronoun** that identifies the noun that is valuable. "Yours" refers to you again and means "your car," which I'm sure is very nice.

REFLEXIVE PRONOUNS

Reflexive pronouns refer to nouns or pronouns that immediately precede or follow them. Because this is a type of personal pronoun, it comes in the same three categories:

- **First person:** "myself" and "ourselves"

- **Second person:** "yourself" and "yourselves"

- **Third person:** "himself," "herself," "itself," and "themselves"

1. We have nothing to fear but <u>fear</u> **itself**.

   "Itself" is a reflexive **pronoun** that refers to the <u>noun phrase</u> immediately before it.

2. However, <u>I</u> **myself** am afraid of more than just fear.

   Doing this adds emphasis to that noun phrase.

3. For example, <u>my dad</u> accidentally nailed **himself** to the roof with his nail gun.

   "Himself" is a reflexive **pronoun** that refers to the subject <u>noun phrase</u> of the same sentence. We use it because the <u>antecedent</u> is doing something to the <u>antecedent</u>.

4. <u>My brother</u> was also working on the roof. Dad accidentally nailed **him** to the roof, too.

   In this case, we don't use a reflexive personal **pronoun** because the *subject* of the sentence is not the <u>antecedent</u> to the **pronoun**.

5. So in addition to fear **itself**, my dad scares *me*.

   Do you see why one **pronoun** is reflexive and the *other* is not?

DEMONSTRATIVE PRONOUNS

Demonstrative pronouns refer to noun phrases that are closer or farther in distance or time:

- **Closer:** "this" and "these"

- **Farther:** "that" and "those"

These are called "demonstrative" because they demonstrate or point out another noun phrase.

1. **This** is for your heartache, and **these** are for your runny nose.

   "This" is a **demonstrative pronoun** that refers to a single noun like "book of poetry," and "these" is another **demonstrative pronoun** that points out a plural noun like "tissues."

2. **That** is for your heartache, and **those** are for your runny nose.

   "That" and "those" are **demonstrative pronouns** that point out the same noun phrases. They suggest that those things aren't as close as they were in Example 1.

3. **This** is Joe, and **that** is the mess he made.

   The **pronoun** "this" refers to Joe, who is standing right beside us, and the **pronoun** "that" suggests that his mess is farther away.

INDEFINITE PRONOUNS

Indefinite pronouns are indefinite — undefined — because they don't connect directly to an antecedent noun phrase. One type doesn't refer to any specific noun phrase:

- anybody, anyone, anything

- everybody, everyone, everything

- nobody, none, no one, nothing

- somebody, someone, something

1. **Everybody** is going to miss me.

    ▌ This category of pronoun always takes a <u>singular verb</u>.

2. **Someone** probably <u>misses</u> me.

3. **No one** <u>misses</u> me?

    ▌ Seriously?

The other type of indefinite pronoun refers to a specific noun phrase, but it doesn't clearly define what portion of that noun phrase is included:

- **Plural:** all, most, many, several, some, few, both

- **Singular:** either, neither, one, none

4. The people here are friendly. **Several** <u>have invited</u> me to dinner.

    ▌ If this type of **indefinite pronoun** refers to more than one thing, it takes a <u>plural verb</u>.

5. **One** <u>has given</u> me cupcakes.

    ▌ If this type of **indefinite pronouns** refers to a single noun, use a <u>singular verb</u>.

6. **None** <u>has abandoned</u> me emotionally like **either** of you <u>has</u>.

    ▌ "None," "either," and "neither" are also considered singular, even though it sounds a little weird sometimes.

INTERROGATIVE PRONOUNS

Interrogative pronouns help us ask questions. We don't know yet what noun phrase they refer to — that's why we're asking. There are only five — "who," "whom," "whose," "what," and "which."

1. **Who** ate one of my cupcakes?

2. **What** were they thinking?

3. Oh. These aren't my cupcakes. **Whose** are they?

D. Verbs

Verbs tell us about the subject of a sentence or clause. Active verbs like "kick" and "narrate" tell us what the subject is doing. Linking verbs like "is" or "has" describe the subject by linking the subject to descriptive information.

VERB FORMS

When it comes to how a verb is spelled in a sentence, **regular verbs** all follow the same general rules. **Irregular verbs** don't follow those same rules very well. They are usually older verbs that are still following outdated grammar rules from *Game of Thrones* days. The rules for verb forms depend on three main characteristics — number (singular or plural), person, and tense.

NUMBER AND PERSON

Just like with nouns, verbs have singular and plural forms. And just like with pronouns, they also come in first-, second-, and third-person forms. You can see how this works most clearly with the irregular verb "to be."

	Singular		Plural	
Person	*noun*	*verb*	*noun*	*verb*
First-Person	I	am	we	are
Second Person	you	are	you	are
Third Person	he, she, it	is	they	are
	Jojo the dog		the gerbils	

Number and person are less obvious but still present with a regular verb like "to sweat":

	Singular		Plural	
Person	*noun*	*verb*	*noun*	*verb*
First Person	I	sweat	we	sweat
Second Person	you	sweat	you	sweat
Third Person	he, she, it	sweats	they	sweat
	Jojo the dog		the gerbils	

For regular verbs, then, the main rule that verbs follow is that you add the letter "s" to the verb when the subject is a third-person singular noun phrase like "it" or "the dog" or "Jojo." Otherwise, leave it alone.

Verb tense shows us when something happens. English changes the spelling of the verb and sometimes adds helping verbs to show readers whether something happened in the past, is happening in the present, or will happen in the future. Here are some of your options:

Tense	Time	Irregular verb	Regular verb
Present	**It happens now.**	**She sings.**	**We listen.**
Present Progressive	It is in the process of happening at this moment.	She is singing.	We are listening.
Present Perfect	It began in the past and ended now or recently.	She has sung.	We have listened.
Past	**It happened before now.**	**She sang.**	**We listened.**
Past Progressive	It began, continued for a while, and ended recently.	She was singing.	We were listening.
Past Perfect Progressive	It began, continued, and ended in the past.	She had been singing.	We had been listening.
Future	**It will happen later.**	**She will sing.**	**We will listen.**
Future Progressive	It will begin and continue for a while in the future.	She will be singing.	We will be listening.
Future Perfect	It will begin and end in the future.	She will have sung.	We will have listened.

HELPING VERBS

Helping verbs — also known as auxiliary verbs — combine with an active verb to provide additional information about that action. These helping verbs always come before the main active verb, but sometimes adverbs will also slip in between them.

Be, Has, and Will

As you can see in the verb tense chart, "be," "has," and "will" can be used to help show when something happens.

1. A grand piano **will** <u>fall</u> from the sky.

   > This **helping verb** shows us that <u>the main verb</u> will happen in the future.

2. A grand piano **will** *probably* <u>fall</u> from the sky.

   > *Adverbs* also affect the meaning of <u>the main verb</u>, but they aren't **helping verbs**. They're just *adverbs*, and *adverbs* go anywhere they want.

3. A grand piano **has** <u>fallen</u> from the sky twice in my lifetime.

   > This **helping verb** and the spelling of <u>the main verb</u> show that this action has happened in the past.

4. A grand piano **is** <u>falling</u> from the sky at this moment.

   > This **helping verb** and the spelling of <u>the main verb</u> show that this action is happening now.

5. A grand piano **will** *not* **be** <u>falling</u> from the sky at this moment.

   > *Negations* before the <u>verb</u> come after the first **helping verb**.

Do

The helping verb "do" can either add extra emphasis to the main verb or allow you to negate the meaning of the main verb without sounding like William Shakespeare.

1. A falling grand piano <u>destroys</u> the car it lands on.

   > Here's a <u>main verb</u> without any added emphasis.

2. A falling grand piano **does** <u>destroy</u> the car it lands on.

   > The **helping verb** asserts the <u>main verb</u> more strongly — just in case anyone has any doubts about this idea.

3. A falling grand piano **does** *not* <u>destroy</u> the car it lands on.

   > If there aren't already any other helping verbs present, you can negate the meaning of a <u>main verb</u> with this **helping verb** and the *adverb* "not."

4. A falling grand piano <u>destroys</u> *not* the car it lands on.

   > Without the **helping verb**, your negation sounds like you live in merry old England.

Modals

Modal verbs change what's called the "mood" of the verb — usually by making the main verb conditional or necessary in some way. You have several modal verbs to choose from — "can," "could," "may," "might," "shall," "should," "will," "would," and "must." Each one puts a slightly different spin on the meaning of the main verb.

1. He **should** <u>move</u> his car before the grand piano destroys it.

   The **modal helping verb** shows that it would be a good idea for the <u>main verb</u> to happen.

2. He **might** <u>move</u> his car before the grand piano destroys it.

   The **modal helping verb** shows that it is a possibility that the <u>main verb</u> will happen.

3. He **can** <u>move</u> his car before the grand piano destroys it.

   The **modal helping verb** shows that the subject is capable of doing the <u>main verb</u>.

4. He **may** <u>move</u> his car before the grand piano destroys it.

   The **modal helping verb** shows that the subject has the choice to do the <u>main verb</u>.

5. He **may** *not* <u>move</u> his car before the grand piano destroys it.

   As with all the other helping verbs, *adverbs* can also slip in between the **modal helping verb** and the <u>main verb</u>, but they are still *adverbs*, not **helping verbs**.

E. Adverbs

Adverbs are words that help to describe verbs, adjectives, and even other adverbs. However, the most common job for an adverb is to provide more information about the main verb of the sentence or clause — usually by explaining how, when, where, or why that verb happens.

1. Kim <u>complained</u> **loudly** about the onions on her salad.

   This **adverb** explains *how* the <u>main verb</u> happened.

2. **Tonight**, Kim <u>complained</u> about the onions on her salad.

   This **adverb** explains *when* the <u>main verb</u> happened. Notice that it comes before the subject. Adverbs are sometimes like that.

3. In fact, Kim *is* **still** <u>complaining</u> about the onions on her salad.

   This **adverb** also explains when the <u>main verb</u> happens. It has slipped in between the *helping verb* and the <u>main verb</u>.

4. **Later,** Kim <u>complained</u> **loudly** about the lack of onions.

   You can pile on the **adverbs**, too. <u>Main verbs</u> can take it.

One thing to remember about adverbs is that you can usually make your writing more effective by not using them. Instead, choose more precise verbs or nouns that already include information the adverb provides.

F. Prepositions

Prepositions are words that show the relationship of a noun phrase to a verb or other noun phrase, or the position of a noun phrase relative to a verb or other noun phrase. At a literal level, prepositions almost always show the location of that noun phrase.

1. Your money is **inside** <u>my wallet</u>.

   This **preposition** introduces <u>a noun phrase</u> that explains the location of your money.

2. My wallet rests safely **under** <u>one of my mother's rocking chairs</u>.

   This **preposition** introduces <u>a noun phrase</u> that explains where the wallet is resting.

3. Her rocking chair **at** <u>home</u> is safer than her rocking chair **at** <u>work</u>.

   These **prepositions** introduce <u>noun phrases</u> that describe the two different rocking chair options.

However, prepositions can also be used to make less literal connections between noun phrases and verbs or other noun phrases.

4. You invested your money **with** <u>me</u>.

   This **preposition** doesn't require the money to be physically present with the <u>noun phrase</u>.

5. I invested your money **in** <u>lottery tickets</u>.

   The money is not literally inside the <u>noun</u>.

6. **For** <u>all practical purposes</u>, lottery tickets are as safe as the stock market.

   This <u>noun phrase</u> is intangible, so the preposition is figurative.

7. Yes, I *can* tell my head **from** <u>a hole in the ground</u>.

   Somebody has to win the lottery.

G. Conjunctions

Conjunctions connect words, phrases, or clauses within a sentence. **Coordinating conjunctions** connect words, phrases, or clauses of equal importance to create a list of two or more equal and similar items. **Correlative conjunctions** also connect words, phrases, or clauses of equal importance, but they do so with a pair of words. **Subordinating conjunctions** connect a dependent clause to a main clause.

COORDINATING CONJUNCTIONS

The coordinating conjunctions are "for," "and," "nor," "but," "or," "yet," and "so." You can remember this by remembering the otherwise meaningless acronym "FANBOYS." Although each coordinating conjunction creates a slightly different relationship between whatever items it connects, the implication is that those items are equally important.

1. I don't like cake, **and** I don't like ice cream.

> This **coordinating conjunction** links two independent clauses to create a compound sentence.

2. I don't like cake **or** ice cream.

> This **coordinating conjunction** links two noun phrases to create a compound noun phrase of things I don't like.

3. I like donuts, fig bars, and coffee, **but** not ice cream.

> This **coordinating conjunction** links a list of a record four noun phrases to create an even longer compound noun phrase of things I do or do not like.

4. Ice cream gives me gas **but** makes me happy.

> This **coordinating conjunction** links two verb phrases to create a compound predicate that describes the two equally important but contradictory things that ice cream does to me.

CORRELATING CONJUNCTIONS

Like coordinating conjunctions, correlating conjunctions connect equally important words, phrases, or clauses. The difference is that they do this as a team of two words. The first word comes before the first item, and the second comes before the last item.

1. **Either** your dog goes, **or** I go.

> This set of **correlating conjunctions** links two independent clauses to create a very difficult choice.

2. **Neither** <u>my dog</u> **nor** <u>you</u> are going anywhere.

> This set of **correlating conjunctions** links two <u>noun phrases</u> to create a definite compound subject.

3. Your dog is **both** <u>stupid</u> **and** <u>ugly</u>.

> This set of **correlating conjunctions** links two <u>adjectives</u> that describe the poor, soon-to-be-going dog.

SUBORDINATING CONJUNCTIONS

Subordinating conjunctions connect two *un*equally important clauses — a more important main clause and a less important dependent clause. Once connected to the main clause, the dependent clause takes on a supporting role, helping to explain something about the main clause.

You have many subordinating conjunctions to choose from, including:

- **Cause:** as, because, in order that, since, so that

- **Condition:** if, even if, in case, unless

- **Concession:** although, even though, while

- **Place:** where, wherever

- **Time:** after, as soon as, before, until, when, while

1. I went to the bathroom **before** <u>you arrived</u>.

> The **subordinating conjunction** connects "you arrived" to the rest of the main clause, creating a <u>dependent clause</u>. Notice that the **conjunction** becomes part of the <u>dependent clause</u>.

2. We should leave soon **because** <u>it's a long drive</u>.

> The **subordinating conjunction** connects "it's a long drive" to the rest of the main clause, creating a <u>dependent clause</u> that explains why we should leave soon.

3. <u>We should also leave in an hour</u> **if we want to avoid rush-hour traffic**.

> There's no comma between the **dependent clause** and the rest of <u>the main clause.</u> That's because dependent clauses like these are considered essential parts of the main clause. Even if you hear a pause when reading it out loud, you don't separate them with a comma.

4. **Although it's a long drive,** <u>I</u> will stop **if you need to go to the bathroom**.

> Both **dependent clauses** help to explain about why I might stop on this long drive. Because the first comes before the <u>subject</u> of the main clause, it's separated from the subject by a comma.

4. Common Problems

A. Sentence Fragments

A sentence fragment is a phrase or dependent clause that is punctuated as if it were a complete, independent sentence.

1. **Fragment:** Because that truck is not worth the money.

   Complete Sentence: <u>You shouldn't buy Kevin's truck</u> **because that truck is not worth the money**.

   > The first "sentence" is a **dependent clause**. A **dependent clause** only make sense when it's helping to explain the idea of <u>an independent clause</u>.

2. **Fragment:** Which is not my definition of true love.

   Complete Sentence: The feelings we have for puppies are based on <u>a hormonal reaction</u>, **which is not my definition of true love**.

   > The first "sentence" is a **relative clause**. A **relative clause** only makes sense when it's used to further explain a <u>noun phrase</u> in the main clause.

3. **Fragment:** Venturing out late into the night on a mission of mercy.

   Complete Sentence: Venturing out late into the night on a mission of mercy <u>is dangerous</u>.

   > The first "sentence" is a **gerund noun phrase**, a thing you might do if you are brave or foolish enough, but it's not a complete thought. In the second actual sentence, the **gerund noun phrase** now makes sense as the **subject** of an independent clause because a predicate verb phrase completes the thought.

Sentence fragments usually happen within paragraphs of several sentences when a supporting clause or phrase within one sentence is separated from the rest of that sentence and punctuated as if it made sense on its own.

4.   Another example of how Rick avoids the truth comes when he goes into the kitchen. He stares sadly at a picture of the two of them hung on the fridge. **Coming as close to actually facing his feelings as he will get in this story.** However, instead of facing the fact that she simply left, he continues to believe Bigfoot stole his wife. He can face that she is gone, but he cannot face the real reason for her going.

   > The **sentence fragment** in this paragraph is a gerund noun phrase that follows up on the previous sentence with a closely related observation about the significance of that prior sentence. It doesn't make sense on its own, but within the flow of the paragraph's ideas, it blends right in.

When you read your own work, it's hard to spot a sentence fragment because the flow of ideas in a paragraph makes sense as a whole. However, if you take the time to read a paragraph backward, sentence by sentence, it becomes easier to check that each sentence makes sense on its own.

5. He can face that she is gone, but he cannot face the real reason for her going.

   ▌ This sentence makes sense as a complete thought.

6. However, instead of facing the fact that she simply left, he continues to believe Bigfoot stole his wife.

   ▌ This one does, too.

7. Coming as close to actually facing his feelings as he will get in this story.

   ▌ Uh-oh. Taken outside of the flow of the paragraph, it's easier to see that this sentence doesn't make sense on its own.

8. He stares sadly at a picture of the two of them hung on the fridge.

   ▌ This is a complete sentence, and it's the one the fragment above should be connected to, using one of the solutions described below.

9. Another example of how Rick avoids the truth comes when he goes into the kitchen.

   ▌ This sentence is fine.

Sentence fragments are a problem because readers expect each sentence to provide a complete idea. A sentence fragment doesn't deliver that complete idea, so readers have to step back, look at the paragraph as a whole, and figure out what idea you are trying to explain with the sentence fragment. This makes your writing less effective, even if readers are able to eventually figure out your idea.

HOW TO FIX SENTENCE FRAGMENTS

To fix sentence fragments, you can either reconnect them to the main idea they should help to explain, or you can rephrase them as independent clauses.

Option 1: Reconnect to a Main Clause

If the sentence fragment was never intended to be a complete idea of its own, the better solution is to reconnect it to the idea it was meant to explain.

1. **Problem:** He stares sadly at a picture of the two of them hung on the fridge. **Coming as close to actually facing his feelings as he will get in this story.**

   ▌ This **sentence fragment** is a **gerund noun phrase** that explains what happens when he stares.

Solution 1: Coming as close to actually facing his feelings as he will get in this story, he stares sadly at a picture of the two of them hung on the fridge.

> If what happens when he stares is the more important idea, the better option is to reconnect the **dependent clause** as **an introductory clause** for the main clause.

Solution 2: He stares sadly at a picture of the two of them hung on the fridge, **coming as close to actually facing his feelings as he will get in this story.**

> The **dependent clause** can also follow the rest of the main clause.

2. **Problem:** The taco truck's chicken tacos have extra cilantro. **Which is my favorite.**

> This **sentence fragment** is a **relative clause** that is meant to add a side comment about a noun in the previous sentence.

Solution: The taco truck's chicken tacos have extra cilantro, **which is my favorite**.

> Because this is an aside, the better solution is to reconnect this to the main clause as a nonrestrictive relative clause, using a comma to show that it's not essential information.

3. **Problem:** This kale provides all the nutrients I need. **And tastes like nutrients, too.**

> This **sentence fragment** is a **verb phrase** with a coordinating conjunction. It doesn't make sense on its own because it refers back to the subject of the previous sentence.

Solution 1: This kale provides all the nutrients I need **and** tastes like nutrients, too.

> Because this verb phrase refers to the previous sentence, one way to reunite it is to use the **coordinating conjunction** to create a compound predicate.

Solution 2: This kale provides all the nutrients I need, **and** it tastes like nutrients, too.

> Another fix is to join the fragment to the previous sentence with the **coordinating conjunction** and then add a second subject noun phrase. That creates a compound sentence — two closely related and equally important ideas.

OPTION 2: REPHRASE AS A COMPLETE SENTENCE

If the sentence fragment was intended to be a complete idea of its own, then rephrase the fragment so that the idea has a subject and predicate that present a complete idea.

1. **Problem:** He stares sadly at a picture of the two of them hung on the fridge. **Coming as close to actually facing his feelings as he will get in this story.**

   ▎ This **sentence fragment** from earlier is still just a **gerund noun phrase**.

   Solution: He stares sadly at a picture of the two of them hung on the fridge. **This** is as close to actually facing his feelings as he will get in this story.

   ▎ In this solution, we keep the two related sentences loosely connected by making the **subject** of the second sentence a **demonstrative pronoun** that refers back to what he does in the first sentence.

2. **Problem:** This <u>kale</u> provides all the nutrients I need. **And tastes like nutrients, too.**

   ▎ The **sentence fragment** from earlier is still just **a predicate verb phrase** without a subject. However, maybe they aren't as closely related as I thought.

   Solution: This kale provides all the nutrients I need. **It** tastes like nutrients, too.

   ▎ Now both of these related sentences have a **subject** and predicate verb phrase of their own. By presenting them separately, you show that they are separate ideas.

3. **Problem::** The feelings we have for puppies are based on a hormonal reaction. **Which is not my definition of true love.**

   ▎ This **sentence fragment** is a **relative clause** that adds an aside about the nature of puppy love.

   Solution 1: The feelings we have for puppies are based on a hormonal reaction. **That** is not my definition of true love.

   ▎ If you think this aside should stand on its own in your paragraph, rephrase it by replacing the relative pronoun "which" with a **demonstrative pronoun** as the **subject** of the new sentence.

   Solution 2: The feelings we have for puppies are based on a hormonal reaction. **A hormonal reaction** is not my definition of true love.

   ▎ You could also replace "which" with **a regular noun phrase** as the **subject** of the new sentence.

B. Run-On Sentences

Run-on sentences are two or more independent clauses that are either punc-tuated as if they were a single main idea or connected with the wrong sort of punctuation.

1. **Run-on:** <u>You looked</u>, <u>I panicked</u>.

> This type of run-on sentence is called a comma splice because it splices (joins) two <u>independent clauses</u> with a single **comma**. Even if it's only four words long, it's still a comma splice.

2. **Run-on:** <u>It rained</u> <u>it poured</u>.

> When two <u>independent clauses</u> are connected by **nothing**, it's called a fused sentence.

Length has nothing to do with this, by the way. As you see, run-on sentences can be very short because it's a problem with the ideas in the sentence, not with the wordiness of it.

3. **Complete Sentence: One of the many problems with so many of the sentences in so many of the college textbooks that a student reads in the course of a year** <u>is that the sentences in these books employ far more words and phrases and dependent clauses than are actually necessary for the presentation of even the simplest of ideas</u>.

> This long sentence has a single **subject noun phrase** and a single <u>predicate verb phrase</u>, so it stands on its own as an independent clause, even though it's a long-winded one.

Run-on sentences are a problem because they confuse readers. Readers expect each sentence to provide a single, complete idea. When a run-on sentence gives readers more than one idea at once, they have to step back, look at the sentence, and separate the two ideas from that single sentence. This delay in understanding your ideas makes the paper as a whole less effective.

HOW TO FIX RUN-ON SENTENCES

There are several ways to fix run-on sentences. With every option, the solution requires you to use the right punctuation to give your readers one complete idea at a time.

OPTION 1: SEPARATE THE INDEPENDENT CLAUSES WITH A PERIOD
If the two ideas in the run-on sentence are not very closely related, or if you don't want to emphasize how the two ideas are related, you should present them separately.

1. **Problem:** <u>I adore pie,</u> <u>it goes well with a cup of coffee.</u>

   This is a comma splice because it splices two <u>independent clauses</u> together with a **comma**.

   Solution: I adore pie. It goes well with a cup of coffee.

   If you replace the comma with a **period**, you make each independent clause its own sentence.

2. **Problem:** <u>My cat's whiskers are long,</u> <u>they tickle my ears when she climbs on my head.</u>

   This is another comma splice. Each <u>independent clause</u> presents an idea about your cat's disgusting whiskers.

   Solution: My cat's whiskers are long. They tickle my ears when she climbs on my head.

   These are related ideas, so you might want to find a different way to combine them, but if you want each idea to stand on its own, replace the comma with a **period**.

3. **Problem:** <u>The rest stop smelled like urine</u> <u>it had a beautiful view.</u>

   This is a fused sentence because two <u>independent clauses</u> are jammed together with **nothing** between them.

   Solution: The rest stop smelled like urine. It had a beautiful view.

   These ideas are so different from each other that they really need to be punctuated as separate ideas. Nothing says "the end of one idea" like a **period**.

OPTION 2: USE A COORDINATING CONJUNCTION
TO CREATE A COMPOUND SENTENCE

If the two ideas in your run-on are equally important, you can connect them with a coordinating conjunction such as "and," "or," "but," or "so." This creates a compound sentence.

1. **Problem:** <u>I adore pie,</u> <u>it goes well with a cup of coffee.</u>

   This is still a comma splice.

   Solution: <u>I adore pie,</u> *and* <u>it goes well with a cup of coffee.</u>

   The *coordinating conjunction* shows that these two <u>independent clauses</u> are equal and related, but that's all. You'll notice that the **comma** can remain in place.

2. **Problem:** <u>I'll buy anything on sale,</u> <u>last week I bought a rest stop.</u>

   Here's another comma splice.

Solution: <u>I'll buy anything on sale</u>, *so* <u>last week I bought a rest stop</u>.

> This *coordinating conjunction* shows that the first <u>independent clause</u> is a reason or condition that leads to the second, equally important <u>independent clause</u>.

3. **Problem:** <u>The rest stop smelled like urine it had a beautiful view</u>.

> This is still a foul-smelling fused sentence.

Solution: <u>The rest stop smelled like urine</u>, *but* <u>it had a beautiful view</u>.

> This *coordinating conjunction* shows that the first <u>independent clause</u> contrasts with the second, equally important <u>independent clause</u>.

When you fix a run-on sentence in this way, you keep the comma before the coordinating conjunction because this is a **compound sentence**. The Commas section of Chapter 3 has more to say about that.

OPTION 3: USE A SUBORDINATING CONJUNCTION
TO CREATE A COMPLEX SENTENCE

If one idea is more important than the other, you should use a subordinating conjunction such as "because," "if," "although," or "when." This combines the two ideas into a single main idea with a dependent clause that helps to explain it.

1. **Problem:** <u>I adore pie</u>, <u>it goes well with a cup of coffee</u>.

> Yes, we've heard about your pie thing. This is a comma splice.

Solution 1: I adore pie *because* <u>it goes well with a cup of coffee</u>.

> The *subordinating conjunction* shows us that the second clause is a reason for the first one. In this revision, it's become a <u>dependent clause</u> that only makes sense when it's explaining about the first and more important idea.

Solution 2: *Because* <u>it goes well with a cup of coffee</u>, I adore pie.

> You can use the <u>dependent clause</u> as an introduction to the main clause, too. It's still a dependent clause, but you're also using it to introduce the main clause.

2. **Problem:** <u>You make me so angry</u> <u>I love you so much</u>.

> Here are two closely related independent clauses, but because there is nothing between them, they become a fused sentence.

Solution 1: *Even though* <u>you make me so angry</u>, I love you so much.

> The *subordinating conjunction* turns the first idea into a <u>dependent clause</u> that now introduces the main clause. This solution decides that love is the more important of the two ideas.

Solution 2: I love you so much *even though* you make me so angry.

> This works, too. If you read it out loud, you'll hear a pause before the *subordinating conjunction*. However, don't add a comma because this is a dependent clause now. It's an essential part of the predicate verb phrase, so no comma should come between it and its verb.

3. **Problem:** I'll buy anything on sale, I'll buy a used rest stop.

> Ah, you're a collector. This is a comma splice.

Solution: I'll buy anything on sale *if* I'll buy a used rest stop.

> The *subordinating conjunction* turns the second idea into a dependent clause that presents a condition that would make the first and more important idea true. Again, because it's a dependent clause, don't separate it from the rest of the predicate with a comma. It's just not done.

OPTION 4: USE A SEMICOLON TO SHOW A VERY CLOSE RELATIONSHIP

If you want to emphasize that the two ideas in the run-on are very closely related, you can join them with a semicolon and keep them as a single sentence.

1. **Problem:** You make me so angry I love you so much.

> Have you two considered counseling? This is still a run-on.

Solution 1: You make me so angry; I love you so much.

> By replacing the comma with a **semicolon**, you tell the reader that these two independent clauses are so closely related you can't bear to put even a period between them.

Solution 2: You make me so angry; *therefore*, I love you so much.

> You can also add a *transitional word or phrase* after the **semicolon** to suggest the relationship of the two independent clauses. Put a comma after the *transition* because it's an introduction.

2. **Problem:** The rest stop smelled like urine it had a beautiful view.

> It's a weird, fused sentence.

Lousy Solution: The rest stop smelled like urine; it had a beautiful view.

> This is a lousy solution because it takes two unrelated independent clauses and joins them with a **semicolon**. This is grammatically correct, but it suggests to the reader that the two ideas are very closely related when they aren't. So don't do this, in other words.

C. Passive Voice

Passive voice — also known as "passive sentence structure" or "passive construction" — disconnects a verb from the noun that is doing that verb. In this way, passive sentence structure obscures or deemphasizes that noun phrase.

Formal writing prefers **active voice** because it makes a clear connection between the action and the actor in a sentence. With active voice, the subject of a sentence is the doer, and the main verb is the action.

1. **Andrea** <u>slept on</u> my couch.

    The **subject** is the **noun phras**e that does something, and the <u>main verb</u> is what it does.

2. **The UPS driver** <u>rang</u> the doorbell seventeen times.

    The **subject** does the <u>verb</u>.

3. **The doorbell** <u>woke</u> Andrea.

    You get the idea.

When linking verbs are involved, the rest of the predicate stays focused on the subject of the sentence.

4. **Andrea** <u>is</u> *unhappy*.

5. **The UPS driver** <u>has been</u> *a bit of a turd lately*.

    The <u>linking verb</u> connects the **subject** to the rest of the predicate, which describes the **subject**.

Passive structure, on the other hand, focuses on the verb and the thing that is affected by that verb. The subject of the sentence is not the doer of the verb anymore.

6. **My couch** <u>was slept on</u> by *Andrea*.

    The **subject** is now the **noun phrase** affected by the <u>verb</u>. The *doer* of the <u>verb</u> is removed from the action in a prepositional phrase.

7. **My couch** <u>was slept on</u>.

    The *doer* of the <u>verb</u> isn't even in this sentence.

8. **The doorbell** <u>was rung</u> seventeen times by *the UPS driver*.

    Again, the **subject** is the **noun phrase** that is affected by the <u>verb</u>. The *doer* of the verb is tucked away in a prepositional phrase.

9. **The doorbell** <u>was rung</u> seventeen times.

    And again, all we have now are the <u>verb</u> and the **noun phrase** affected by the <u>verb</u>.

Sometimes Passive Voice Isn't a Problem

If you don't know who or what did the verb, then passive voice makes a lot of sense. It still allows you to state that something has happened.

1. **My car** <u>was broken into</u> last night.

   > You don't know who did the <u>verb</u>, so it makes sense to make the **affected noun phrase** the **subject**.

2. **My cassette tapes** <u>were stolen</u>.

   > We don't know who did this <u>verb</u>, either, but we do know what **noun phrase** was affected.

3. **Cassette tapes** <u>can't be replaced</u>.

   > That might not be the worst thing.

Sometimes you may know the doer of the verb, but that information isn't important to the idea or is implied by the context.

4. **The park** <u>was rumored</u> to be haunted.

   > The key is that the <u>verb</u> is happening and clouding the reputation of the **subject**. The nouns responsible for the <u>verb</u> don't matter as much.

5. **The rumors** <u>were</u> widely <u>thought</u> to be false.

   > The **subject** of these sentences is an implied consensus of everyone who has heard the rumors.

6. **Our thinking** <u>was changed</u> by *the jogging ghost of Bush Pasture Park*.

   > Finally, we have the *doer* of the <u>verb</u>, but with this passive structure, the **subject** and the focus of the sentence remain on affected by the <u>verb</u>.

Passive Voice Is Usually a Problem

One simple reason that passive voice is usually a problem is that it requires more words than active voice to state the same information.

1. **Active:** Andrea slept on my couch.

   Passive: My couch was slept on by Andrea.

   > This passive sentence uses seven words to present the same information.

2. **Active:** The UPS driver rang the doorbell seventeen times.

   Passive 1: The doorbell was rung seventeen times by the UPS driver.

   > Two more words.

   Passive 2: The doorbell was rung seventeen times.

   > Yes, the second passive sentence used two *fewer* words, but hang on. It's shorter because it removes the doer of the verb entirely. So it's not the same information. So it's not really shorter, is it?

A more important problem with passive voice is that it obscures the subject of the verb, which justifiably raises questions for readers.

3. The dishes have been washed.

> Who washed the dishes? They didn't wash themselves — though that would be nice.

4. The robber was apprehended.

> By whom? The police? A citizen militia? The League of Dishwashers?

When the doer is important to the idea and missing from a sentence, passive voice makes readers wonder about the full meaning of the sentence. That moment of distraction makes your writing less effective. However, even if you include the doer later in the sentence, passive sentence structure still disconnects the subject from the verb.

5. **Passive: Chemicals** <u>were released</u> into the water supply late last night by *the Corporation for Corporate Freedom.*

> This sentence names the *doer* of the <u>action</u>, but this sentence tucks that information away at the end of the sentence, far from the <u>verb</u>. It makes the *doer* seem less guilty.

Active: The Corporation for Corporate Freedom <u>released</u> chemicals into the water supply late last night.

> Do you see how much worse the action seems when active structure connects the **doer** to the <u>verb</u> by making it the **subject** of the sentence?

6. **Passive: This call** <u>is being recorded</u> for quality assurance.

> This idea seems harmless enough. With passive structure, the **subject** is what is affected by the <u>verb</u>, not who is doing it.

Active: The Corporation for Corporate Freedom <u>is recording</u> this call for quality assurance.

> Not them again! The idea is more alarming when active structure uses the **doer** as the **subject** of the <u>verb</u>.

The final problem with passive sentence structure, then, is that it can deliberately hide the doer of the verb in order to purposely confuse or withhold important information from readers. That makes for good advertising but dishonest writing.

When the subject next to the verb isn't the doer of the verb, you probably have passive verb structure. If that's a problem — as it usually is — then fixing the problem is straightforward: make the doer of the verb the subject of the sentence.

1. **Problem: Snails** <u>are considered</u> a delicacy by *the French*.

   The **subject** of this sentence is not the thing that does the <u>verb</u>. The *doer* of the verb comes at the end of the sentence.

   Solution: The French <u>consider</u> snails a delicacy.

   In this active sentence structure, the **doer** of the <u>verb</u> is now the **subject** of the sentence.

2. **Problem: Oxygen** <u>was discovered</u> in 1774.

   The **subject** of this sentence is not the thing that did the verb. So the doer of the verb is missing, and that information seems to be important.

   Solution: **Joseph Priestly** <u>discovered</u> *oxygen* in 1774.

   In this active sentence structure, the **doer** of the <u>verb</u> is now the **subject** of the sentence. (Thank you, Wikipedia.)

3. **Problem: Sales in the Northwest Region** <u>were observed</u> to be 10 to 30 percent higher than last month.

   The **subject** of this sentence is what the <u>verb</u> observed, not the doer of the <u>verb</u>.

   Solution 1: I <u>observed</u> sales in the Northwest Region to be 10 to 30 percent higher than last month.

   In this active sentence structure, the **doer** of the <u>verb</u> is now the **subject** of the sentence. However, it's not a great solution. The important information in this sentence is *not* that you did some observing.

   Solution 2: Sales in the Northwest Region <u>increased</u> 10 to 30 percent from last month.

   Nice work. What matters is what you observed, and that's the **subject** of this sentence. There's no inherent evil in using "I" in formal writing. The problem with "I" is just that it usually draws readers away from the more important information.

4. **Problem: Mistakes** <u>were made</u>.

   Solution: I <u>made</u> mistakes.

   Okay, fine. It was me. I am **subject** of this active sentence. I am **doer** of this <u>verb</u>.

Punctuation and Mechanics

In formal writing, punctuation and mechanics help to clarify the meaning of sentences. With informal writing, punctuation is often used to create sound effects. Commas create, the sound, of, pauses. Ellipses create the sound... of a voice... trailing away... That's fine for notes to friends and heart-wrenching poetry, but in formal writing, punctuation and mechanics are only used to present ideas more clearly. There are no sound effects.

Punctuation clarifies the ideas within a sentence. It shows readers how the parts of a sentence are organized and connected to each other. It separates the items in a list. It identifies any words that you're quoting directly from outside sources. In this way, readers see how the phrases and clauses of a sentence work together to create the main idea of the sentence.

Mechanics focus mostly on the meanings of words and phrases within a sentence. They distinguish between the official names of things and the general names for types of things. They let readers know when words have been combined to make a new compound word. In this way, mechanics show your readers exactly what you mean by those words or phrases.

The more complex your ideas become, the more carefully you must use punctuation and mechanics to show readers exactly what you mean. In this chapter, we will start by looking at the main rules that guide punctuation:

- ending punctuation

- commas

- semicolons

- colons

- apostrophes

- quotation marks

- other punctuation marks

Then we'll look at some important guidelines for sentence mechanics.

- capitalization

- italics

- abbreviations

- hyphens

We'll end by looking at some common errors with punctuation and mechanics and then how to fix them.

1. Ending Punctuation (. ? !)

All writing requires complete sentences, and complete sentences require some form of ending punctuation before a new sentence can begin. Ending punctuation tells readers that a sentence has ended in one of three ways — a statement (.), a question (?), or a shout(!).

A period is the most common ending punctuation mark. It tells s reader that this sentence is a statement of an idea or information. A question mark indicates that the sentence asks a question. Finally, an exclamation mark signals a level of surprise or excitement that warrants a shout.

1. Here is a sentence that ends in a period.

   It's a statement of fact.

2. The first known use of the period is thought to be in a cave painting in Mongolia circa 25 B.C.

> This may not actually be a fact. However, notice that the sentence ends with the abbreviation "B.C.," which itself uses **periods**. When a sentence ends with a period as part of an abbreviation, use only the single period to also end the sentence.

3. When should a sentence end in a question mark?

> That's the question, which always ends with a **question mark**.

4. Should all sentences end in question marks?

> No — only the questions.

5. That's remarkable!

> It's just a basic rule of punctuation. There's no need to shout.

6. I never realized just how stimulating it is to use an exclamation point properly.

> Yes, it's quite a revelation.

2. Commas (,)

Commas divide, and in formal writing, that's all they do. You may have been taught to "put a comma where you hear a pause," but that sound-based tip doesn't work well in the idea-based world of formal writing. In your college papers, you should only put a comma where a comma rule applies to the ideas in the sentence.

A. Items in a List

In a list of three or more items, put a comma after every item except the last one. The items can be anything — nouns, adjectives, phrases, or clauses — that are similar. In most cases, you use a **coordinating conjunction** such as "and" or "but" to hold the list together as a group.

1. Travis, Steve, *and* Bethany attacked the wolverine.

> In this list of nouns, **commas** separate each item in the list except the last one, "Bethany." The *coordinating conjunction* holds the list together.

2. This foolish display of bravery surprised, annoyed, *but* also impressed the unsuspecting wolverine.

> This list of verbs is also held together by a *coordinating conjunction*. There's no **comma** after "impressed" because it's the final item on the list.

3. The wolverine could have <u>chased them back to camp,</u> <u>torn them to pieces,</u> *and* <u>eaten them</u>.

> Here's a list of three <u>verb phrases</u> in the past tense. Do you notice how the items in the list all use the same verb tense (past)? All the items on the list are the same type of grammatical thing.

4. The wolverine could have <u>screamed in terror,</u> <u>run away,</u> <u>climbed a tree,</u> *or* <u>simply died of fright</u>.

> This is a list of four <u>verb phrases</u>. You can see how the rule still applies, even when the number of items in the list increases.

5. The wolverine could have hidden under <u>the branches of a tree</u> *or* <u>a rotten log</u> *or* <u>a couch</u>.

> Here's a comma-free variation to the rule. Here we have a list of three <u>noun phrases</u> where the wolverine might hide. However, because we have a *coordinating conjunction* between each of them, no commas are required.

6. The <u>ferocious,</u> <u>unpredictable,</u> <u>sneaky</u> creature simply laughed.

> This is a variation without the use of a conjunction. With a list of adjectives before a noun, we still put a **comma** after each <u>adjective</u> (except the last one), but we don't need a coordinating conjunction to hold the list together. No one knows why.

7. The wolverine then <u>smiled to herself</u> *and* <u>trotted away</u>.

> This list of <u>verb phrases</u> is held together by a *coordinating conjunction*, but there are only two items in this list, so we don't use any commas here, either.

You may have been taught to omit the comma that comes after the next-to-last item on the list and before the coordinating conjunction. This next-to-last comma goes by many names — such as **Oxford comma** and **serial comma** — and its use is the subject of one of grammar's most contentious and nerdy debates. If you were taught to use it, your teacher was probably taught the same as a student.

In your own college writing, you will often get to decide whether you use the serial comma or not. As long as you use it (or not) consistently in your paper, you should be fine. However, there are rare situations where the absence of the serial comma creates confusion, suggesting the final two items in the list describe the first item.

Consider how the meaning of this sentence changes when we remove the serial comma:

8. I admire my parents, God, and Carrie Underwood.

> This makes sense. All three items in the list seem to be admirable.

9. I admire my parents, God and Carrie Underwood.

   > Now the meaning is unclear. This *might* mean the same idea as the first sentence, but without the serial comma to clearly divide the items in this list, it might mean that your parents are God and Carrie Underwood.

10. The donor pledged her support, financial assistance and time.

    > Is the donor pledging three things (support, financial assistance, and time) or just two forms of support (financial assistance and time)?

11. The donor pledged her support, financial assistance, and time.

    > With the **second comma**, it is now clear that in addition to financial assistance and time, you can count on the donor's support. Maybe she'll introduce you to her rich friends.

B. Clauses in Compound Sentences

A **compound sentence** is a list of two or more **independent clauses** — ideas that could stand on their own as complete sentences. Treat a compound sentence like any other list by putting a comma after each independent clause except for the last one. The only difference is that you use a comma even if there are only two independent clauses in the list. A coordinating conjunction such as "and" or "but" holds the compound sentence together.

1. I like the accordion, *and* the accordion likes me.

   > In this compound sentence, a **comma** separates the first independent clause from the second one. The *coordinating conjunction* holds the sentence together.

2. A lot of people don't like the accordion, *but* a lot of people are wrong.

   > This example works just like the first example. Both clauses could stand alone as complete sentences. This *coordinating conjunction*, however, shows that the ideas are contrasting.

3. Accordion music is fun to listen to, accordion music is fun to make, *but* accordion music does cause hair loss.

   > Here we have a list of three independent clauses that are separated by **commas** and held together by a *coordinating conjunction*.

4. Accordions are not cheap, *and* accordion lessons are not cheap, *but* I really want to play this beautiful instrument, *so* I plan to spend the money

   > This list of four independent clauses are separated by **commas**. In this example, the relationship between independent clauses keeps changing, so we use more than one *coordinating conjunction*.

65

Technically, you can use the list rule to create a grammatical compound sentence with any independent clauses. However, just like with any other list, it should be a list of *similar* items. In other words, the independent clauses should be closely related:

5. <u>My new accordion is beautiful</u>, *but* <u>the music I make with it is pretty ugly</u>.

   > The two <u>independent clauses</u> here are focused on the same topic and have a clear, contrasting relationship that the *coordinating conjunction* captures.

6. <u>I will soon learn to make beautiful accordion music</u>, *and* <u>my foot itches</u>.

   > This sentence is a compound sentence, but in spite of the *coordinating conjunction*, these two <u>independent clauses</u> don't seem to have anything in common. This should *not* be a compound sentence.

C. Introductory Words or Phrases

Use a comma to separate any introductory words or phrases from the subject of the sentence.

1. <u>In the morning</u>, *my homework* is due.

   > In this sentence, the <u>introductory phrase</u> tells us *when* the main idea happens. The **comma** separates that <u>introduction</u> from the *subject* of the main sentence — my homework.

2. <u>However</u>, *I* have not yet started my homework.

   > There are many ways to introduce the main clause. This <u>introduction</u> is a transitional word that connects this sentence to a previous sentence. It tells us this is a contrasting idea.

3. <u>Because I care about my education</u>, *my homework* is important.

   > This <u>introduction</u> is a dependent clause that provides a supporting reason for the main idea of the sentence.

4. <u>Unfortunately</u>, *I* had to work all afternoon in the dining hall.

   > This <u>introduction</u> is an adverb that tells us what the author thinks about the main idea — in this case, it was unfortunate.

5. <u>My dear professors</u>, *you* need to understand that I have an actual life outside your classrooms.

   > Here the <u>introduction</u> is a direct address that tells the readers this sentence is directed at them. This is used in informal writing rather than formal writing. It's also kind of whiny in this case.

6. <u>In fairness to me</u>, <u>however</u>, *the homework* was only assigned this morning.

If there's more than one <u>introduction</u> before *the subject* of the sentence, put a **comma** after each <u>introduction</u>.

7. <u>Then</u> *I* went right to work.

Here's an exception to the rule. With many single, time-related adverbs like "now," "then," or "today," you don't separate the <u>introduction</u> from the *subject* of the main sentence. That's because adverbs don't follow rules. They just do whatever they want.

The key with this rule is being able to identify the subject of the main sentence. So who or what is doing something or being described by this sentence? That thing is usually the subject of the sentence. If any words or phrases — other than time-related adverbs — come before that subject, this rule applies.

D. Interruptions to the Main Clause

Writers often interrupt their sentences to add additional information or transitions that refer back to prior sentences. Use commas to separate the main clause from this additional information or transitions.

1. Standardized testing**,** <u>however</u>**,** is not an accurate measure of knowledge.

The <u>interruption</u> is a transitional word. Because this comes in the middle of the main sentence, **commas** come before and after it. Notice that if you cut out the interruption, the sentence still makes sense. That will be true for all interruptions.

2. Standardized testing**,** <u>which was first used in 1682</u>**,** is not an accurate measure of knowledge.

The <u>interruption</u> here is a dependent clause that provides nonessential information about the subject. Notice the **commas**.

3. Standardized testing**,** <u>my child</u>**,** is not an accurate measure of knowledge.

This <u>interruption</u> is a direct address to the reader. This is too informal for college writing, though. Don't try this at home. Actually, you can try it at home, but don't try it at school.

4. Standardized testing**,** <u>tragically</u>**,** is not an accurate measure of knowledge.

This <u>interruption</u> is a judgment of the main idea of the sentence that it interrupts. It's not essential information for this idea.

5. Standardized testing**,** <u>unlike individualized testing</u>**,** is not an accurate measure of knowledge.

The <u>interruption</u> is a negation of the term that comes before it. It highlights that term but isn't essential for explaining the main idea.

6. Standardized testing is not an accurate measure of knowledge**,** <u>however</u>**.**

> When the nonessential information or transition comes at the end of the main sentence, you still separate the <u>interruption</u> from the main sentence with a **comma**, but you don't put a comma after it. Use **ending punctuation** instead.

7. Standardized testing is not an accurate measure of knowledge**,** <u>is it</u>?

> This type of <u>interruption</u> is called a tag question. It refers back to the main idea and asks the reader to consider it, but it doesn't add new information to that main idea.

8. Standardized testing is not an accurate measure of knowledge**,** <u>which makes many scholars question its use</u>.

> This <u>interruption</u> adds a follow-up observation about the main idea.

E. Direct Quotations and Attributions

Use commas to separate direct quotations from **attributions** — statements that identify the source of the quotation.

1. <u>William Shakespeare writes</u>**,** *"All the world's a stage, and all the men and women merely players."*

> In this example, the <u>attribution</u> comes first, then the **comma**, and then the *direct quotation*.

2. *"All the world's a stage, and all the men and women merely players***,***"* <u>writes William Shakespeare</u>.

> The <u>attribution</u> can also follow the *direct quotation*, but that's more common in informal writing. Notice how in this case the **comma** goes inside the second quotation mark.

3. *"All the world's a stage***,***"* <u>according to William Shakespeare</u>**,** *"and all the men and women merely players."*

> The <u>attribution</u> can also interrupt the *direct quotation*. In that case, the interruption rule applies, so you put a comma before and after the interruption. Pay attention to the **comma** placement. With sets of quotation marks, any commas usually stay outside of the first set and inside of the second set.

4. Shakespeare says the world is like *"a stage."*

> However, when the *direct quotation* is just a word or phrase and is needed to complete the sentence's idea, this comma rule doesn't apply.

F. Multi-Part Numbers and Nouns

Commas also separate the parts of **multi-part nouns** — like "Portland, Oregon" — that are made up of more than one thing. This helps readers to keep those parts straight while reading.

NUMBERS

With large numbers, separate every three digits with a comma.

1. I won 10,000 dollars at the casino.

   > With large numbers, use a **comma** to separate the number after every three digits.

2. I had 100,000,000 ideas about how to spend my winnings.

   > This rather larger number has three sets of three digits, so it requires two **commas**.

3. Then I lost 11,800 dollars at the casino.
   > Bummer.

4. I had to borrow $1200 from my mom to make rent.

   > With four-digit numbers, the **comma** is optional.

CITIES

Use commas to separate contextual information that is closely related to a particular city.

1. Powell's Books is located in Portland, *Oregon.*

   > Use a **comma** to divide the name of the city from its *state*.

2. Portland, *Oregon,* is also where my cat now lives.

   > When the city is in the beginning or middle of the sentence, put a **comma** before and after the *state*.

3. My cat and I often visited Washington, *D.C.*

   > The contextual information isn't limited to states.

4. Seattle was just okay as far as cats are concerned.

   > When the city doesn't need contextual information because there's only one well-known city by that name, you don't need to include it.

5. Paris, *France,* was a virtual paradise for cats.

   > This differentiates it from Paris, Texas, or Paris, Kentucky, or Paris Hilton.

ADDRESSES

Use commas to separate the main parts of an address.

1. You can mail my check to <u>Chemeketa Community College</u>, <u>4000 Lancaster Drive NE</u>, <u>Salem</u>, <u>Oregon 97305</u>.

    Use a **comma** to divide the <u>name</u>, <u>street address</u>, <u>city</u>, and <u>state</u>. However, you *don't* need a **comma** to separate the zip code from the state.

PEOPLE

Use commas to separate the name of a person from any degrees, titles, or other suffixes that are closely connected to their name.

1. Have you ever read the work of <u>Kurt Vonnegut</u>, *Jr.*?

   This works with names like it did above with cities. You separate the *suffix* from the <u>name</u> with a **comma**.

2. <u>Kurt Vonnegut</u>, *Jr.*, used to be my favorite author.

   When the <u>name</u> is used in the beginning or middle of the sentence, use **commas** before and after the *suffix*.

3. Then I discovered <u>James Jones</u>, *Jr.*, *MBA*, *PhD*.

   When there is more than one *suffix* for a <u>name</u>, separate each with **commas**.

DATES

When you use the full date as a noun, use commas to separate the year from the rest of the date.

1. My uncle moved to Tigard on <u>March 22</u>, *1958*.

   Separate the *year* from the <u>date</u> with a **comma**.

2. On <u>March 22</u>, *1958*, Tigard only had 800 people living in it.

   When the <u>date</u> is used in the beginning or middle of the sentence, use **commas** before and after the *year*.

3. <u>March 22</u> was the spring equinox that year.

   If you don't provide the year, don't use commas with the <u>date</u>.

4. Tigard has grown more than 5,000 percent since <u>March 1958</u>.

   Likewise, if the date consists of just the month and year, don't separate the year from the date with commas. It feels like you should, but here's one more example where your feelings are trying to betray you.

G. To Avoid Confusion

There are times when the phrases within a sentence look awkward or confusing when placed side by side with other parts of a sentence. When that happens, you can separate one part from another with a comma. However, you may be better off simply rephrasing the sentence to avoid the awkward structure in the first place.

1. <u>Whatever will be</u>, will be.

   > In this case, the <u>subject</u> ends with a verb, and that looks weird when it's placed next to the main verb, so we separate the two verbs with a **comma**.

2. <u>Many people who like to sing</u>, sing while in the shower.

   > Here's another example of the same problem. You can reword this, "Many people who like to sing do so while in the shower."

3. <u>What I think it is</u>, is a moth.

   > Here's another example. How about rephrasing it to "I think it is a moth"? Isn't that better?

3. Semicolons (;)

Semicolons have two purposes. They join two complete sentences to indicate a relationship between the ideas, and they separate items in a list when some or all of the items contain commas.

A. Join Independent Clauses

Semicolons join two or more closely related independent clauses to form a more complex idea. Adding a transitional word or phrase like "however," "therefore," or "on the other hand" will show readers how these two independent ideas are related.

1. <u>The professor was late to class</u>**;** <u>the students waited outside the door</u>.

   > Here we have two <u>independent clauses</u>. There's an implied cause-and-effect relationship here, so joining the two clauses together makes sense. The <u>independent clause</u> after the **semicolon** is not capitalized.

2. <u>The professor was late to class</u>**;** *however*, <u>she had a good reason</u>.

   > Here, a *transitional word* after the **semicolon** shows the relationship between the two <u>independent clauses</u>. A comma separates the introductory transition from subject of the second <u>independent clause</u>.

3. Dustin was also late to class; his excuse, *however*, was obviously a lie.

> In this example, the *transitional word* occurs in the middle of the second independent clause. The **semicolon**, however, must always go where the two independent clauses meet.

4. Dustin's excuses for tardiness are usually lies; *for example*, he once claimed he had been detained by Martians.

> These independent clauses are related, as the *transitional phrase* indicates, so a **semicolon** is okay. However, they aren't *that* closely related, so a semicolon is probably not the best option.

5. Dustin's excuses for tardiness are usually lies. *For example*, he once claimed he had been detained by Martians.

> Letting the independent clauses stand as separate sentences allows each idea to be considered on its own.

B. Separate Multi-Part Items in a List

The other purpose of a semicolon is to separate multi-part items in a list when some of those items already contain commas. Sometimes it may be better to try rewording the sentence so that these semicolons are not needed.

1. Over the years, I have lived in Springfield, Oregon; Springfield, Kentucky; Springfield, Georgia; and Springfield, Vermont.

> The multi-part items in the list are a series of cities and state abbreviations that are already separated by commas. The **semicolons** work just like the commas in Comma Rule A. That way you can tell that I've lived in four places and not eight.

2. Over the years, I have lived in Springfield, Oregon; Springfield, Kentucky; Springfield, Georgia; **Paris**; and Springfield, Vermont.

> Not all the items in the list need to be multi-part nouns for **semicolons** to apply. It can be matched set of **single** and multi-part nouns.

3. The family reunion included my uncle, Homer Simpkins, a retired vet; my aunt, Marge Simpkins, a retired nurse; my cousin, Lisa Andres, a doctor; and her brother, Bartholomew Simpkins, a pathologist.

> Each item in this list consists of three parts, and each part is separated from the others by commas. Without **semicolons** to separate these items, readers would have a hard time sorting out who was who.

4. The picnic table was packed with kids eating cake, parents wiping cake off of the kids' clothes, and grandparents laughing knowingly.

> Notice how no semicolons are used here? That's because the items in the series don't include commas.

4. Colons (:)

The colon is a bridge between an independent clause and a list, definition, explanation, quotation, or some other elaboration of the opening statement. They tend to emphasize the follow-up elaboration. In addition to this use in sentences, colons also have some special technical duties to perform.

A. Introduce Elaborations

When a statement introduces a more detailed elaboration of that same idea, use a colon as a bridge between the idea and the elaboration. The statement before the colon must always be an independent clause because it must always be a complete idea.

1. For some, <u>the definition of love is simple</u>: *unconditional sacrifice.*

   The **colon** here is a bridge between the <u>independent clause</u> and a short *definition* that elaborates upon <u>the first idea</u>. Notice how the **colon** focuses attention on that definition.

2. <u>Others see love as a composite of three necessary qualities</u>: *empathy, passion, and just a little lunacy.*

   This **colon** here introduces a *list* of three qualities that provides details about the <u>independent clause.</u>

3. <u>No one needs to live without love</u>: *Healthy, enriching relationships are available to all who seek them sincerely.*

   The **colon** introduces a *restatement* of the <u>independent clause.</u> Because the *restatement* is also an independent clause, it's capitalized.

4. <u>My uncle has his own idea about love</u>: "It ain't a bowl of jellybeans on a Sunday afternoon. It's damned hard work."

   In this sentence, the **colon** introduces a quotation that elaborates on the <u>independent clause.</u> The quotation marks show us that these are your uncle's actual words.

B. Technical Clarity

Colons also have smaller and more technical roles to play in formal writing, usually with the goal of clarifying the meaning.

1. Dear Mrs. Steuck:

   Here the **colon** comes after the greeting in a formal letter. It becomes a bridge to the body of the letter.

2. This letter is in reference to your recent order of the book <u>Batboys</u>**:** *The True Story of Baseball's Unsung Heroes.*

> The **colon** divides the <u>main title</u> from its *subtitle*, which is an elaboration of the <u>title</u>.

3. At <u>4</u>**:** *30* p.m. yesterday, your bank informed us that your ratio of debt to credit is <u>4</u>**:** *1*.

> The **colon** separates the <u>hour</u> from the *minutes*. It also shows the relationship of two numbers. Poor Mrs. Smith outspent her account four times over.

5. Apostrophes (')

Apostrophes have three specific functions in formal writing. They show that some letters or numbers are missing, they help to create possessive adjectives, and *on rare occasions*, they help to resolve confusion when letters become plural nouns.

A. Missing Words or Numbers

An apostrophe shows readers that letters or numbers have been removed from a word — like a bookmark that shows where the missing characters once belonged. The resulting word is called a **contraction** because the word contracts into a shorter version of its formerly expansive self.

1. I <u>didn'</u>t answer your phone call last night.

> This is a <u>contraction</u> of the words "did" and "not." Because the "o" is omitted, the **apostrophe** goes between the "n" and the "t."

2. To get me to answer, <u>you'</u>ll need to call before midnight.

> This is a <u>contraction</u> for "you" and "will." The **apostrophe** shows where "wi" are missing.

3. I **won'**t bother to explain why midnight is too late for a phone call.

> This is a <u>contraction</u> for "will" and "not." The **apostrophe** represents the missing "o" from "not." "Willn't" never really caught on, so for some reason, we instead say "won't."

4. You can reach me any time before ten **o'clock**.

> This is an old <u>contraction</u> for "of the clock." In this case, the **apostrophe** shows where whole words have disappeared from the original phrase.

5. **It'**s also fine to email me.

> This <u>contraction</u> is commonly misused as a possessive adjective. Anytime you write "it's," substitute the words "it is" or "it has" in your head as a test. If that makes sense, use the **apostrophe**.

6. I prefer email because I am not stuck in the ʼ80s like some people I know.

   > The full word for this <u>contraction</u> is "1980s." The **apostrophe** indicates that "19" has been omitted.

7. How ʼ<u>bout</u> you stop <u>whininʼ</u> ʼ<u>bout</u> it?

   > You can also use **apostrophes** to create informal <u>contractions</u> that sound like a spoken dialect. This is an informal style of writing, though, so don't use it in a formal paper.

Contractions make your writing sound more like spoken language, so they tend to be less appropriate for formal papers. It's like wearing sweatpants on a date. Yes, sweatpants are more comfortable — everyone knows that — but taking the time to get dressed up for someone sends a message that he or she is important. Writing out the full phrase shows the same kind of respect for the readers of a formal paper.

B. Possessive Adjectives

Apostrophes also show ownership or close association between two noun phrases by turning one of the noun phrases into a **possessive adjective** for the other.

SINGULAR NOUN PHRASES

With singular noun phrases, add an apostrophe and "s" to the end of a noun phrase to convert it into a possessive adjective.

1. I approve of <u>my sisterʼs</u> *husband.*

   > By adding an **apostrophe** and "s" to "my sister," it becomes a <u>possessive adjective</u> that describes who owns the *noun phrase*. It tells us the husband belongs to my sister. Kind of.

2. I borrowed <u>my brother-in-lawʼs</u> *truck* for the week.

   > With a compound noun like "brother-in-law," add an **apostrophe** and "s" to the end of the last word to create a <u>possessive adjective</u> that now describes who owns the *noun phrase*. You wouldn't write "brother's-in-law."

3. I borrowed <u>Jamesʼs</u> *truck*, in other words.

   > Even if a singular noun ends with an "s," you add an **apostrophe** and "s" to create a <u>possessive adjective</u>.

4. Technically, it became <u>my sister and Jamesʼs</u> *truck* when they married.

   > With a compound noun phase like "my sister and James," add an **apostrophe** and "s" to the end of the whole noun phrase to create a monster <u>possessive adjective</u> that now describes who owns the *noun phrase*.

5. Technically, my sister *and* James both owned the *truck* when they married.

> If a complicated possessive adjective becomes too hard to follow, however, you can rephrase the idea to show who owns the *noun phrase* without using a possessive adjective.

6. They have a cat named Socrates, so they are also <u>Socrates'</u> *owners*.

> When the noun doing the owning is a proper noun, ends in "s," and is more than one syllable long — which is admittedly pretty rare — you only need to add the **apostrophe** to create a <u>possessive adjective</u>.

PLURAL NOUN PHRASES

With plural noun phrases, you have two options for creating possessive adjectives. When the main plural noun ends with an "s," as most do, add an apostrophe after the "s." When it ends with another letter, add an apostrophe and an "s."

1. <u>Dogs'</u> *best friends* are not people.

> When the <u>plural noun phrase</u> ends in "s," just add the **apostrophe** without the additional "s" to show who owns the *noun phrase*.

2. However, <u>my friends'</u> *dogs* sure act like they are.

> Adding the **apostrophe** without the additional "s" tells readers that you have more than one friend who own the *noun phrase*. If you mean the dogs of one friend, you would use "friend's" as the <u>possessive adjective</u>.

3. <u>The men's</u> *room* is off limits to dogs.

> When the plural noun doesn't end in "s," add the **apostrophe** and "s" to create a <u>possessive adjective</u> for the *main noun*.

C. Plural Letters

You can also use an apostrophe and "s" to make a word plural, but you only do that when the word is a single letter and only when it helps to avoid confusion. This is rare.

1. I got straight A's this term.

   I got straight As this term.

> Use an **apostrophe** and "s" to make a single letter a <u>plural noun</u> when the absence of an apostrophe would cause confusion. Leaving out the **apostrophe** here makes the <u>plural noun</u> confusing because it looks like a different word.

2. It's harder to get good grades now than it was in the 1990s.

> However, don't use an **apostrophe** to make a <u>number plural</u>. Just add the "s" because this is not confusing.

3. I don't have time to listen to CDs or watch DVDs.

  > Just add the letter "s" to make an acronym a <u>plural noun</u>, too.

4. Last week, I studied with my friends, the Woffords.

  > Do not use **apostrophes** to turn last names into <u>plural nouns</u>. People love
  > to do that, but it's a mistake. You'll regret it.

6. Quotation Marks (" ")

In formal writing, quotation marks primarily show readers that the words
you are using come from someone else. They also are used to talk about
words as words, to set off the titles of short works, and to act like air quotes
to make a word or phrase ironic.

A. Direct Quotations

Quotation marks note the beginning and end of actual words from a source
outside the formal paper. Within the boundaries of the two sets of quotation
marks are words coming from someone other than the author. When a word or
phrase that requires quotation marks is used *within* a set of quotes, the interior
quotation marks change from double quotation marks to single.

1. Koeby said, "<u>Public speaking is a lost art.</u>"

  > The **quotation marks** go at the beginning and end of the <u>quotation</u>. Capi-
  > talize the first letter inside of **quotation marks** when the <u>quotation</u> is a
  > complete sentence (or longer).

2. Holly said that the country needed "<u>another Martin Luther King, Jr.</u>"

  > Do *not* capitalize the first letter inside of the **quotation marks** when the
  > <u>quotation</u> is a word or phrase that completes the rest of the sentence.

3. Shaeny agreed: "<u>I love that speech!</u>"

  > If the <u>quotation</u> is a question or exclamation, the punctuation mark goes
  > inside the **quotation marks**.

4. Is Shaeny being honest when she says, "<u>I love that speech!</u>"?

  > If the <u>quotation</u> is part of a larger question or exclamation, the ending
  > punctuation marks go outside the **quotation marks**.

5. Torrey replied, "She is. The repetition of '<u>I have a dream</u>' really got her."

  > When a <u>word or phrase</u> that requires **quotation marks** goes inside a larger
  > quotation, use **single quotation marks** for the <u>inner quotation</u>.

B. Words as Words

Quotation marks also show readers that you are writing about words as words and not as the things that those words represent.

    1. One of my favorite words is "sluice."

> The **quotation marks** show that you are talking about a word and not an actual sluice, whatever that is.

    2. I hate to use the word "hate."

> The first "hate" is you being a hater. The **quotation marks** show that the second "hate" is a word that you maybe don't hate as much as you think.

    3. A common error is the use of "anxious" to mean "eager."

> Again, the **quotation marks** show that we're talking about how to use two words, not the emotions they represent.

C. Titles of Shorter Works

Quotation marks also mark the beginning and end of titles for shorter created works — works that are usually parts of some larger work. Newspapers, for example, contain articles, and quotation marks set off the titles of those articles.

    1. Conrad's favorite song on the album *Let It Be* is the song "Let It Be."

> **Quotation marks** set off the title of a shorter work within *an album*.

    2. Caelin read "Where the Sidewalk Ends" from Shel Silverstein's *Where the Sidewalk Ends*.

> **Quotation marks** set off the title of a shorter work within *a book*.

    3. "Which Rock Star Will Historians of the Future Remember?" is a fascinating article in this week's *New York Times Magazine*.

> **Quotation marks** set off the title of this shorter work within a *magazine*.

D. Ironic Meaning

Quotation marks can also work like air quotes to show that a word or phrase is being used ironically. Formal writing doesn't do a lot of this, but some "scholars" can't help themselves.

    1. I really "love" working in the lab all weekend.

> The **quotation marks** show that the literal meaning of the word has been reversed.

2. Sure, I have a "goal" in life — to avoid anything involving responsibility.

> These **quotation marks** overturn the conventional meaning of the word, as if to say, "That's your word, not mine."

3. *Nietzsche's* idea of "superman" is super overrated.

> With formal writing, **quotation marks** can show readers that this is an important word or phrase from *an outside source*. The **quotation marks** also tend to challenge the validity of that term.

7. Other Punctuation Marks

A. Parentheses ( )

Parentheses work as a team of two to enclose information that is good to know — and usually related to the main idea — but not a part of the main clause.

1. *Standardized testing* (first used in 1682) *has never been an accurate measure of knowledge.*

> The **parentheses** show that the enclosed information is related to the *main clause* but not a direct part of that idea.

2. *I read an article about it in a journal* (Childhood Education) *that my teacher assigned.*

> The information inside the **parentheses** adds detail to the *main clause* that is not essential to that main idea.

3. *The author teaches at a small college in Springfield* (Illinois).

> The information inside the **parentheses** clarifies which Springfield we're talking about. It is not a necessary part of the *main clause.*

4. I can't remember the name of the article because the *dek* (the subtitle that comes after the main title) was very long and stuffed with fancy words.

> **Parentheses** can also provide a short definition of a *word* that is likely to be unfamiliar to the readers.

5. Graydon works for the *Downtown Emergency Service Center* (DESC).

> **Parentheses** can provide an acronym or abbreviation for a *longer term*. By doing this, you can use the abbreviation in future sentences.

6. I gave Graydon *four hundred dollars* ($400) as a charitable donation.

> You can clarify a *written number* by adding the numerals in **parentheses**.

7. In the fourth paragraph you wrote, "*I defiantly* (sic) *believe the author's claim.*"

   You note an error inside a *quotation* with **parentheses**. "Sic" means "thus" in Latin, so it shows readers that you see the error but have not corrected it.

8. In the fourth paragraph you wrote, "*I defiantly* (definitely) *believe the author's claim.*"

   If you're a nice person, you can also use **parentheses** to fix an error.

B. Dash (—)

Dashes can separate, introduce, interrupt, or omit words, phrases, and clauses within a sentence. They can do just about anything, in other words. However, all of those jobs are done more precisely by other punctuation marks, so in formal writing, which requires precision, you should avoid dashes. The only exceptions to that rule are for introductions or interruptions that require extra — some would say dramatic — emphasis.

DRAMATIC INTRODUCTION

Use a dash to separate an introductory noun phrase from an idea about that noun phrase.

1. Unconditional sacrifice —— for some, this is the definition of love.

   The **dash** separates an important introductory noun phrase from the full idea about that noun phrase.

2. Love, love, love —— I am sick to death of reading examples about love.

   The **dash** can also separate a list of important introductory noun phrases from the full idea about them.

DRAMATIC INTERRUPTION

Use dashes to add extra emphasis to an interruption to the main clause. This is more typical in informal writing, so only do this when the interruption really needs to stand out. Otherwise, use commas or parenthesis to separate the interruption.

1. *Standardized testing* —— first used in 1682 —— *has never been an accurate measure of knowledge.*

   The **dashes** before and after the interruption make it clear that this is not part of the *main clause*. The extra emphasis also suggests that this side fact is important. If it's not, then use commas to separate the interruption.

2. *Louis Armstrong's claimed date of birth* — July 4, 1900 — *is probably untrue.*

> When there are commas within an <u>interruption</u>, the **dashes** are better than commas at separating the <u>interruption</u> from the *main clause.* If the interruption isn't worthy of extra emphasis, use parentheses instead.

3. *I prayed* — but dared not hope — *that this day would come.*

> The **dashes** indicate a sudden <u>interruption</u> of thought in the middle of the *main clause.* Dashes make more sense in informal sentences like this one.

C. Ellipses (. . .)

Ellipses are a series of three successive periods that indicate the author has removed words from a direct quotation. They replace words from the original text that the author doesn't believe are relevant to the purpose of the quotation. They thus make the quotation easier to understand.

1. Prof. Slemenda maintains that "<u>The Rabid Bats are</u> . . . <u>well on their way to the highest levels of rock status.</u>"

> The **ellipses** indicates an omission of words within a <u>direct quotation</u>.

2. Slemenda claims that the band "will break even newer ground if rumors pan out about . . . a virtual reality interaction . . . technology, called 'Bats in Your Brain'."

> You are welcome to use more than one set of **ellipses** in a single <u>quotation</u> as long as it doesn't change the meaning of the sentence.

3. Slemenda claims that the band "<u>will break even newer ground</u>" with new technology.

> When you omit words before the <u>quotation</u>, don't add **ellipses**.

4. Slemenda also observes, "<u>The Bats have long been popular among the young</u> . . . . <u>Now that their earliest fans are old, they appeal to all ages.</u>"

> If the omitted words include the ending punctuation of a sentence within the <u>quotation</u>, add an extra **period** to the **ellipses** — but only one, even if more than one sentence ending is omitted.

5. Slemenda concludes, "<u>This is just one example of the sort of dangerous show-manship that</u> . . . <u>suggests that the Rabid Bats are no mere flash in the pan</u> . . . ."

> If you end a <u>quotation</u> before the sentence you're quoting is complete, add an **ellipsis** to the ending punctuation to indicate the author's thought continues in the original.

8. Capitalization

Capitalization means putting an upper case or capital letter at the beginning of a word. Capitalization also helps readers distinguish between proper nouns and common nouns.

A. The First Word of a Sentence

1. **The** White House is a white house.

   > Capitalize **the first word** of every sentence.

2. My uncle always says, "<u>**You** could live in the White House some day</u>."

   > Capitalize **the first word** of <u>a complete sentence within quotation marks</u>.

3. My uncle says that I have "<u>the mind of **President Bush**</u>."

   > If <u>part of a sentence</u> is within quotation marks, only capitalize **words that are capitalized in the original**.

4. However, I don't want to live in the White House: <u>**White** is a boring color for a house</u>.

   > Capitalize **the first word** of a complete sentence that follows a colon.

B. Proper Nouns

Capitalize the official name of any person, place, thing, or idea.

1. The **White House** is a white house.

   > Capitalize the **official name** of a specific place.

2. People who live in **Oregon** are called *Oregonians*, which is kind of boring.

   > Capitalize the **names** of cities, states, countries, and regions of a country. Also capitalize *words that are formed from those names*.

3. **Aunt Anita** said she was my *aunt*, but **Mom** and **Doctor Dye** both said that she was actually my *grandmother*.

   > Capitalize the **names of people**. Capitalize the titles of people when they're used as part of **names** or in place of their **names**, but don't capitalize them when they used as *common nouns*.

4. I suffer from **Trabue Syndrome**, a *syndrome* that includes a grave fascination with whales.

   > In short, capitalize the **official name** of any particular thing. Don't capitalize *common nouns*.

5. I live in **Southern Oregon**, which is *north* of **Northern California** but still part of the **West**.

> Capitalize directions when they are used as **names** or as **part of names** but not when they are used as *general terms*.

6. The <u>State</u> **of** <u>Jefferson</u> is not an actual state, but it too is part of the West.

> However, do not capitalize **short prepositions, conjunctions, or articles** within a <u>name</u>.

C. Major Words in Titles of Created Works

Capitalize the first word and other major words in the titles of songs, books, articles, films, and other created works.

1. I was listening to "<u>Smells</u> Like *Teen* **Spirit**" on the oldies station.

> Capitalize all the **nouns**, <u>verbs</u>, and *adjectives* or *adverbs* in titles.

2. That song reminds me of *The Wind* <u>in</u> **the** *Willows*.

> Don't capitalize <u>articles</u>, **prepositions**, or conjunctions unless one is the first word of the title. Always capitalize the first word of a title.

D. Days, Months, and Holidays

Always capitalize the names of days, months, and holidays, but only capitalize seasons if you are talking about a specific season in a given year.

1. Next **Monday**, I plan to spend most of the day planning out what to do on **Tuesday**.

> Capitalize **days** of the week.

2. I plan to spend most of **October** planning for **Halloween**.

> Capitalize **months** and **holidays**.

3. The **spring** is a great time for planning, but <u>Spring 2005</u> still stands out as the best planning season of all time.

> Don't capitalize the names of **seasons** unless you refer to a <u>specific season</u>.

E. The Pronoun "I"

For some reason, always capitalize the pronoun "I."

1. **I** don't understand why **I** can't capitalize all the other pronouns.

> Capitalize the **first-person singular pronoun** whenever it shows up as a **subject** in a clause.

2. It's probably not because **I** am more special than <u>you</u>, but it does make <u>me</u> wonder.

> Don't capitalize any <u>other pronouns</u>.

9. Abbreviations

Abbreviations are shortened versions of words — like "Dr." for "Doctor" or "km" for "kilometers." They were invented back when everything was handwritten so that copyists didn't have to write out full words, which wasted precious ink, paper, and years of their lives. In this age of computers, the ink, paper, and years of our lives are less precious, so we should now use the full word instead of its abbreviation most of the time. However, many abbreviations are still used regularly in formal writing.

A. Abbreviations with Names

It is acceptable to abbreviate the titles of people that come before or after their names and to abbreviate first and middle names.

1. <u>Rev.</u> *Brown* and <u>Mrs.</u> *Brown* both see <u>Dr.</u> *Smith* in <u>St.</u> *Paul* for their elbow problems.

   When you abbreviate <u>titles</u> before a *name*, be sure to add a **period** to the abbreviation.

2. <u>Dr.</u> *Smith* is a doctor of philosophy in linguistics, as is *Joe Jerry Smith*, <u>Jr.</u>, <u>Ph.D.</u>, his eldest son.

   When you abbreviate <u>titles</u> that follow a *name*, separate them from the name with commas and add a **period**. Some guides prefer no periods with abbreviations for degrees like "PhD." That's fine. Just be consistent.

3. *Joe Jerry* Smith, Jr., usually goes by <u>J.</u> <u>J.</u> Smith to avoid embarrassment.

   You can abbreviate *first and middle names* by using the <u>initial letter</u> of the *name* followed by a **period** and a space.

B. Acronyms

Acronyms take the first letter of multiple words to create a quick abbreviation. Do not use periods or spaces in abbreviations that consist of all capital letters, with only a few exceptions.

1. She tried to teach me the difference between <u>HTML</u>, <u>XML</u>, and <u>PHP</u>.

   Do not use periods or spaces with the <u>acronyms</u> for well-known terms.

2. We really should have bought stock in <u>IBM</u>, <u>ATT</u>, <u>CBS</u>, and <u>GM</u>.

   Do not use periods or spaces with <u>acronyms</u> for corporations.

3. The <u>FBI</u> and <u>CIA</u> are recruiting agents at <u>PSU</u> and <u>MIT</u>.

   Don't use periods or spaces with the <u>acronyms</u> for schools and familiar institutions.

4. Some idiot put a <u>CD</u> in the <u>DVD</u> player, and it wasn't me this time.

   ▌ Don't use periods or spaces with <u>abbreviations</u> for very familiar objects.

5. <u>FDR</u> and <u>JFK</u> were born in the <u>USA</u>.

   ▌ Don't add periods or spaces to <u>acronyms</u> for famous people or countries.

6. <u>U. S.</u> relations with Cuba seem to be warming up.

   ▌ Here's your exception. With the abbreviation of "United States," use **periods** after both <u>initials</u> but without a space in between.

C. Technical and Scientific Terms

In most cases, use technical and scientific abbreviations only when writing technical and scientific papers. Otherwise, spell out the full word.

1. The frog weighed 15 <u>kg</u> and was 25.7 <u>in.</u> tall.

   ▌ Do not use **periods** with most <u>abbreviations</u> of measurements. However, put a **period** after "in" to avoid confusion with the preposition.

2. The frog traveled at 30.4 <u>mph</u>.

   ▌ Do not use periods with <u>abbreviations</u> for commonly used terms like this, "mpg," "rbi," and so on.

3. The frog died at 2:30 <u>a. m.</u> from exhaustion.

   ▌ Use **periods** but not spaces for <u>abbreviations</u> of words used with numbers like "a.m." (*ante meridiem* — before noon) "B.C.E." (before common era), and so on.

4. We dissected the frog, examined the muscles, ran tests, <u>etc.</u>

   ▌ Use **periods** but not spaces with abbreviations for <u>common Latin terms</u>, such as "etc." (*et cetera* — and so on), "e.g." (*exempli gratia* — for example), and "i.e." (*id est* — that is).

In formal writing, do *not* abbreviate normal words such as "through" (thru), days of the week, months of the year, words at the beginning of a sentence, states' names, people's names, (such as "Jas." for "James"), or academic courses (such as "econ" for "economics").

Do not use abbreviations that your reader may not understand, either. If you must use an unfamiliar abbreviation, write out the full name the first time you use the term and then give the abbreviation in parentheses. After that, you can use the abbreviation.

Never use texting abbreviations such as "LOL," "IMHO," or "LMAO," either. That's just embarrassing.

10. Italics

Italics are letters set in a typeface that slants to the right — *like this*. They add emphasis to words or phrases, set off the titles of long works or of vehicles, and indicate non-English words or sounds used in English. If you are writing by hand or are using a typewriter because you still live in 1989, <u>underline</u> words you would otherwise *italicize.*

A. Emphasis

With informal writing, italics create a sound effect. They show readers when to pronounce a word more loudly, as in "You're not my best friend anymore — you're my *worst* friend." With formal writing, however, italics should only be used occasionally to highlight important words when it is necessary to make the meaning clear.

1. The doctor did not say that her elbow *would* not recover but that it *might* not recover.

   The *italics* add extra emphasis to highlight an important distinction.

2. We wondered why they saw a doctor of *linguistics* for tendinitis of the elbow.

   The *italics* add extra emphasis to draw attention to an important term that might otherwise be missed. What were they thinking?

B. Titles of Larger Created Works

Italicize the titles of created works that are complete in themselves. This includes books, movies, music albums, television shows, magazines, newspapers, websites, and computer software. For the titles of shorter works, see the Quotation Marks section earlier in this chapter.

1. *To Kill a Mockingbird* is a great movie but an even better book.

   Italicize the *titles* of books and movies.

2. You can download the *El Capitan* upgrade free from *apple.com.*

   Italicize the *titles* of software and website.

3. "<u>Let It Be</u>" is probably the worst song in *Let It Be.*

   Set off the *titles* of albums with italics. Set off the <u>titles of shorter works</u> within an album with quotation marks.

C. Names of Vehicles

Italicize the names of any specific vehicles that have been given names.

1. We were riding on *The City of New Orleans*, one of the most famous trains ever.

   ▮ Italicize the *name* of a specific train or ship.

2. *Greased Lighting* is the name of my <u>Ford Focus.</u>

   ▮ Italicize the *names* of specific cars but not the general <u>brand names</u> of vehicles.

D. Non-English Words and Sounds

Italicize non-English words and sounds that appear in your sentences.

1. *Radix lecti* sounds so much classier than its English translation: couch potato.

   ▮ Italicize *Latin terms*.

2. A rose by any other name is still a member of the *rosoideae* plant family.

   ▮ The *genus and species of plants* are usually italicized.

3. Because she had grown up in Germany, my sisters and I called our grandmother *grossmutter*.

   ▮ Italicize *non-English words*.

4. When she dropped me, my head hit the sidewalk with an ominous *thunk*.

   ▮ Italicize *words that reproduce sounds*. It's hard to imagine when this would show up in a formal paper.

11. Hyphens (-)

Hyphens connect two or more words to create a compound word that combines the meanings of both into a single unit. Hyphens also allow you to divide a word at the end of a line and continue on the next line.

A. Compound Adjectives

Use hyphens to combine two or more words into a single adjective before a noun.

1. I drove *Greased Lightning* the wrong way down a <u>one- way</u> *street*.

   My <u>fourth- grade</u> *teacher* saw me.

   ▮ The **hyphen** combines separate words to create a <u>compound adjective</u> that describes the *noun*.

2. This <u>fifteen-</u> <u>year-</u> <u>old</u> *bourbon* is fifteen years old.

My <u>tenth-</u> <u>grade</u> *daughter* is in tenth grade.

> The **hyphen** creates a <u>compound adjective</u> when it comes before the *noun*, but when the terms come after the *noun*, they remain separate and unhyphenated.

B. Compound Nouns and Numbers

Use hyphens to combine two or more nouns or numbers into a single term or to combine a noun with certain prefixes.

1. The opening of your essay was a real <u>attention-</u> <u>grabber</u>.

> The **hyphen** combines separate words to create a <u>compound noun</u>.

2. I felt like a <u>three-</u> <u>year-</u> <u>old</u> watching cartoons.

> You aren't limited to combining only two nouns. Here we combine three.

3. I'm <u>thirty-</u> <u>six</u> now, so that was a nostalgic feeling.

> Use **hyphens** to write <u>numbers</u> from twenty-one to ninety-nine.

4. The feeling stayed with me for <u>three-</u> <u>quarters</u> of an hour.

> Use a **hyphen** to write out <u>fractions</u>.

5. Even at this age, I lack <u>self</u>-*control* when it comes to a good essay opening.

> Many <u>prefixes</u> connect to *nouns* with a **hyphen** to create a compound noun. "Self-," "all-," and "ex-" usually require a hyphen. Other prefixes like "semi" rarely do. It's a good idea to check the spelling of compound nouns with a dictionary.

C. Line Breaks

If necessary, use a hyphen to divide words at the end of a line.

1. The road to Silverton was full of <u>pot-</u>
<u>holes</u> that made driving dangerous.

> Make the break only between <u>syllables</u>. Use the **hyphen** to show that the word continues on the next line.

2. In the back seat, my screaming <u>third-</u>
<u>grader</u> begged me to slow down.

> If there's already a **hyphen** in a word, use it to divide the word into <u>parts</u>.

12. Common Problems

A. Excessive Ending Punctuation

In informal writing it's not uncommon to register shock with more than one exclamation point:

> You have to see this!!!!

Similarly, you can register grave curiosity with more than one question mark:

> What were you thinking????

This excessive use of ending punctuation creates a sound effect. It shows readers how emphatically to shout these statements or ask these questions. This type of excess is a problem in formal writing because it distracts readers from the purpose of sentences — to present ideas clearly.

A second type of excess is overusing single exclamation points within an essay, usually because the writer is trying to emphasize the point rather than actually convey the need for a shout:

> Credibility is Rick's problem! He's proven himself to be unreliable! He tells tall tales about Bigfoot stealing his wife! He has a wild imagination, and he lets it get away from him! Rick needs to take responsibility for his actions or no one will ever believe him again!

In formal writing, there may be rare occasions when you appropriately register shock or surprise with an exclamation point, but they really are rare. When you add an exclamation point after many sentences, the punctuation ceases to denote shock or surprise.

HOW TO FIX EXCESSIVE ENDING PUNCTUATION

Use just one period after almost all statements. Use just one question mark after any question. And if, from time to time, the idea of a sentence is so startling or outrageous that you cannot contain yourself and simply must shout, you may use a single exclamation point.

A better way to convey emphasis, however, is to use italics. This is better because italics provides a most precise emphasis. An exclamation point emphasizes the entire idea. Italics emphasize the part of that idea that is most startling or surprising.

1. **Problem:** Why are people so violent???

   > That's a good question, but the excessive question marks make this informal and a little whiny.

   Solution: Why are people so violent?

   > That's better. Now we can focus on the question.

2. **Problem:** We have to change now!!!!!

   > That's true, but all those exclamation points make it seem like you're screaming. That distracts from your point, and it isn't professional.

3. **Solution:** We have to change *now*.

   > Now the idea stands on its own for consideration. Italicizing the *key word* makes it clear that you wish to emphasize the urgency of the moment.

B. Misusing Apostrophes to Form Plural Nouns and Third-Person Verbs

In spoken English, most single nouns become plural nouns by adding the sound "s" to the end of them. Similarly, with third-person singular subjects, most verbs add the sound "s" at the end. In written English, however, it's not enough to just add the *sound* "s." You also have to spell that sound correctly or else you will confuse the meaning of those nouns and verbs for your readers.

HOW TO FIX MISUSED APOSTROPHES

Get rid of them and spell these nouns and verbs correctly.

WITH PLURAL NOUNS

To form most plural nouns, add a single "s" directly to the end of the noun. If the noun already ends in "s" or a something that sounds like "s," such as "sh" or "ch," add "es" to the end of the noun.

1. **Problem:** I misuse my **apostrophe's**.

   > When you add an apostrophe and "s" to the end of a noun, it converts that noun into a **possessive adjective**. Because there's no noun following that adjective, readers think, "You misuse your apostrophe's *what?*"

   Solution: I misuse my **apostrophes**.

   > By adding a single "s" to the noun, it becomes a **plural noun**. Now the sentence makes sense, but it's also ironic now because you're not misusing your apostrophes anymore.

2. **Problem:** The environmental science **class's** went to the landfill.

   The apostrophe and "s" have again turned a singular noun into a **possessive adjective**. The environmental science class's *what* went on a field trip? Its mascot? Its professor?

   Solution: The environmental science **classes** went to the landfill.

   Oh, more than one class went on the field trip. Now we understand. By adding an "es" to the singular noun, it becomes a **plural noun**.

3. **Problem:** My **friend's** help me with math.

   Your friend's *what* helps you with math?

   Solution: My **friends** help me with math.

   By adding a single "s" to the noun, it becomes a **plural noun**. Now we know that you have more than one friend who help you with math.

4. **Problem:** The **fly's** are terrible this summer.

   The fly's *what* is terrible?

5. **Solution:** The **flies** are terrible this summer.

   If the singular noun ends in a consonant followed by a "y," replace the "y" with "ies" to form a **plural noun**.

WITH THIRD-PERSON VERBS

To form verbs that go with third-person singular subjects such as "she," "LeAnna," and "the alligator," add a single "s" directly to the verb. If the verb already ends in "s" or something that sounds like "s," add "es" directly to the end of the verb.

1. **Problem:** The dog **run's** after the garbage truck.

   When you add an apostrophe and "s" to the end of a **verb**, the word sounds right but doesn't make any sense. Is this a contraction? The dog run *is* after the garbage truck? Is it a possessive adjective?

   Solution: The dog **runs** after the garbage truck.

   By adding a single "s" to the **verb**, the sentence now makes sense. It's a dumb dog, and it's running after a garbage truck.

2. **Problem:** *World Weekly News* **publish's** some questionable garbage.

   Because this **verb** can't also be a noun like "run," this spelling makes no sense at all.

   Solution: *World Weekly News* **publishes** some questionable garbage.

   By adding a single "es" directly to the **verb**, the sentence makes sense.

3. **Problem:** The bird **fly's** into the window.

> This apostrophe and "s" at the end of a **verb** makes the verb look like a contraction. The bird fly — whatever that is — is into the window? That *sort of* makes sense, but it's not what you mean.

Solution: The bird **flies** into the window.

> It was only stunned, though, and then it flew away. Anyway, if the **verb** ends in a consonant followed by a "y" — like with the word "fly" — replace the "y" with "ies" to form a third-person verb.

C. Using Punctuation for Sound Effects

The goal of *informal* writing is to write how you speak so that your readers will be able to "hear your voice." To create the right sound effects, then, you use commas to create, short, pauses. You can use periods to create. Longer. Pauses. Ellipses will create the sound of a voice trailing off... These tricks help to make your writing sound like talking, and that "voice" creates a personal connection between you and your readers. With informal writing, that kind of connection is a key to success.

With formal writing, however, the sound of your voice doesn't matter. The ideas in your brain are what matter. If you use ellipses to create a sound effect, you will confuse the meaning of your sentence because ellipses are only meant to do one thing — show readers where words have been omitted from a direct quotation. If you use commas whenever you hear a pause as you read aloud, you will confuse the meaning of your sentences because sometimes you're pausing to catch your breath rather than to show where parts of a sentence begin and end.

In short, using punctuation for sound effects will make your formal paper less effective.

HOW TO FIX PUNCTUATION FOR SOUND EFFECTS

Stop it. That's the first thing.

Then study and practice the actual rules of commas, colons, ellipses, and other punctuation marks. People learn how to do this every day. There's no reason you can't be one of those people.

D. Errors with Titles of Created Works

Most writers don't have any trouble capitalizing the title of a created work because they know it's a proper noun — the official name of the book, play, painting, TV show, movie, magazine, or poem. The problem comes from trying to decide whether to set it off with italics or quotation marks or nothing.

1. I really like *Let it Be*, but I hate "Let it Be."

   ▌ I really like the *album*, but I hate the song.

2. I really like "Let it Be," but I hate *Let it Be*.

   ▌ I really like the song, but I hate the *album*.

If you don't format the title correctly, you give readers the wrong idea about the created work. That's a problem.

HOW TO FIX ERRORS WITH TITLES

The way to make sure you format titles correctly is to keep this in mind at all times:

- For the titles of larger works, use *italics*.

- For the titles of smaller works, use "quotation marks."

Now all you need to know is what "larger" and "smaller" means. It's not usually a matter of length. Larger works are usually works that contain many stand-alone parts:

- A book contains many chapters

- A magazine or newspaper contains many articles

- A poetry anthology contains many poems

- A TV series contains many episodes

- A movie contains many scenes

- A full-length play contains scenes and acts

Smaller works are usually part of some larger works:

- A chapter is a part of a book

- An article is a part of a magazine or newspaper

- A poem is a part of a poetry anthology

Use italics for the titles of larger works. Use quotation marks for the titles of smaller works.

1. My favorite song on *Let it Be* is "Let it Be."

   The smaller work is a song that appears on the *larger work*, an album of the same name.

2. Did you read "Still I Rise" by Maya Angelou in *The Complete Poetry*?

   The smaller work is a poem that appears in the *larger work*, a book of poetry.

3. Many high school classes study *The Odyssey*.

   This *larger work* is also poem, but it's a book-length poem made up of many stanzas, so we treat it like we would a chapter book, a play, or any other larger and more complex work.

4. The main character in *Hamlet* is Hamlet.

   "Hamlet" is the name of a person in the *larger work*, which is a play about that person. His name is capitalized as a proper noun, but it's not formatted with italics or quotation marks when it refers to the person.

5. I love *David*.

   The italics indicate that you love Michelangelo's sculpture, which is considered a *larger work*, and not the David who makes you coffee every morning.

6. "Room for Debate" is my new favorite *New York Times* feature.

   Articles, columns, and website pages all considered smaller works, even if they are very long, and the newspapers, magazines, and websites that publish them are all considered *larger works*, even if they are fairly short.

Word Choice

The words you choose within each sentence allow you to present your ideas clearly and professionally. Whenever you're writing in a formal situation — at school, work, court, and so on — your audience expects you to choose words that are appropriate and precise:

- **Appropriate:** You must choose words that are fitting for a formal audience such as a professor, boss, or judge. They must be respectful, objective, and in no way distracting from the ideas you present.

- **Precise:** Your words must also mean exactly what you think — not just *kind of* what you think — so that your readers will understand your ideas clearly and efficiently.

Some student writers suppose that choosing the right word is a matter of sounding like a boring, long-winded textbook. They use lengthy words and elaborate phrases that they think will make them sound intelligent. But that's not how college writing works. The goal is not to sound like something you are not. The goal is simply to present ideas precisely and seriously so that your readers will better understand them. Careful word choice is one of your best tools for doing that.

1. Appropriate Words

Whether you are writing a research paper for a professor, a report for your boss, or a letter to a traffic court judge, your words must be appropriate for the situation in three important ways:

- Your words must be the correct words for what you mean.

- Your words must be objective toward the topic at hand.

- Your words must be more formal in style.

A. The Correct Words

Every word in a formal paper should be correctly spelled, and it should mean what you think it means. In practice, this means that you should not guess about spelling or meaning — and you shouldn't trust your spell-checker, either, because your spell-checker is also guessing.

Spelling matters. In formal writing, misspellings distract from the idea you are trying to explain. Misspellings make you look stupid — or at best, lazy — in the eyes of a careful reader. That may be unfair, but that's life. If you're not sure about the spelling of a word, look it up in a dictionary.

Spell-checkers are unreliable. If you're typing and see that your spell-checker has found a misspelling, don't let it choose the correct spelling for you. The spell-checker is only looking at the letters in your misspelled word and guessing at what you probably mean. That's why it often offers you several words to choose from. You must always choose the word that means what you are thinking. Consider these spell-checker options for the misspelled word "opinun" (opinion) in this sentence:

A thoughtful opinun is worth sharing.

Suggested Replacement	Actual Meaning	Used in the Sentence
opining	verb, expressing an opinion	A thoughtful <u>expressing an opinion</u> is worth sharing.
opium	noun, a narcotic drug	A thoughtful <u>narcotic drug</u> is worth sharing.
opinion	noun, a reasoned judgment	A thoughtful <u>reasoned judgment</u> is worth sharing.
opine	verb, to express an opinion	A thoughtful <u>to express an opinion</u> is worth sharing.

If you trust your spell-checker's first or fourth guess, the sentence is confusing. If you trust the spell-checker's second guess, the sentence becomes a joke that your readers will tell others over dinner. If you trust your spell-checker's third guess, you get the correct word for this idea. So don't trust your spell-checker. Look up your options and choose the correct one.

Homonyms are words that sound the same when spoken but are spelled differently and — more to the point — have different meanings. You must again make sure you use the correct word for your sentence, or you will confuse your readers and look unintelligent. Consider the following examples:

1. The pirate <u>bares</u> his chest.

   > Here, the pirate <u>uncovers</u> his upper torso. Careful there, pirate. Keep your shirt on.

2. The pirate <u>bears</u> his chest.

   > In this sentence, he <u>carries</u> his treasure chest, which is a thing pirates do.

3. Charlotte <u>defiantly</u> disagrees with the author.

   > Here, Charlotte disagrees <u>with bold disobedience</u>, which seems a little much.

4. Charlotte <u>definitely</u> disagrees with the author.

   > Now she disagrees <u>without doubt</u>, which is still bold but more appropriate to the situation.

If you're not sure which word you need, show enough respect for your audience and their opinion of you to look the options up in a dictionary and choose the correct one. Many common homonym errors are listed and explained at the end of this chapter, so check that out, too.

B. An Objective Attitude

How you discuss your subject must also be appropriate for the formal writing situation.

Your word choice must consider not only the literal, or denotative, meaning of words but also the figurative, or connotative, meaning. Word smay have positive or negative connotations, depending on the cultural, historical, and personal attitudes attached to the words.

Consider the difference between the words "cheap" and "affordable." At a literal level, both words mean that an item or service is inexpensive. However, "cheap" comes with negative associations, which suggests that the item or service is of poor quality. "Affordable," on the other hand, suggests that it's of sound quality and reasonably priced.

Consider the attitudes expressed by the words chosen in the following examples. We'll start with positive connotations, which express a favorable attitude toward the subject:

1. This **cozy** and **affordable** <u>rental home</u> is located in the heart of a **vibrant** <u>urban area</u>.

> These **adjectives** all suggest positive qualities about the <u>nouns</u>, which are also positive terms that suggest comfort and safety.

2. Many <u>individuals</u> have been **unfairly displaced** in this city.

> There's no positive way to describe living without a home, but this phrase suggests that these individuals are not to blame.

Negative connotations express negative attitudes toward the subject:

3. This **cheap, tiny** <u>hole-in-the-wall</u> is for rent in the **chaotic** <u>inner city</u>.

> These **adjectives** carry negative associations, first in describing an apartment and then the location of that apartment. The <u>nouns</u> are both negative, too. The second suggests neglect and poverty.

4. This city is full of <u>bums</u>.

> This <u>noun</u> suggests the individuals are lazy and a public nuisance, putting the blame for homelessness squarely on the people experiencing it.

Neutral associations express an objective attitude toward the subject. This is best for formal writing because it allows readers to make up their own minds about how to view a subject:

5. This **400-square-foot studio** <u>apartment</u> is now available <u>downtown</u>.

> These **adjectives** provide direct information about the size and style of the <u>noun</u> without adding any positive or negative judgments. The <u>nouns</u> are also informational and neutral.

6. There are 1,850 thousand <u>individuals who are experiencing homelessness</u> in Marion and Polk Counties.

> In the same way, this <u>noun phrase</u> provides descriptive information about the subject without pointing blame toward or away from them.

Formal writing almost always presents a judgment of yours to your readers — that's what a thesis is, after all. However, that judgment must be supported with objective information and reasons based on objective information, not with judgmental words.

C. A Formal Style

You must also choose words that are appropriate for your relationship with a formal audience. Just as you would not talk to an ancient and some-what angry grandmother with the same style of words that you use with your closest friends or your three-year-old cousin, you must carefully match the style of words you use to the audience you're addressing. With a formal audience, that means using a more formal or professional style.

Consider the levels of formality in the following examples, first from a cover letter to a future employer and then from a short essay.

1. **You know**, this project manager <u>gig</u> is **basically** perfect *cuz* I **totally** have a <u>handle</u> on that <u>stuff</u>.

   > In this example, some words are **conversational words** that we often use when talking but that add no actual information. Some words are <u>informal nouns</u> that don't define their meaning except in the broadest sense. And one word is a *phonetic spelling* of spoken language, which is just embarrassing in a cover letter. This is a personal and informal style of language.

2. **Well**, <u>I think</u> we all have to fight for freedom *nowadays*.

   > **Verbal pauses** are useful as transitions in conversation, but they don't explain how sentences are related in the way that regular transitions do. <u>Self-references</u> are common in conversation but draw attention away from the subject in written works. *Colloquialisms* bring a folksy sound to a sentence, but that also draws attention away from the information they provide.

You can see that an informal style sounds a lot like conversation. At first glance, that might appeal to you because it's personal and friendly. While that's true of this style, it's also true that a conversational style tends to be more focused on making that personal connection than actually presenting useful information. That makes it inappropriate for formal writing where the whole purpose is to efficiently present ideas.

Here are two examples of a semi-formal style:

3. **Thanks** for meeting with me to discuss the project manager position. I now feel more <u>in the loop</u> about the company's needs and look forward to applying for this position.

   > **Conversational phrasing** within otherwise formal style can make that formal style a little more personal. Similarly, <u>idioms</u> can bring a little liveliness to an otherwise businesslike style.

4. Freedom of speech allows **me** to communicate **my** opinions and ideas without fear of government retaliation or censorship. Therefore, **I'm** well within **my** rights to express grievances with the establishment.

> Sometimes **self-references** are relevant to the subject. The subject of personal rights, for example, includes the rights of the author. Warranted **self-references** and <u>contractions</u> may occasionally appear in a formal paper, but they still make the style more personal and less formal.

In some professional situations — such as an email to a colleague, a letter to your senator, or a blog entry on a company website — semi-formal language is appropriate. In general, however, the personal element of semi-formal style undercuts the professionalism that's expected in most formal writing situations.

Finally, here are two examples of a more formal style:

5. A good project manager fulfills all obligations in a timely, well-organized fashion. <u>My</u> objectives for this project, therefore, are to **assess past records**, **compile data on our demographic**, and **correspond with team leaders**. In this way, the team will be able to develop a more efficient business model for this company.

> This is a much less personal style. Aside from a single <u>personal pronoun</u>, the author focuses on the ideas at hand, providing **specific information** about what he or she will do in this role.

6. Freedom of expression is one of the cornerstones of democratic systems. For this reason **the American Civil Liberties Union of Oregon** <u>is correct</u> in its aggressive protection of **the free speech rights** of **exotic dancers at Cheetah's**.

> This style of language also focuses specifically on the subject at hand. It provides **specific information** about the topic, and even though the core idea is an opinion, that <u>opinion</u> is stated as a direct assertion without using "I think" phrasing that brings attention back to the author.

Using clear, formal writing is appropriate when applying for a job. It's also important to focus on the issues at hand, like why you would do a good job, rather than on your personality. This is even more important in the formal writing required with college papers. With college papers, you've already gotten the job — to explain one idea clearly — and a more formal style is the appropriate way to share that idea with your readers.

2. Precise Words

Precision means choosing the words that mean *exactly* what you think.

General words like "good" and "effective" do tell readers what you think, but they are ambiguous. They can be understood in more than one way — and sometimes in dozens of ways. The lack of precision from a general term prevents readers from being able to correctly interpret your ideas. Yes, they can see that you think freedom is good, but good *in what way*?

Is it good in the sense of moral goodness according to a particular religious code? Is it good in the sense of financial profitability? Is it good in the sense of personal well-being?

We naturally gravitate toward general words because they are so easy to think of and use. They also allow us to not have to do the hard work of being more precise. We can get away with that in conversation where even a grunt will do ("The burrito was like so *ugh*, you know?"). But the formal writing situation expects more from us. It expects us the writers to take the time to choose precise terms so that our readers can spend less time working to understand us.

When you review what you've written and come across a general term that can be understood in more than one way, invest some time in replacing that general term with a more precise alternative that only allows one understanding. In that way, your readers will know exactly what you mean.

1. My sister **met with serious misfortune** today.

   Did she **stub her toe**? Did she **lose her job**? Did she **get shot**? How serious is this misfortune?

2. I missed class because **I wasn't feeling well.**

   Were you **throwing up**, **feverish**, or just **tired and hungover**? All of these would be examples of not feeling well but vary significantly in their severity.

3. The concert was **awesome**. I was <u>very tired</u> the next day, but it was worth it.

   Empty superlatives substitute scale for precision, making the term even more general than it needs to be. Similarly, <u>intensifiers</u> amplify a general word instead of making it more precise. We have a word for "very tired" — "exhausted." Use it. And while you're at it, offer a more precise term that tells us more clearly what you mean by "awesome."

When you're writing about real-world events, ask yourself if the words will create a clear visual image in the reader's mind. If not, then change them.

4. The <u>red</u> **car** drove quickly past the house.

> This general **noun** could mean any kind of that **noun**. The only precision is the <u>color</u>. When I think of a "red car," I picture a mid '80s Corvette. My friend George pictures a Pontiac Vibe for some reason. Tell us which car you saw, so we can picture that instead.

5. The **red** Pontiac Vibe drove quickly past the house.

> I don't mean to be picky here, but there are many different shades of this general **adjective**: cherry red, blood red, ruby red, scarlet, and crimson to name a few. Tell us which shade you're talking about, and that's what we'll picture.

6. The cherry red Pontiac Vibe **drove** <u>quickly</u> past the house.

> This general **verb** and <u>adverb</u> tell us a little about the nature of the car's passage past the house, but not much. How quick is "quickly"?

7. The cherry red Pontiac Vibe raced past the **aqua and orange ranch house** at 74 miles per hour.

> Nice work. You could tell that I was about to complain how the general noun phrase, "the house." This is more precise — ugly but more precise.

The more precise your words are, the more effectively they will show readers exactly what you think. Because a clear presentation of ideas is the primary goal of formal writing, precision becomes one of your best tools for achieving that goal.

3. Common Problems

A. Slanted Language

Slanted language adds negative or positive judgments to your writing by choosing words that come with negative or positive associations. This asks readers to feel positively or negatively about an idea that hasn't necessarily been defended by sound evidence or reasoning. Slanted writing may also leave out or downplay information about other viewpoints of an issue, giving readers a false impression that all the evidence is on the side of the writer. By doing so, the word choice "slants" toward a particular judgment instead of remaining neutral and objective.

Slanted language is a problem because it encourages readers to react to information emotionally. Emotions aren't necessarily a bad thing, but they cloud issues that require a more intellectual, logic-based approach. Especially within argumentative papers, your argument must be presented directly to readers through the use of reasoning and evidence rather than quietly slipped into the paper through slanted language.

In addition, a careful reader will see slanted language for what it usually is — bias on the part of the author — and take the argument less seriously or with skepticism.

HOW TO FIX SLANTED LANGUAGE

To recognize slanted language in your own writing, you must step back from what you've written and look at it with the eyes of a critical reader.

Are your judgments supported by evidence? If not, then you will probably need to replace those terms with more objective ones.

Is your paper hiding evidence to make your ideas look stronger? That's not cool. Let's look at all the evidence and let it lead us to the most thoughtful conclusion.

Is the paper or any of its paragraphs over- or under-emphasizing evidence? Then try organizing that evidence so that equally substantial evidence gets equal emphasis.

1. **Problem:** Although the pit bull has a history of fighting with other dogs, he has been a **loyal companion** to his owner for fifteen years.

   While both negative and positive information is included in the incorrect example, a few **slanted words** slant the information to the positive. Ending the sentence with positive information also adds a slight slant.

Solution: Although the pit bull has a history of fighting with other dogs, he has been with his owner for fifteen years.

▌ Removing the slanted terms makes this sentence more neutral.

2. **Problem:** The **vicious beast** has a history of **picking fights** with other dogs.

   ▌ Not only does the writer omit the positive information in the first example, the writer also uses **slanted words** to create a negative slant.

   Solution: The pit bull has a history of fighting with other dogs, but it has been with his owner for fifteen years.

   ▌ The sentence now includes both positive and negative information and does not include any slanted language. Much better.

3. **Problem:** The **zealots** supporting this **costly** bill **foolishly imagine** that it will provide jobs and environmental benefits.

   ▌ The **slanted words** ridicule the bill and its proponents instead of focusing on the information that would allow readers to come to their own conclusions.

   Solution: Supporters of this bill assert that it will provide jobs and environmental benefits.

   ▌ By using neutral language, the sentence now focuses on the central point that supporters make this assertion about the bill. Now it's time to look at the facts of the bill so that readers can decide for themselves whether this is a sound assertion.

4. **Problem:** At a **bargain** price of $1.5 million, the bill will provide **amazing** job benefits for 800 **hardworking** citizens and replace an <u>addiction</u> to <u>planet-killing</u> fossil fuels with clean, renewable energy.

   ▌ Most of the **slanted language** provides a positive judgment of the bill that has not been backed up by facts yet. When the focus turns to fossil fuels, the <u>negative slanted language</u> gives a negative spin to the information. Even saying that the bill "will" provide the job benefits is a kind of slanting because it states a possibility as an established fact.

   Solution: The $1.5 million bill expects to provide 800 new jobs and a source of renewable energy for the city.

   ▌ The neutral version presents a realistic and straightforward presentation of the idea. Now readers can focus on that idea and decide what to think about it as they take in more information.

B. Exclusionary Language

Exclusionary language is any word or phrase that excludes, devalues, or judges a person or group of people, often on the basis of gender identity, race, color, age, and religion. A prominent example is the so-called "generic he," which means using the masculine pronoun "he" to refer to men or women, as in a sentence like this:

> When a student chooses which class to take, he sometimes bases his decision on how late he wants to sleep in.

The generic he just excluded half of all students from the conversation.

Exclusionary language is a problem for several reasons. First, it causes harm to those it excludes. There is direct harm in the form of the hurt feelings or frustration your words cause. There is also indirect harm from the harmful ideas and value judgments about others that your words perpetuation within your community — and within *you*.

This is also a practical problem for your formal writing because excluding others reduces the effectiveness of your paper. It's likely to anger or irritate those you happen to exclude, and it might do the same with readers who may not themselves be excluded but who also don't approve of excluding others. It also undercuts your credibility as a writer. That makes it much harder for readers to take you or your ideas seriously — even if they should.

HOW TO FIX EXCLUSIONARY LANGUAGE

Fixing exclusionary language begins by you choosing to be careful about the words you choose to describe people and situations. Exclusionary attitudes have a way of sneaking into our thinking and then our language, but when we choose to care about how we phrase ideas, we expose those attitudes for what they are and can avoid the phrasing that perpetuates them.

Is this "political correctness"? Yes. Is that a bad thing? Not when it exposes and contends against attitudes that harm others.

Here then are some practical problems and solutions for exclusionary language.

Problem 1: The Generic He

1. **Problem:** If <u>a student</u> signs up for this writing class without having the prerequisite skills, **he** will have to work twice as hard.

    > Using the **masculine pronoun** to refer to a gender-neutral <u>antecedent</u> excludes everyone who is not male.

Solution 1: If <u>a student</u> signs up for this writing class without having the prerequisite skills, **he** or **she** will have to work twice as hard.

> English doesn't have a gender-neutral singular third-person pronoun, so when the gender-neutral <u>antecedent</u> is singular, your only option is to include both the masculine and feminine **third-person pronouns**.

Solution 2: If <u>students</u> sign up for this writing class without having the prerequisite skills, **they** will have to work twice as hard.

> A more graceful solution is to use a plural <u>antecedent</u> and **third-person pronoun**. English does have a **gender-neutral plural third-person pronoun**.

2. **Problem:** If <u>a student</u> signs up for this writing class without having the prerequisite skills, **he** will have to work twice as hard.

> It's back!

Not-a-Solution 1: If <u>a student</u> signs up for this writing class without having the prerequisite skills, **he/she** will have to work twice as hard.

> You see this in some of the forms you have to fill out, but it's a dated and clumsy way to address the problem. Slashes also belong to informal writing. Use one of the solutions above.

Not-a-Solution 2: If <u>a student</u> signs up for this writing class without having the prerequisite skills, **s/he** will have to work twice as hard.

> Even worse. Out of curiosity, how would you read that out loud? Never mind. Just use one of the solutions above.

Not-a-Solution 3: If <u>a student</u> signs up for this writing class without having the prerequisite skills, **they** will have to work twice as hard.

> The formal writers of the future will probably use "they" as both a singular and plural pronoun (like "you" is now), but in these times of ours, "they" is still a **plural pronoun**. So don't use it for a <u>singular antecedent</u>. Use one of the solutions above instead.

PROBLEM 2: THE GENERIC MAN

Like the first problem, it's also been common to use "man" in place of "person."

1. **Problem:** That's one small step for a man, one giant leap for **mankind**.

> Neil Armstrong's famous words as he first set foot on the moon includes a **exclusionary word** that ignores or devalues half the population. Come on, Neil. You're better than that.

Solution: That's one small step for <u>a man</u>, one giant leap for **humanity**.

> This **inclusive word** is more accurate. The <u>reference to himself</u> is okay, too, because it is also accurate.

2. **Problem:** Who's going to **man** the lemonade stand?

   ▎ The same **exclusionary word** can also be used as a verb.

   Solution: Who's going to **work** the lemonade stand?

   ▎ That's better.

3. **Problem:** Jane is the **chairman** of the committee.

   ▎ Many words use "man" in this general sense of "person." When they do, the
   whole word becomes an **exclusionary term**.

   Solution: Jane is the **chair** of the committee.

   ▎ The **inclusive term** means the same thing and saves you having to type three
   letters. Today, there are many common gender-neutral terms for traditional
   "man" terms — fire fighter, mail carrier, police officer, salesperson, and so on.

PROBLEM 3: IRRELEVANT GENDER DISTINCTIONS

Many gender-based nouns or titles are also exclusionary because they make
an irrelevant distinction between men or women doing the same thing, which
usually suggests a difference in the value of work done by women.

1. **Problem:** Jane is also a promising **actress** at our community theater.

   Solution: Jane is also a promising **actor** at our community theater.

   ▎ The **inclusive term** used to refer to men only, but now it means anyone
   who acts, regardless of their gender identity.

2. **Problem:** My uncle is a **male nurse**.

   ▎ Does a male nurse do anything different because of his maleness?

   Solution: My uncle is a **nurse**.

   ▎ I didn't think so.

PROBLEM 4: STEREOTYPES

Stereotypes are broad and usually oversimplified judgments about individuals
that are based on the general groups they belong to — profession, religion,
gender identity, age, race, color, and so on. When these ideas affect our word
choices, the words become exclusionary.

1. **Problem:** Doctors don't get to spend enough time with their **wives** and **children**.

   ▎ This sentence contains the **exclusionary words** that assume that all doctors
   must be married and have children. It excludes those who don't fit that
   stereotype.

   Solution: Doctors don't get to spend enough time with their **families**.

   ▎ By using a more **inclusive term**, the idea no longer excludes doctors with
   husbands.

2. **Problem:** Salvatore is **confined** to a wheelchair.

> This **exclusionary term** assumes that people who use wheelchairs are trapped in them and defined by them. However, a disability is simply one part of who a person is.

Solution: Salvatore **uses** a wheelchair.

> This **word** is factual.

C. Wordy Sentences

Wordy sentences use more words than necessary to present their ideas. They may become wordy by repeating themselves or by using long phrases when a more precise word or two could do the same work.

This is a problem because it makes your writing less effective. Readers have to work harder to figure out your ideas when those ideas are not stated clearly. They may also become confused by the wordiness and never quite understand your idea.

HOW TO FIX WORDY SENTENCES

The key to fixing a wordy sentence is to closely examine the meaning of each word or phrase. If the word or phrase adds no new meaning to the sentence, it is unnecessary. Out it goes.

1. **Problem:** Technology is something <u>we</u> **as humans** all use.

> This **wordy phrase** repeats an idea inherent in an <u>earlier word</u>. If "we" means the author and readers, then let's hope both are human. Because it adds no additional information, out it goes.

Solution: Technology is something <u>we</u> **all** use.

> It could be argued **this word** is also implied by the <u>earlier word</u>, but it adds the additional information that the "we" includes everyone, no exceptions. It can stay.

2. **Problem: In my opinion, I think that** college should be free of charge to college students.

> These **wordy phrases** mean the same thing, so we know that one can go. However, any time you present an opinion, readers can see that it's an opinion without you having to point out that it's an opinion, so both can go.

Still a problem: College should be free **of charge to college students**.

> These **wordy phrases** don't add any additional meaning to the sentence, so out they go. "Of charge" is already part of "free." And because only college students are paying (or not) for college, we already understand that this applies to them.

Solution: College should be free.

▌ Here's the same idea in just four words. It's a much more effective sentence.

3. **Problem: It is clear that excessive verbiage associated with communication can contribute in great part to the institutional failure of participating parties to transmit information across various media platforms.**

▌ *Oy vey.* Sometimes a sentence is so flatulent with **wordy phrases** that you need to retrieve the idea and start over with new words.

Solution: Wordy sentences impede communication.

▌ Here's the same idea in four words. Nice work.

D. Clichés

Clichés are phrases and metaphors that were once memorable and original ways of expressing an idea, but now — through overuse — they have become automatic and boring.

Clichés are a problem for two reasons. First, they may not capture your idea very clearly. If you write that the college's failed anti-smoking policy is now "dead as a doornail," we get the idea that it won't survive, but what's a doornail? And why are doornails so illustrative of death? The cliché has a nice ring to it, perhaps, but it's not precise or vivid.

The second problem, as you can see from the same example, is that clichés are usually inefficient. This one takes four words to say what could be said just as clearly with one — "dead." Because the cliché has ceased to bring vividness to the meaning of the sentence, it now only brings wordiness. It makes the sentence less efficient.

HOW TO FIX CLICHÉS

In a nutshell, don't use them.

Instead, choose words that mean exactly what you think. If you can do so in a unique and colorful way, that's great. Go for it. Someday your originality will become a cliché for later generations to avoid. Otherwise, just focus on presenting your idea precisely and avoiding all clichés.

1. **Problem:** I encourage you to think **outside the box** for this project.

▌ It's doubly painful to use an uncreative **cliché** to describe creativity.

Solution: I encourage you to think <u>creatively</u> for this project.

▌ This is the same idea in <u>one word</u> instead of three.

2. **Problem:** Dexter slept **like a baby** after his long night of rampage.

> This **cliché** is supposed to mean untroubled sleep, but anyone who's spent much time with babies knows that there's nothing untroubled about sleep that's interrupted every two hours to exchange food for dirty diapers. This **cliché** is both wordy and inaccurate.

Solution: Dexter slept <u>peacefully</u> after his long night of rampage.

> That's better.

3. **Problem:** His clothes **look like they were thrown on with a pitchfork**.

> This **cliché** was a classic three hundred years ago when pitchforks were a thing. Who knows what this even means now?

Solution: His clothes look like they were put on in a hurry.

> This phrasing actually means something to readers who are now unfamiliar with pitchforks.

4. **Problem:** By replacing clichés with your own original illustrations, you can **kill two birds with one stone**: presenting your ideas more clearly and engaging readers with new creativity.

> This **cliché** means to accomplish two outcomes with one action, and it's been so overused that we don't even notice the violence anymore.

Solution 1: By replacing clichés with your own original illustrations, you can **achieve two goals at once**: presenting your ideas more clearly and engaging readers with new creativity.

> Replacing the cliché with a **clear statement of the idea** makes the sentence more direct and effective.

Solution 2: By replacing clichés with your own original illustrations, you can **feed two birds with one biscuit**: presenting your ideas more clearly and engaging readers with new creativity.

> Replacing the cliché with **a new illustration** — or revision of the cliché — gives readers both the concept and a new mental image. These two effects make the sentence more effective.

E. Unnecessary Self-Reference

In formal writing, the focus must remain on your ideas and evidence, not on you the writer. This is why you have been told in the past that you should never use "I" in a formal paper. That's not quite true, but it's at least pointing you in the right direction. If you are part of the evidence in your paper, then you can refer to yourself because your experience is a necessary part of the paper. However, any other self-references are unnecessary.

Unnecessary self-reference is a problem for two reasons. First, it draws attention away from your ideas and evidence. Second, it's informal in style — chatty — and that quickly becomes annoying for serious, careful readers, such as writing professors.

HOW TO FIX UNNECESSARY SELF-REFERENCE

Eliminate statements where you announce what your writing is doing, reflect on the writing process, or refer back to your own writing. No one needs to watch home movies of your mental process. Instead, state your point simply, clearly, and succinctly.

1. **Problem: In this paper, I will talk about** photosynthesis, and **I will hopefully explain** the key steps involved, including light-dependent reactions and the Calvin cycle.

   > These **self-references** have nothing to do with the ideas at hand. It's the author talking about his or her own experience, and because the author is presumably not a green plant, that experience has nothing to do with photosynthesis.

   Solution: Photosynthesis involves several key steps, including light-dependent reactions and the Calvin cycle.

   > Now the point is clear. We know what to expect.

2. **Problem: When we first got the assignment sheet, I wasn't sure what to write about. Then I thought about** my grandma. **I want to talk about her and** her life **and how she** influenced **me.**

   > Whoa. The writer records his or her process in this passage. That has nothing to do with poor old Grandma.

   Solution: My grandma has had a colorful life, and she has also had a huge influence on my life.

   > Now the focus is on the grandma's life story and her influence on the writer — not the writing process or the writer's uncertainty. In this paper, the writer's experience is part of the evidence, so it's okay to refer to him- or herself as the recipient of Grandma's influence, but any other self-references should still be cut.

3. **Problem: I think that** Hamlet's greatest problem is his inability to let go of his dead father.

   > You don't need to preface an opinion by stating that it's your opinion. That's an **unnecessary self-reference** because we can tell from the sentence that it's an opinion, and we can tell that it is your opinion because you wrote the paper, right?

Solution: Hamlet's greatest problem is his inability to let go of his dead father.

> You might feel like you have to add an "I think" to soften a bold assertion like this. You don't. Be as bold as your evidence allows you to be, and don't apologize for that.

4. **Problem: I feel that** Hamlet's greatest problem is his inability to let go of his dead father.

> You *feel* it? Really?

Solution: Hamlet's greatest problem is his inability to let go of his dead father.

> Keep your feelings out of this, too. Focus on your ideas.

F. Jargon

Jargon is wording that is only familiar to people within a specific field where that wording is typically used. Specialized scientific, medical, and engineering fields are often prone to jargon, but no field is immune.

Jargon isn't a problem when it is appropriate for the formal writing situation. If you are only writing to experts in a field, then it makes sense to use the more precise, technical terms that those experts understand. The problem is when part or all of your readers are not experts. In that case, jargon can become incomprehensible and make the paper highly *in*effective.

HOW TO FIX JARGON

When you are not writing exclusively to experts, you can fix jargon in one of two ways. The first option is to replace specialized terms with more universally understood terms. If jargon is unavoidable — like it is at times in a writing handbook, for example — then your second option is to help out the non-experts by introducing the specialized terms and offering a brief definition that will make the terms meaningful for all your readers.

1. **Problem:** I couldn't send an email because I wasn't **getting a ping** to my **LAN.**

> Someone who understands computers may appreciate the **jargon** here, but to others, the meaning isn't clear.

Solution: I couldn't send an email because I **couldn't connect to the Internet.**

> Most people understand this **general term** that means the same thing.

2. **Problem:** Applicants will be provided time to do their **due diligence** after submitting their **LOI**.

> Acronyms are common **jargon** terms.

Solution: Applicants will be provided time to do their necessary research after submitting their **letter of intent** (LOI).

> Even in technical writing, it's a good idea to introduce the **full term** that an acronym abbreviates followed by the acronym the first time you use it. You can then use the acronym in the rest of the paper without fear of alienating a non-expert.

3. **Problem:** Within our **logframe**, the behavior-change activities fall under intermediate result two, but the health outcomes are all tied to intermediate result one.

> Some **jargon** may be truncated versions of a larger term. Other jargon may be truncated versions of longer phrases. This is efficient when the entire audience is familiar with the terms, but it's otherwise it's a barrier to understanding.

Solution: Within our **logical framework**, the **activities likely to change behaviors** fall under **the second intermediate result category**, but the health outcomes are all tied to **the first intermediate result category**.

> Jargon is efficient, so there's a tradeoff when you replace it with **the full terms**. The writing requires more words. However, if that's what your readers need, then there's no getting around that tradeoff.

4. **Problem: I'm dragging a mid-well top to sell my lead, going with a happy fish dying on the pass.**

> Don't even try to decode the **jargon** used in the restaurant industry.

Solution: A medium well-done top sirloin steak is the only item unfinished on an order, and it's running longer than it should be. Meanwhile, the happy-hour fish that goes with it is getting cold in the serving window.

> If you say so.

4. Commonly Confused Words

The English language is full of words that sound or look similar to each other but have vastly different meanings. However, that doesn't give you an excuse to keep making these mistakes. Every time you choose a word that sounds or looks similar to the word you actually need, you end up looking less intelligent than you are, and that makes your formal paper less effective.

The key to avoiding this error is to learn from your mistakes. Your readers will tell you when you make one of these mistakes because they're often funny mistakes. When that happens, make a note and then do a little checking to make sure you have the meanings of "bear" and "bare" figured out.

Becoming more aware of common mistakes like using "accept" when you need "except" will also help you to slow down and check the meanings when you need to choose one of those words. Grammar or spell-checking software won't catch this sort of error, so this is on you — you and your dictionary.

ACCEPT / EXCEPT

The thrift store will **accept** all children's items except car seats.

> **Accept** is a verb that means "to welcome or admit." Except is a preposition that means "not including."

ADVISE / ADVICE

I **advise** you to take your mother's advice.

> **Advise** is a verb that means "to recommend." Advice is a noun that is a recommendation.

AFFECT / EFFECT

Adding chlorine will **affect** the experiment. The effect will be a catastrophic decline in the frog population.

> **Affect** is a verb that means "to have an impact on something." Effect is the noun for that impact.

ALREADY / ALL READY

We already were **all ready** in case the hurricane reached land.

> **All ready** is a phrase that means "fully prepared." Already is an adverb that means "done previously."

CAPITAL / CAPITOL

The **capitol** building in the capital city was paid for with capital raised from a bond measure.

> **Capitol** is a noun that refers to a building where lawmakers meet. Capital is a different noun that refers to the city where that building is located or other things such as monetary resources.

CONSCIOUS / CONSCIENCE / COUSCOUS

Jenny was **conscious** of how much her conscience bothered her when she lied about how much *couscous* she ate.

> **Conscious** is an adjective that means "aware or awake," but the noun conscience mean "an inner sense of right and wrong." *Couscous* is a delicious grain that's often served with stew. It's also a frequent spell-check solution to misspelled versions of the other two words.

EVERY DAY / EVERYDAY

Every day in our modern lives we take advantage of <u>everyday</u> innovations.

> **Every day** is a phrase that means "each day," while <u>everyday</u> is an adjective that describes a noun as being commonplace or ordinary.

IT'S / ITS

It's too bad that Shannon's favorite necklace lost <u>its</u> clasp.

> **It's** is always and only a contraction of "it is" or "it has." <u>Its</u> is always and only the possessive adjective form of the pronoun "it." If you're not sure which word to use, read the sentence with "it is" in place of the word. If that makes sense, use **it's**. If it doesn't, use <u>its</u>.

LOSE / LOOSE

Did you **lose** some of your <u>loose</u> change?

> **Lose** is a verb that means "to give up or misplace something." <u>Loose</u> is an adjective that means that something is not gathered or doesn't fit very well.

PRINCIPAL / PRINCIPLE

The **principal** embodies all the <u>principles</u> of good education.

> **Principal** is a noun that means "the main person" or "the head of a school." <u>Principle</u> is a different noun that means "a rule or standard."

QUITE / QUIET / QUIT

It is **quite** <u>quiet</u> in here, so I won't *quit* writing yet.

> **Quite** is an adverb that means "truly" or "to a large degree." <u>Quiet</u> is an adjective that means "not loud." *Quit* is a verb that means "to stop."

THAN / THEN

If you have more money **than** I have, we can go to the movies and <u>then</u> have waffles and chicken.

> **Than** is usually a conjunction that's used to compare two things. Then is usually an adverb that refers to a point in time.

THEY'RE / THEIR / THERE

They're parking <u>their</u> car over *there*.

> **They're** is the contraction for "they are." <u>Their</u> is the possessive adverb for the pronoun "they." And *there* is most often an adverb that explains where you are doing something.

THOROUGH / THROUGH / THREW / THRU

In a show of **thorough** domination <u>through</u> eight innings, Colby **threw** strike after strike.

> **Thorough** is an adjective that means "complete." <u>Through</u> is another adjective with many meanings, including "from the beginning to the end." *Threw* is the past tense form of a verb that refers to throwing or tossing something. "Thru" is an informal abbreviation of "through" that shows up almost exclusively in the term "drive-thru." Don't ever use this word in formal writing.

TO / TWO / TOO

If you liked the first **two** *Dumb and Dumber* movies, you should come <u>to</u> the third one, *too*. It's *too* funny for words.

> **Two** is always a number that means "one more than one." <u>To</u> is a preposition that shows direction or movement. *Too* is an adverb that either means "also" or "excessively."

WHERE / WERE / WE'RE

We're going to the same place <u>where</u> they *were* last night.

> **We're** is the contraction for "we are." <u>Where</u> is an adverb conjunction that refers to a place. *Were* is the past-tense form of the verb "to be."

WHETHER / WEATHER / WETHER

Whether we are able to attend the concert will depend on the <u>weather</u>, not the *wethers*.

> **Whether** is a conjunction that usually introduces a choice. <u>Weather</u> is a noun that means that it's raining — again — and should not be confused with *wether*, which is a castrated sheep or goat.

WHO'S / WHOSE

Who's going to <u>whose</u> house tonight?

> **Who's** is the contraction for "who is" or "who has." <u>Whose</u> is the possessive adjective form of the pronoun "who." If you're not sure about which version to use, read the sentence with "who is" in place of the word. If that makes sense, use who's. If it doesn't, use <u>whose</u>.

YOUR / YOU'RE

You're not going to put <u>your</u> phone in the refrigerator, are you?

> **You're** is the contraction for "you are." <u>Your</u> is the possessive adjective form of the pronoun "you." A refrigerator is a bad place for a phone.

WORD CHOICE
Commonly Confused Words

116

PART TWO
Research Basics

Research

Research is the process of finding information to help you figure things out. This is important because knowing more about a topic helps you arrive at better conclusions.

In your day-to-day life, even the simplest decision — like choosing which shoes to wear — usually involves a little research. You look out the window or check the weather forecast before deciding on rain boots or sneakers or flip-flops. If your beloved asks you to pick a movie to watch, you check online to see what's available, read a few reviews, watch a movie trailer or two, and then choose the least apocalyptic of the bunch.

In your college classes, the goal of research is also to find information that will help you figure things out. If you're assigned a paper in your history class that requires you to analyze the effects of the American Civil War on the educational systems in Confederate states, you'll need to gather information about those educational systems before and after the war so that you can understand what changed and whether it was the war or something else that led to those changes.

Whether at home or in college, then, the research process follows the same basic process:

1. Ask a good question.

2. Gather and assess information.

3. Form a conclusion.

In this chapter, we'll take a brief look at this three-step process and then introduce you to the basics of formal documentation, which is how you show your readers which information and ideas come from you and which come from other sources.

1. The Research Process

A. Ask a Good Question

Research always starts with a question, and it's a good question if you don't already have the answer figured out from the start.

Sometimes, when information is lacking, these can be questions of fact: What really happened? What's really happen*ing*? With college writing, you more often want questions of meaning: Why did that happen? How was it possible? What causes that? These types of questions require both sufficient evidence and thoughtful interpretation of that evidence.

Sometimes research questions start pretty simple. For example, you might ask your college biology professor, "Do cows really have four stomachs?" The answer might have a lot of scientific information about biology and cud-chewing, but the first part of the answer will immediately teach you something new: Cows have one stomach, but it has four compartments. Answering that simple question now allows you to ask better questions about why and how.

If you already have a strong suspicion about the answer to a question, it's important that you don't then use the research process to back up that idea. That's not gathering information to help you figure something out. That's you defending yourself against better alternatives to your current way of thinking. Instead, you can ask yourself how good that current idea is and then gather information to *test* your current thinking and improve upon it.

You can find a good question in any topic, by the way, even the seemingly boring ones that you're assigned in some classes. No matter what's assigned, do some light exploration of the topic by reading a little about it or talking to your professor until you uncover some little issue or controversy that makes you curious. You will always find something like that because there's never enough information for us to be sure about everything.

Another method is simply to narrow your focus to some small part of a larger topic so that you can get into more detailed information. Once you get into the details, your imagination has something to work with, and that's more enjoyable than trying to make sense of broad ideas and summarized information.

So start asking questions and look for a good one — a question that doesn't have an obvious answer and one that interests you in some way. Once you get moving in a good direction, the rest of the process will go much smoother.

B. Gather and Assess Information

Gathering information begins with your research question. You identify the keywords in that question and use them to search for information. The second step is then to assess the reliability of that information so that you don't rely on *un*reliable information to make up your mind.

IDENTIFY KEY TERMS

To find information on the Internet, you need to search for it with keywords. That's what you use when you need to find a good place to eat. You tell your phone: "Thai food. Inexpensive. Downtown Salem." Your phone then searches the Internet for websites that contain those keywords so that you can gather information from those sites and make up your mind about where to eat.

That's also what you do when you research more complex questions using more reliable sources of information in your college library. You identify the keywords in your research question and then use those words to start searching for information in library catalogs and databases.

Consider this pretty good question, for example:

> What impact has the reintroduction of wolves had on ranching operations in the Western United States?

That question gives us the following key terms:

- wolves

- reintroduction of wolves

- impact of wolves on ranching

- western United States

That's enough to get you started. As you begin to search for information about this question, you can then experiment with the terms to see which ones seem to pull in the most valuable evidence. Perhaps wildlife managers use "restoration" rather than "reintroduction." If so, then go with that.

FIND YOUR INFORMATION THROUGH THE LIBRARY

When you turn to the general Internet for information, you will find that there are some pretty good organization and government agency websites that provide free access to valuable information. However, you'll also find that these are rare exceptions and not easy to track down. So while the general Internet is great for helping you find affordable Thai food, it won't be much help when it comes to answering college research questions.

For college writing, you need to go to your college library. College libraries pay large sums of money for access to scholarly research and high-quality publications that are not available for free on the Internet. These publications get into the deep details of information about topics — the sort of details that professional scholars need to answer their questions. This information is carefully edited and tested by other professionals, too, so it's much more reliable than the average website, which anyone can create with about three clicks of a mouse.

You might be able to use Google or Google Scholar to learn that there's an academic journal called *Journal of Wildlife Management* and that it published an article on wolf restoration in Idaho and Oregon. But without the library access, you'd have to pay $19.95 for access to that article — and that's before you even know how useful it will be with your research question. Two or three of these articles, and we're starting to talk about real money.

If you struggle to locate or access a specific article or journal, your library also comes with librarians, and librarians are experts at finding information. They're also efficient at helping you improve your search terms so that it will be easier to find more and better information on your own. And finally, they are much nicer than their reputation. Rather than shushing you, they will jump at the chance to help you and smooth out any bumps you might have in your research process.

EVALUATE THE QUALITY OF YOUR SOURCES

No matter where you find your information, you must test the reliability of that information and its source before you allow it to influence your thinking. A Google search for "reintroduction of wolves in the western United States" yields almost 400,000 potential sources of information. You don't have time to read them all, so you need to carefully choose which sources to consider and then give them your attention.

A Google search will typically list its sources by popularity, which may or may not yield reliable sites. A library search may offer more reliable sources in general, but it typically does little to distinguish between the timeliness or depth of evidence in one source or another. This means that you have to be the judge about what to read and what to take seriously.

When evaluating the quality of your sources, it's important to keep four key criteria in mind: currency, reliability, authority, and point of view.

- **Currency:** Depending on the information you are looking at, *when* the information was created tells you about its usefulness for your paper. If you're looking into the history of wolf reintroduction, older information may be necessary to demonstrate a trend over time. But an article from 1970 complaining about the lack of compensation for Oregon ranchers whose cows have been slaughtered by wolves is outdated. It may be written by an authority in the field and have reliable information, but those ranchers receive compensation now, so the currency dramatically limits the source's usefulness.

- **Reliability:** To test a source's reliability, you need to examine the way the author is presenting the ideas. Does the author logically connect the paper's claims to properly-cited evidence? Does the author address and treat fairly any counterarguments to the paper's claims? Does the author provide a list of sources? Authors of reliable work will have done these things — just like you have — because reliability is important.

- **Authority:** Smart people are not equally qualified to speak on all topics. This means you'll have to do a little research on your research to understand the author's qualifications to provide the information you find in the source. You can often tell a lot about people's credentials based on what jobs they've had, accomplishments they've achieved, or education they've received. Your research should extend to the publisher as well. By running the piece, the publisher provides its

123

endorsement of the material, and publishers have reputations just like individuals.

- **Point of view:** If you notice **slanted language** or suspect claims in a source, you may need to stop and research it for evidence of a bias. Does the author or publisher have anything to gain or lose based on the findings of the source? Recognizing and questioning your own biases is one of the cornerstones of academic work. Hold your sources to the same standard if you're going to use them in a formal research paper.

TAKE NOTES

It doesn't matter who you are, your memory isn't good enough on its own. As you gather information, you must keep track of what you find from each source.

Keep a separate note for each source you consider, even if you don't like it or don't plan to use the information. At a minimum, jot down the author's name, the title of the work, the main point in your own words, and where you found it, including the page number, if any. With simple notes like this, you won't need to reread sources to track down an important idea or piece of information. That particular headache is a good one to avoid.

C. Form a Conclusion

You've asked a good question. You've carefully gathered reliable information that will help you figure out an answer to that question. Now it's time for you to form your own conclusion, the best answer that you can figure out from the information you've gathered.

This above all is a matter of honesty. Only conclude what your evidence allows. You may want to conclude more than that — to be bold and emphatic because you care so much about a topic, or to tear down the ideas of others because you dislike them so much, or just to show off a little. But formal writing requires objectivity, and that means taking your evidence for what it is and working within those boundaries.

If your evidence only shows that the best answer is that something might be valid, then explain why something might be valid. Back that position up with the evidence that led you there. Be fair and objective. What matters in formal writing is not the boldness of the idea but the honesty of the idea.

2. Documentation

Documentation in formal writing is a system for showing readers which words, ideas, and information in your paper come from outside sources. This is how formal writers give credit to one another.

Failure to document your sources accurately is called **plagiarism**, one of the high crimes of college writing. People tend to think of plagiarism as intentionally stealing the ideas of others. That's certainly one kind of plagiarism, but most plagiarism in student writing comes from sloppy or uninformed forms of documentation. Sources aren't given proper credit because the writers either haven't taken the appropriate care or simply don't understand how to document them properly. So pay attention to what follows. You will be held responsible for understanding it.

Proper documentation involves two intertwined processes: in-text citations and end-of-paper citations.

A. In-Text Documentation

In-text documentation uses small pieces of information within the body of your paper to show readers that an idea belongs to someone else. The information varies with documentation styles. MLA style requires the author's last name and a page number if page numbers are available. APA style requires the author's last name, the date of publication, and page numbers when available. Chicago style uses a superscript number that points to further information in a footnote. In-text documentation points readers to specific works listed in more detail in your end-of-paper documentation.

You must include in-text documentation whenever you incorporate outside ideas in any of three different ways:

- direct quotation

- summary

- paraphrase

No matter how you happen to incorporate the work of others, it's vital that you do so ethically. Be careful to *not* remove or add any words that would change the meaning or otherwise misrepresent the source.

There will always be at least two and sometimes three components each time new material enters the paper. The first part is an introduction to the outside material, which often includes a **signal phrase** that identifies the author. That's followed by the quotation, summary, or paraphrase. And then, if the introduction didn't identify all of the information required by the documentation, there will usually be a parenthetical citation at the end of the borrowed material.

Let's take a look at how this works, starting with direct quotations.

DIRECT QUOTATION

Direct quotation is taking the exact words of an outside source and including them in your paper. This is the most straightforward way to document an idea from an outside source. You repeat the exact words of your source, placing quotation marks where those words begin and end — or in the case of a long quotation, using block formatting to show when those words begin and end. Omit unnecessary words within the quotation by using an ellipsis. Use brackets to improve readability and maintain rules of grammar.

Consider this passage from Marcus Aurelius's "On Getting Out of Bed" for the examples that follow:

> In the morning, when you rise unwillingly, let this thought be present — I am rising to do the work of a human being. Why then am I dissatisfied if I am going to do the things for which I exist and for which I was brought into the world? Or have I been made for this, to lie in bed and keep myself warm?
>
> "But this is so pleasant!"
>
> Do you exist then to take your pleasure, and not at all for action or hard work? Do you not see how all other things in the world are — all trees and plants, sparrows and ants, spiders and bees? They are all working together to put in order their various parts of the universe. And are you unwilling to do the work of a human being? Do you hold back from doing the work appropriate for your nature?
>
> "But one must rest, too!"
>
> Rest is necessary, but nature has set boundaries for this, too. She has set boundaries both for eating and drinking, yet you go beyond those boundaries, beyond what is sufficient. However, in your actions, this is not so. You stop short of what you can do. Thus you do not love yourself, for if you did, you would love your human nature and its will.
>
> Others — as many as take pleasure in their trade and profession — will exhaust themselves for that work. But you value your own nature less than the carpenter values his craft, less than the dancer values his dancing, less than the greedy man values his money, less than the vain man values his applause. These people, when they have a strong attraction to a thing, choose

to go without food or sleep for the sake of the things they care about. Do actions taken for the common good of human society appear more vile to you or less worthy of your respect and labor?

Now let's consider some ways to include parts of this passage in a college paper, starting with direct quotation.

1. **In "On Getting Out of Bed," Marcus Aurelius puts a series of pointed questions to the reader:** "Do you exist then to take your pleasure, and not at all for action or hard work? Do you not see how all other things in the world are — all trees and plants, sparrows and ants, spiders and bees? They are all working together to put in order their various parts of the universe. And are you unwilling to do the work of a human being? Do you hold back from doing the work appropriate for your nature?" (10).

   The **introduction** to this direct quotation cites the author and title as it states the purpose of the quotation that follows. It ends with a parenthetical citation that include the page number in the publication where the quotation appears. It's important to directly quote the author here because the point of the quotation is to share the specific questions from the original text.

2. **In discussing the nature of work in "On Getting Out of Bed," Marcus Aurelius claims,** "Others . . . will exhaust themselves for that work . . . . These people, when they have a strong attraction to a thing, choose to go without food or sleep for the sake of the things they care about" (11).

   This **introduction** uses a signal phrase to identify the title and author. Within the quotation, the first ellipsis shows that a word or phrase has been omitted from the sentence. The second ellipsis, which follows a period, shows that a sentence or more has been omitted.

While this method is the easiest way to bring ideas and information into your paper, it should also be the one you use the least. The only time to directly quote a source is when the words that the source uses to present an idea is as important as the idea itself. The paper should primarily be your explanation of your own idea, so the main way to incorporate outside information should be through summary and paraphrase of that information.

SUMMARY

Summary is taking a set of detailed information and compressing it into a shorter statement that describes what that information means or adds up to. Instead of listing all of the free-ranging wolves in Idaho, for example, you could summarize that there are currently 872 free-ranging wolves in Idaho. Summary strips the original passage down to its meaning, allowing readers to stay focused on your ideas.

To summarize outside ideas or information, begin with a reference to the original work. Describe the author's main ideas in fewer sentences than the original used and without commenting on the content or changing the author's meaning by overemphasizing one idea over another. In each case, an in-text citation must follow the last sentence of the summary. When possible, provide a page number or page range to direct readers to the part of the text you summarize.

3. **In "On Getting Out of Bed," Marcus Aurelius** weighs the pleasures of life against the importance of work, reconciling a love of self with a love for the greater needs of humanity (10–11).

> This **introduction** to this summary notes the original author and title. The summary itself is much smaller than the original material, as you would expect. It doesn't include any of your ideas about the work, either. It just states the author's ideas as clearly as possible. Finally, the summary ends with another parenthetical citation that provides the page numbers where these ideas are explained.

You might think you don't need a citation when you summarize. After all, you put the idea in your own words — and you agree with the idea. Why credit the author for something you wrote and you believe? The answer is that coming up with the idea and gathering the evidence deserves credit. After all, just because you understand how your toilet works, it doesn't mean you deserve credit for indoor plumbing. Always cite the original work. Always.

PARAPHRASE

Paraphrase is appropriate when you need to incorporate an idea someone else has expressed — but in a way that may be potentially confusing to your readers because of technical terms or overly complex sentence structure. The goal of paraphrase is to make the idea more understandable to your specific audience, which is probably different from the audience of your source.

You must always give credit to the original source who came up with the ideas you paraphrase. Just as with summary, putting someone else's ideas into your own words does not make those ideas your own. An in-text citation must follow the last sentence of the paraphrase. When possible, provide a page number or page range to direct readers to the part of the text you paraphrased.

4. **In "On Getting Out of Bed," Marcus Aurelius describes** *the difficulty of waking up* in the morning, exploring the tension between *the satisfaction inherent to work against the satisfaction of personal comfort* (10).

> The paraphrase begins with an **introduction** that notes the author and title while also compressing the original quotation. In this case, the author of the paper has *rephrased the rhetorical questions into statements*. In addition, the paraphrase uses simpler terms, exchanging "rise unwillingly" for "difficulty of waking up." The paraphrase ends with the page number in a <u>parenthetical citation</u>.

When you paraphrase, you should address both the ideas and the evidence the author employs, but your wording of those ideas shouldn't mirror the phrasing or sentence structure of the original. Simple word rearranging is called **patchwriting**, a common problem that we'll look at later in this chapter. You can occasionally include unique or specialized language in your paraphrase, but that information should still appear within quotation marks.

COMMON KNOWLEDGE

Ideas that fall under common knowledge are the only ideas — other than your own — that you don't need to cite with in-text documentation. But what is common knowledge? Once upon a time, finding an idea cited in five credible sources was considered a reliable test for common knowledge. These days, knowledge spreads so quickly on the Internet that this rule is less useful. Instead, it's important to understand what common knowledge means instead of simply being able to recognize it.

Common knowledge is what we call ideas that are no longer up for debate. Society settled the argument and moved on. We didn't know, in the first few minutes after his assassination, who shot President John F. Kennedy. In the hours that followed, authorities had a pretty good idea that it was Lee Harvey Oswald. Ultimately, he didn't stand trial where society could "prove" his guilt or innocence, due to his own assassination by Jack Ruby. As a result, a commission led by Supreme Court Chief Justice Earl Warren had to settle the matter with a thorough investigation that led to a ruling that Oswald, in fact, committed the crime. History now remembers Oswald as the shooter. Until new evidence — not to be confused with new *theories* — comes forward to reopen the argument, Oswald's guilt is considered common knowledge.

When an idea or piece of information is considered common knowledge, it does not need to be cited, even if the knowledge is something you didn't personally know until you came across it. Common knowledge is about society's knowledge, not your own. These are simultaneously the results of our society's creative inquiry and the building blocks that make future inquiry possible. They'll similarly be the building blocks of your own ideas and will be a major part of the logic you use to prove your thesis.

B. End-of-Paper Documentation

End-of-paper documentation provides all of the publication information that readers will need to track down the exact source that you used in your paper. This allows readers of your writing to test your ideas by examining your support. It also allows them to build upon your ideas and further their own understanding. This is how cultures develop knowledge over time, and documentation makes this task much easier.

The documentation at the end of the paper varies among different types of documentation styles, but it almost always includes these key pieces of information:

- author

- title

- publisher

- how you accessed it

It would be distracting to put all this information into the body of the paper, especially in cases where you cite the same work many different times. To avoid that, the relatively brief in-text citations alert readers that you are using material from an outside source and then point readers toward a single, complete listing at the end of the paper.

This is similar to the way hypertext functions on a web page. Highlighted hypertext words show readers that highlighted ideas or information can be found in more detail at an outside source. When you click on the link, the computer instantaneously reads the publication information necessary to bring the reader to the website where the original idea is located. In the same way, the in-text citation shows readers where to look at the end of your paper for information about finding the full source that you are using.

3. Common Problems

A. Poor Note-Taking

Poor note-taking means failing to keep track of each piece of information and where it comes from *as you gather it*. In the moment, your brain can remember clearly where each piece of information comes from because it just happened. Over time, memories fade and quietly disappear.

This is a problem because formal writing requires accurate and precise handling of information. If you don't have accurate and precise notes, your paper won't deliver accurate and precise information. Your brain will try to help out with its fading memories, but that will only make things worse by bringing broad summaries and vague references to "studies" or "reports" without any in-text citations of where that information came from. Conscientious students may simply leave out the evidence they can no longer cite, but that's not a big improvement. Their papers will contain little outside evidence, which makes the papers look like guesswork rather than well-supported ideas.

Poor note-taking is also a problem because the lack of accurate notes often results in incorrect or absent documentation. Without accurate documentation, readers will not be able to track down your resources and use them to build upon your work.

HOW TO FIX POOR NOTE-TAKING

Use a note-taking method — *any* note-taking method — that allows you to connect useful ideas and information to the sources they come from. It can be a spreadsheet. It can be notes on your phone. One of the easiest and best systems is still the little index cards that your grandparents used when they were reading this book. The key, though, is to just do *something*.

The results will be dramatic:

1. **Problem:** Sexual harassment is a big problem in lots of places. Women say they get in trouble when they report problems. **The head of Fox News got fired** for sexual harassment because it is illegal (<u>"Sexual Harrassment"</u>).

   > You read over a couple of sources on your topic, but wrote nothing down. Now your paper is due in a few hours, so you try to pull together what you remember, but you have very little to go on. You find <u>an article from a government website</u> that describes sexual harassment and stick it in. But you lack specific examples, specific points, or citations to back up your thinking. Your ideas are disorganized, and **you're getting facts wrong**. Things are not looking good.

Solution: Even though it is illegal ("Sexual Harassment"), recent news accounts make it clear that sexual harassment remains a big issue in the workplace. In 2016, it became clear that the problem was rampant at Fox News. Former news anchor Gretchen Carlson sued Fox News Chairman Roger Ailes for sexual harassment (Koblin). Within a month, an internal investigation at Fox News found at least six other women attesting to Ailes harassing them, and he resigned (Rutenberg et al., "Internal Inquiry"). Days after his resignation, floods of reports of similar behavior by men across the Fox News network came out in a *New York Times* investigation (Rutenberg et al., "At Fox"). The most common reason that the 18 women interviewed cited for not reporting harassment was "embarrassment and fear of retribution."

> You must have taken good notes this time. Nice work. You have specific sources and concrete examples to help you make specific points and prove a claim. Careful note-taking not only helps you remember where you got your information, it can help you see why the information is particularly interesting and help you realize other research you might need to do. In this case, it was surprising that such a prominent organization has this happening all the time and that people are not reporting it. Specific points and the examples that illustrate them are your tickets to success with a researched argument like this.

B. Missing Citations

Missing citations are any in-text and end-of-paper citations that fail to show up along with the outside ideas and information. Any quotation, summary, or paraphrase from an outside source that is not common knowledge must be cited. It doesn't matter if you put it into your own words. *Any* quotation, summary, or paraphrase from an outside source that is not common knowledge must be cited.

Omitting citations is a problem because it's dishonest, which is bad for your soul, and because it's plagiarism, which is bad for your academic career. It's also unprofessional to not give credit where credit is due.

HOW TO FIX MISSING CITATIONS

The way to fix uncited information is to correctly cite it in the body of the paper and with an end-of-paper citation for that same source. Taking good notes will help with this.

1. **Problem:** The famous Japanese family film *My Neighbor Totoro* quickly reveals that it is different from American family movies. A dad and two little girls move into a house in the country and go about their lives among the people and spirits of their new neighborhood. That's essentially it. American films seem

to focus on adventure, conflict, and danger. This movie depends on situation instead of a plot, and suggests that the wonder of life and the resources of imagination supply all the adventure you need.

> You've clearly seen the movie and have an observation about what it's like. You found a great source that helps you expand on your idea — but you aren't introducing the idea in this paragraph at all. This makes it look like you are pretending to be the one who came up with these thoughts, which in fact come from Roger Ebert. Not only that, it looks like you're pretending that you wrote that final sentence, which Ebert actually wrote.

Solution: The famous Japanese family film *My Neighbor Totoro* quickly reveals that it is different from American family movies. A dad and two little girls move into a house in the country and go about their lives among the people and spirits of their new neighborhood. That's essentially it. In his review of the movie, Roger Ebert notes that **American films seem to focus on adventure, conflict, and danger**, but not this film: "This movie depends on situation instead of a plot, and suggests that the wonder of life and the resources of imagination supply all the adventure you need."

> Now we see what you wrote and thought and then what your source wrote and thought. When you started writing about Ebert's ideas, you cited him with an introductory signal phrase and then, after you **paraphrased** part of his ideas, you put quotation marks around his actual words. Because this is an online source without page numbers, you didn't need to include a parenthetical citation with page numbers.

C. Unquoted Quotations

Whenever you use the exact words from an outside source, you must put those words inside quotation marks and cite the author in the text of the paper. If you use those words without correctly identifying them or citing them, you're taking two things that don't belong to you — the other author's idea *and* the other author's exact words.

This is a problem because it's dishonest, because it's plagiarism, and because it's unprofessional.

HOW TO FIX UNQUOTED QUOTATIONS

To fix this error, you have two options. First, if the words are really great and deserve to be quoted, you can show that you are quoting by placing quotation marks around the exact words you are using and then citing your source. In most cases, however, it's the ideas or information that matter more than the phrasing. When that's the case, your best option is to summarize the information or paraphrase the idea and then cite that correctly.

1. **Problem:** Clutter is a problem in many people's households. The **best criterion for choosing what to keep and what to discard is whether it will make you happy, whether it will bring you joy**.

   > You started with your own idea, but you then used **someone else's idea and words** without identifying the author or putting the words into a quotation. The words in the second sentence are from a best-selling book, *The Life-Changing Magic of Tidying Up* by Marie Kondo.

   Solution 1: Clutter is a problem in many people's households: "The best criterion for choosing what to keep and what to discard is whether it will make you happy, whether it will bring you joy" **(Kondo 42)**.

   > The words are the same as before, but now you've noted the quotation and cited the author with a parenthetical citation. That's the art of the research paper — not showing what an expert you are but using your sources honestly and displaying your own creativity and critical thinking in applying them.

   Solution 2: Clutter is a problem in many people's households. **In her best-selling book, *The Life-Changing Magic of Tidying Up*, Marie Kondo** has a solution for this problem that is radical — get rid of everything you don't love. She writes, "The best criterion for choosing what to keep and what to discard is whether it will make you happy, whether it will bring you joy" (42).

   > This solution also credits the author but uses the **introductory signal phrase** to introduce her, helping the reader understand why Kondo is someone to listen to on this matter. The parenthetical citation at the end adds the page number of the quotation.

2. **Problem:** However, the obsession with clearing up clutter can also lead to self-righteousness about clean spaces. **People suggest that learning to keep your surroundings in order and take responsibility for your messes is important to becoming a competent, socially mature adult**. But **there is no correlation between keeping a neat room and leading a functional, goal-oriented life**.

   > You have a further point to make, that messiness isn't necessarily a bad thing, and you've found someone to help you make that point, but you use **her ideas** without giving her credit.

   Solution: However, this cultural obsession with clearing up clutter can also lead to self-righteousness about clean spaces. One tidy mother explored this issue in an essay in the *New York Times* because her daughter was a messy, creative girl, and she tried to figure out why this drove her crazy: "People suggest that learning to keep your surroundings in order and take responsibility for your messes is important to becoming a competent, socially mature adult" (Batalion). After much research, Batalion concludes that "there is no correlation between keeping a neat room and leading a functional, goal-oriented life."

> Now you are <u>giving credit</u> where credit is due, and your paragraph is more interesting. Giving credit to a source does not make you look like you can't come up with ideas by yourself. It shows that you are playing in the world of ideas and giving credit to the other players you found to be on your team.

D. Patchwriting

Patchwriting is paraphrasing someone in a way that too closely mirrors the punctuation, vocabulary, and sentence structure of the original author. Rather than providing a precise restatement of the original idea, patchwriting uses most of the original wording, only swapping out a few words — the patches.

This isn't as big of a problem as unquoted quotations, which take 100 percent of the original author's words without given credit, but taking 80 or 90 percent of the original author's words without giving credit is still a Class C misdemeanor.

HOW TO FIX PATCHWRITING

There are many ways to change the grammar and sentence structure of paraphrased material while maintaining the original meaning. Start by putting the core idea into your own, unique words. Then set aside the original and just explain that idea more clearly.

The real challenge is feeling confident enough in your own writing to do that without leaning so heavily on your outside sources. It's reasonable for you to feel shy about your abilities when you are new to this style of writing, but you have to get over that, and the only way to get over that is with practice. So suck it up. Do your own work. Pretty soon you'll feel good about it, too.

Even if you don't feel confident, the surest way to avoid patchwriting is to condense the original passage into a smaller summary of thought. If the passage is a paragraph long, make it a sentence. If it is two paragraphs, make it one paragraph. And then give credit where credit is due.

Problem:

Obama: "Barack and I were raised with so many of the same **values: that you work hard for what you want in life; that your word is your bond and you do what you say** you're going to do; **that you treat people with** dignity and **respect**, even if you don't know them, and even if you don't agree with them."

Trump: "From a young age, my parents impressed on me the <u>values that you work hard for what you want in life, that your word is your bond and you do what you say</u> and keep your promise, <u>that you treat people with respect</u>."

> Notice how close the sentence patterns and word clusters in Melania Trump's 2016 speech are to Michelle Obama's speech from eight years earlier. This is patchwriting.

Solution: As Michelle Obama has said of her own upbringing, from a young age, my parents impressed on me a strong work ethic, a sense of personal responsibility, and respect for others.

> These are the same common sentiments Trump was trying to express, but now they are clearly different from Obama's phrasing. The solution uses some alternate phrases ("work ethic" instead of "work hard for what you want") and by condensing some similar ideas (like combining the ideas of keeping your word and following through on promises into "personal responsibility"). As a result, this version is not only distinctive from the original, it's also more concise. Still, it's best to cite the source to avoid any embarrassing claims of plagiarism.

E. Quote Bombs

Just as a photo bomb is when a person jumps into a photo where he or she doesn't belong, a quote bomb is when a quotation occurs in a paragraph where it doesn't belong. The quotation (or summary or paraphrase) is typically related to the topic in some way but doesn't support the central idea of the paragraph.

Seeing a stranger making a funny face at the camera in your precious family photos is distracting. Similarly, a quote bomb will distract from the specific idea the paragraph is attempting to express.

HOW TO FIX QUOTE BOMBS

It's hard to fix a photo bomb, but in writing, it's fairly easy to fix a quote bomb. The delete key leaves behind no trace of what came before. With copy and paste, you might even be able to relocate that quotation to somewhere more appropriate.

Problem: Running marathons requires hard work and a life-long dedication. **"At times, Rio must have felt impossibly far away to Linden, but she maintained her confidence even at the beginning of what turned out to be a year away from racing"** (Heald 37). But with the right mindset, runners can overcome any obstacle and achieve their goals.

> This **quotation**, from a 2016 *Runner's World* article by Oregon writer Michael Heald, is cited, which is nice, but why is it here? Who is "Linden" and what is "Rio," and what do either have to do with the hard work and right mindset of running marathons? No quote is an island. Either this quote doesn't belong here, or we need a better introduction to connect it to this passage.

Solution 1: Running marathons requires hard work and a life-long dedication. But with the right mindset, runners can overcome any obstacle and achieve their goals.

> Because this paragraph is simply making general statements, the Heald quotation is unnecessary. It's a nice enough quotation, but it's not directly tied to our purpose here, so we can cut it altogether. Problem solved.

Solution 2: Running marathons requires hard work and a life-long dedication, even through hard times like training delays and injuries. **This was the case for Olympic marathon runner Desiree Linden, who suffered an injury while training for the Rio Olympics.** In a profile of Linden in *Runner's World*, <u>Michael Heald</u> explains that "at times, Rio must have felt impossibly far away to Linden, but she maintained her confidence even at the beginning of what turned out to be a year away from racing" (<u>37</u>). With this kind of determined mindset, runners like Linden can overcome any obstacle and achieve their goals.

> But perhaps our purpose is less general and more complex. Perhaps we're writing about the kinds of obstacles a runner might need to overcome with determination, and we need an example of that. The Heald quotation provides that, so we can use it if we connect it more directly to the idea at hand. In this version, we have not only provided **context** for the Heald quotation, we have also enriched the passage by adding more information regarding our own topic. And, as required by law, we've <u>cited</u> our source.

MLA Style

The Modern Language Association (MLA) is a professional organization that supports disciplines in the humanities, including literature, art, music, philosophy, religion, and foreign languages. MLA style is a set of agreed-upon guidelines for scholars in these disciplines to follow when writing for classes or for publication. When we follow these guidelines, our readers can easily gather important reference information like who wrote something and on what pages, while remaining focused on the ideas in the writing.

Most of the MLA disciplines study visual or printed texts from throughout history, and MLA style reflects that focus. In the body of papers, MLA cites the author and page number from the text rather than the author and date of publication. That's because knowledge is considered timeless in the humanities. Therefore, when you talk about the ideas you cite in MLA, you use present-tense verbs. To the MLA scholar, the lioness forever "pounces" upon Chronos on page 69 of Jennifer Egan's *A Visit from the Goon Squad*. Furthermore, a scholar's interpretation of that pounce is as valid now as it would have been five years ago or as it will be five, ten, or even fifty years from now.

MLA style consists of three main categories — in-text citations, lists of works cited, and paper formatting. In the body of the paper, you will cite outside sources with MLA-style in-text citations. At the end of your paper, you will add an MLA-style bibliography called a Work(s) Cited page. The paper as a whole uses MLA-style formatting to set margins, line spacing, page-numbering, and so on.

Think of MLA style as a filter. When your ideas pass through this filter, your paper will conform to MLA guidelines and emerge looking like every other MLA manuscript. The two things *different* about your paper will be the two most important ingredients — the idea you present and how you explain it to your readers.

1. In-Text Citations

In-text citations show readers that an idea belongs to someone other than the author and usually show where that idea can be found within the original source. They do so by providing readers with the author's last name and, if available, the page number where the information or ideas came from.

The two places where you cite your sources in the text are in the introduction of that information and in a trailing **parenthetical citation**. The introduction might consist of an introductory statement or a **signal phrase**, and depending on the size of any direct quotations, some punctuation will also be involved.

It's typical to name the author of the work in this introduction, but you can cite the author and page number in the introduction, or you can cite both in the parenthetical citation. The thing you can't do is cite the information more than once. If you put it in the introduction, don't put it in the parentheses.

A. Author in the Introduction

1. <u>Shamah</u> **argues that it's not just one specific or even one type of out-of-school activity that matters:** "Out-of-school activities of all kinds appear to support the development of a sense of purpose" (56).

   The author's <u>last name</u> in the **introduction** tells us who this idea belongs to. The number inside the parenthetical citation tells us which page of the journal this idea appears on. Notice that **the period** goes after the citation and not inside the quotation marks, even if the original quoted material used a period there.

2. **In his review of** *Mouse Guard: Winter 1152 for PopMatters*, <u>Walter Biggins</u> *writes*, "Because a talking animal wearing human clothes is a ridiculous concept to begin with, most funny-animal comics tend toward exaggeration."

> When there's no page number, as with online articles, you only need to report the author's <u>name</u>. If you do that in the **introduction**, you won't have a parenthetical citation. Notice that now the **period** is tucked inside the closing quotation marks.

3. **Biggins writes that** "most funny-animal comics tend toward exaggeration."

> When you quote just a part of a sentence, and when that direct quotation completes the sentence, there's no punctuation between the **introduction** and the quotation unless it's already there for other reasons. In the same way, the first letter of the quotation should be lowercase unless it's uppercase for other reasons.

4. **As <u>Shamah</u> has shown**, there's a clear relationship between out-of-school activities and a student's sense of purpose (56).

> The same patterns apply to paraphrased material. If you name the <u>author</u> in an **introduction**, don't put that information in the parenthetical citation.

B. Author Absent from the Introduction

If you don't cite the author in an introduction, the last name must then be mentioned in the parenthetical citation:

1. It's not just one specific or even one type of out-of-school activity that matters: "Out-of-school activities of all kinds appear to support the development of a sense of purpose" (**<u>Shamah</u>** 56).

> Here the **last name** and page number go inside the <u>parenthetical citation</u>. This information can be in the introduction or the parentheses but not both.

2. Most comic artists understand and maximize the conventions of their form: "Because a talking animal wearing human clothes is a ridiculous concept to begin with, most funny-animal comics tend toward exaggeration" (**<u>Biggins</u>**).

> When there's no page number to cite and the author is not named in the introduction, the author's **last name** is the only information in the <u>parenthetical citation</u>.

3. At least one expert claims that there's a clear relationship between out-of-school activities and a student's sense of purpose (**<u>Shamah</u>** 56).

> And it's the same deal with citations of paraphrases or summaries. If you don't name the **author** in an introduction, then put the **last name** in the <u>parenthetical citation</u>.

C. More than One Work by an Author

If you use more than one work by the same author, the author's last name will no longer point to just one work on the works cited list. You must add a reference to the title to the in-text citation to properly distinguish which work you mean. Use the full title if it's short, and use key words if it isn't short.

1. In support of this position, **Shamah** asserts that out-of-school activities "appear to support the development of a sense of purpose" (<u>"Supporting"</u> 56).

   > The author's **last name** is in the introduction, so only the shortened title and page number appear in the <u>parenthetical citation</u>. Because this is a short work, the title is marked with quotation marks, but because the full title is kind of long, we only use a key word to identify it.

2. It's not just one specific or even one type of out-of-school activity that matters: "Out-of-school activities of all kinds appear to support the development of a sense of purpose" (**Shamah, "Supporting"** 56).

   > If you don't name the author in the introduction, the author's last name, a shortened title of the work, and a page number all go inside the <u>parenthetical citation</u>. Note that in this case, you need to separate the **name** and **title of the article** with a **comma**.

3. Most comic artists understand and maximize the conventions of their form: "Because a talking animal wearing human clothes is a ridiculous concept to begin with, most funny-animal comics tend toward exaggeration" (*Biggins*, **"Coffee Table Mice"**).

   > Because this is a short **title**, we put **the full title** inside the parentheses. The **comma** remains between the *author* and **title** even though there are no page numbers for this online work.

4. At least one expert claims that there's a clear relationship between out-of-school activities and a student's sense of purpose (Shamah, "Supporting" 56).

   Shamah claims that there's a clear relationship between out-of-school activities and a student's sense of purpose (<u>"Supporting"</u> 56).

   > And it works the same way with <u>citations</u> of paraphrases or summaries.

D. Authors with the Same Last Name

When you use works written by different authors who happen to have the same last name, use the first initial of the author to make it clear which of the works you're referring to on your works cited page.

1. <u>D.</u> **Shamah** claims that there's a clear relationship between out-of-school activities and a student's sense of purpose ("Supporting" 56).

   It's not just one specific or even one type of out-of-school activity that matters: "Out-of-school activities of all kinds appear to support the development of a sense of purpose" (<u>D.</u> **Shamah**, "Supporting" 56).

   > Whether it's in the introduction or the parenthetical citation, include the <u>first initial</u> with the **last name**. Of course, that only works if the other author with the same last name has a different first initial.

2. At least one expert claims that there's a clear relationship between out-of-school activities and a student's sense of purpose (*Devora* **Shamah**, "Supporting" 56).

   > If the first initial is also shared with a different author, write out the author's entire *first name* and **last name**.

E. Two or More Authors

For citing multiple authors, follow the same basic rules that you use with one author. List the authors as they are listed in the original citation — not alphabetically. The first author listed is considered the primary author.

1. Growing up in a small town affords some important benefits to kids. <u>According to</u> **Shamah** and **MacTavish**, "The smallness and safety of rural communities promotes the development of place-based knowledge among the youth" (1).

   > The <u>introduction</u> maintains the original order of the authors' **names**.

2. Growing up in a small town affords some important benefits to kids: "The smallness and safety of rural communities promotes the development of place-based knowledge among the youth" (**Shamah** *and* **MacTavish** 1).

   > Note that the **last names** are separated with the *coordinating conjunction* "and" when there are two authors.

3. Things are not always as they seem: "On the surface of things, the place seems to be about as far from the history of race in America as one could get" (**Baldwin, Shatz,** *and* **Banks** 250).

   Baldwin, Shatz, *and* **Banks** write that this city appears to be "about as far from the history of race in America as one could get" (250).

   > With three or more authors, list all their **names** and separate each **name** with a **comma**, adding the word "and" before the final last name.

4. George Orwell, never a healthy man, wrote his masterpiece *Nineteen Eighty-Four* in the last years of his short life while struggling with tuberculosis. Scholars suggest that the dark mood of the book is in part a reflection of the strain he was under while grappling with this terrible illness that ultimately led to his death (**Symons xix; McCrum**).

> When the same idea is conveyed by two different works, separate the two **citations** with a **semicolon** within a single set of parentheses.

F. Organization or Agency as Author

When the ideas you cite are found within official materials coming from an organization or government agency and are not attributed to a specific author, cite the organization or government agency as the author.

1. According to the **U.S. Census Bureau**, "The official poverty rate in 2006 was 12.3 percent, down from 12.6 percent in 2005."

   The **U.S. Census Bureau** reported that the official poverty rate dropped by 0.3% between 2005 and 2006.

   > The **name** of the government agency is cited in the introductory signal phrase just like an individual author would be cited.

2. The official poverty rate dropped by 0.3% between 2005 and 2006 (**U.S. Census Bureau**).

   The economic recovery was starting to show results: "The official poverty rate in 2006 was 12.3 percent, down from 12.6 percent in 2005" (**U.S. Census Bureau**).

   > When an organization or agency is not named in the introduction, put that **name** in the parenthetical citation. If this were a print source, the page number would follow the **name**.

G. Unknown Author

If you don't know the author of your source, and it isn't an organization or government agency, use the title of the work (if it's short) or a key word from the title (if it's not short) in your citation. Many newspaper articles are published without a named author.

1. The original source material deserves a close examination. Grendel is described as a "brutish demon who lived in darkness" (***Beowulf* 4**).

   Grendel is described in ***Beowulf*** as a "brutish demon who lived in darkness" (4).

   > The author of the epic poem *Beowulf* is unknown, so we use the **title** of the work where the author would typically go in either the introduction or the parenthetical citation. Because this is a long work, the title is italicized.

2. Ten years ago, the City of Portland set in motion an ambitious plan to end homelessness in this city, but today there are even more homeless men, women, and children living in Portland (**"Crisis"**).

As reported in **"Crisis,"** there are more homeless men, women, and children living in Portland than there were ten years ago — in spite of the city's ten-year plan to end homelessness.

> The author of this online news article is unknown, so we use a **key word** in place of the full title. Because this is a shorter work within a larger publication, the title is marked by quotation marks.

H. Indirect Citation

Within her article, Dr. Shamah cites an idea from a book by William Damon. If you want to cite the same idea from Damon that Dr. Shamah cites in her article, what do you do?

You go to the library, of course, and get Damon's book, that's what you do. If it has *one* idea worth incorporating into your paper, it might have more and better ideas for you to consider. However, if you don't have time to get that book or your library can't access it, you can use an indirect citation. Give credit in the introduction to the person who came up with the idea, and use the parenthetical citation to show readers that this came from within one of the works on your works cited list.

1. **Damon** claims that "finding one's place in the world is a developmental process that spans the life course" (qtd. in *Shamah* 45).

> The **indirectly cited author** appears in the introductory signal phrase while *the author whose work you actually read* appears within the citation. Note that you must include the phrase "qtd. in" — quoted in — before the author's name in the citation.

2. At least one expert claims that "finding one's place in the world is a developmental process that spans the life course" (**Damon,** qtd. in *Shamah* 45).

> If the **indirectly cited author** is not mentioned in the introduction, then **that author** and *the author whose work you read* both go in the parenthetical citation. Note where the **comma** goes, too.

I. Block Quotations

Use block quotations for those rare occasions when you must quote more than three lines of poetry, more than four lines of prose, or dialogue between characters. You still need to introduce the quote in your own words, but the quotation is separated from your text by more space than you're used to.

1. Roy K. Humble argues for the use of note cards:

> If you're using note cards, you simply unleash their awesome, low-tech power. You lay the note cards on the dinette table and move them around. I know that doesn't sound like much, but trust me — it's awesome and powerful. Note cards allow you to visually arrange the evidence into its natural patterns. (97)

Despite the logic of the argument he presents, many students refuse to try the technique.

> Block quotations use formatting instead of quotation marks to show that this is a direct quotation. Typically, you should introduce a block quotation with a statement and a **colon**. Indent a block quote one inch from the left margin. Unlike other in-text citations, the parenthetical citation sits just *outside* the **ending punctuation** of the block quotation. If the paragraph continues after the block quote, do not indent the sentence that follows the block quote. That shows readers that this enormous quotation is supporting information within a longer paragraph.

2. There are good reasons to use note cards while researching:

> If you're using note cards, you simply unleash their awesome, low-tech power. You lay the note cards on the dinette table and move them around. I know that doesn't sound like much, but trust me — it's awesome and powerful. Note cards allow you to visually arrange the evidence into its natural patterns. (**Humble** 97)

Despite the logic of this argument, however, many students refuse to try the technique.

> If you don't name the **author** in the introduction, then name the **author** in the parenthetical citation. But you know that by now.

2. List of Works Cited

The MLA list of works cited is a complete list of the works that are used — cited — in your paper. This list presents two important pieces of information:

- how the work was used in your paper.

- how readers can find the works.

With MLA style, you can document the same work in several different ways. This allows you to show how you use it in your paper. For example, if your writing addresses the differences in the translations of Pablo Neruda's poetry, you would list the translator in the author's place within the citation. If you're writing about the *meaning* of Pablo Neruda's poetry, you would list Neruda in the author's place.

The complete publication information also allows your readers to find any work that you used and study it themselves. MLA divides that publication information into three mandatory sections and one optional section, presented in this order:

A. Author

B. Title

C. Container (publication)

D. Other information

Because an MLA works cited citation is divided into its key elements, you build it by gathering and presenting the information that fits into each element. MLA style then guides you in how to format the variations that occur within each.

A. Author

The author is the person or people or organization responsible for creating the source. This is the first piece of information you must find to build your citation.

With books, the author's name is usually on the spine. Magazines, newspapers, and journals typically put the author's name near the title of the article. However, the name may also appear at the end of short articles. If the source is a corporate or governmental publication and a specific author is not given, the organization itself is usually the author.

ONE AUTHOR

1. **Todd,** <u>David</u>. *Feeding Back: Conversations with Alternative Guitarists from Proto-Punk to Post-Rock.* Chicago Review Press, 2012.

   > List the author's **last name** first, followed by a **comma** and then the author's <u>first name</u>. End the author section with a **period**.

2. Williams, John <u>Sibley</u>. *Controlled Hallucinations.* FutureCycle Press, 2013.

   > Include the <u>middle name</u> or middle initial if it is listed in the original text.

3. Churchill, Winston. *Triumph and Tragedy.* Houghton Mifflin, 1953.

   > That's *Sir* Winston Churchill to you and me, but in a citation, don't include titles like "Sir," "PhD.," "M.S.W.," "King," "Saint," or "Dr."

TWO AUTHORS

Ede, Lisa, **and** <u>Andrea A. Lunsford</u>. *Writing Together: Collaboration in Theory and Practice.* Bedford/St. Martin's, 2012.

> Use a **comma** and the **conjunction** "and" between the authors' names. Note that the <u>second author's name</u> is written with the first name followed by the last name. Always list the authors in the order they appear in the text, not alphabetically, because libraries list authors this way, and readers who want to find the work may not be able to if you don't list them the same way.

THREE OR MORE AUTHORS

Murray, Robin M., <u>et al</u>. *The Epidemiology of Schizophrenia.* Cambridge UP, 2002.

> When there are three or more authors for a text, list the first author listed in the source. Follow the name with a **comma** and "et al.," a Latin phrase that means "and others."

ORGANIZATIONAL OR GOVERNMENTAL AUTHOR

Business and professional documents are often considered a work product and property of the company rather than that of the poor, nameless authors who work for that organization. In that case, list the organization as the author.

U.S. Census Bureau. *Strength in Numbers: Your Guide to 2010 Census Redistricting Data from the U.S. Census Bureau.* U.S. Dept. of Commerce, Economics and Statistics Administration, U.S. Census Bureau, 2010.

> Abbreviate commonly understood terms like "U.S." instead of writing out "United States." More complex acronyms should be written out.

SCREEN NAME

Many online authors write under a screen name. You don't have to go searching for the author's secret (true) identity. You can use the screen name.

> chewingofthecud. "What Currents or Movements Are Currently Happening in Literature?" *Reddit*, 2014, www.reddit.com/r/literature/comments/20by05/what_currents_or_movements_are_currently.

> Simply list the screen name in the author's place.

NO AUTHOR

If no author is listed for the text, skip the author's place and begin the citation with the information for the next element — the title of the source. Do not use the word "Anonymous" in place of the author.

> 1. *The Qur'an.* Oxford World's Classics Edition, edited by M. A. S. Abdel Haleem, Oxford UP, 2005.

> If there's no author listed for the text, as is common in ancient texts, skip the author's place and begin the citation with the information for the next element — the title.

> 2. "Facetious." *Vocabulary.com*, 2016, www.vocabulary.com/dictionary/facetious.

> Do not cite the editor of a reference work unless the specific entry is signed by an author. Most won't be. Instead, begin with the title, which in this case is the word you looked up.

OTHER CONTRIBUTORS

Sometimes the person or organization most important to your use of a work is someone other than an author. Some terms you are likely to use in your documentation are "performer," "director," "editor(s)," and "translator."

> 1. Bevington, David, and David Scott Kastan, editors. *Macbeth*. By William Shakespeare, Bantam, 2005.

> A discussion of *Macbeth* where the emphasis isn't on the play itself but rather the specific edited collection in which it appears — such as this work's essay about Shakespeare film adaptations included after the main text — would require listing the editors in the author's place in the citation.

> 2. Low, Amanda Kissin, producer, and Bob O'Brien, writer and reporter. *The Hoboken Sound*. Metromedia Telecenter, 1985. https://www.youtube.com/watch?v=clNuALHa_6E

> Only list the most important contributors in the author's place and note their roles in the work by following their names with **a comma** and a description of their contribution.

B. Title

The second key section in an MLA citation is the title of the work. MLA style requires you to capitalize the first word and all nouns, verbs, adjectives, and adverbs in the title. MLA also requires you to format the title to distinguish between larger and smaller works.

Look for the title of the source near the author's name, usually at the beginning of the work.

LARGER WORKS

MLA uses formatting to quickly indicate whether the title of the source is a larger, self-contained work or a smaller work within a larger one. Larger works include books, anthologies, magazines, newspapers, websites, book-length poems, movies, and so on. Italicize the titles of these larger works.

1. Georges, Nicole J. *Calling Dr. Laura.* Houghton Mifflin Harcourt, 2013.

   This is a full-length book, so the title is italicized. Put a **period** at the end of this section.

2. *The Walking Dead.* Created by Frank Darabont, performance by Andrew Lincoln, American Movie Classics, 2010–2016.

   This television series is a larger work that contains episodes within it. Because it has no single author, we leave the author section blank.

3. Bartow, Rick. *After the Fall III.* Paint on clay, 1975, Portland Art Museum, Portland, OR.

   MLA considers works of art to be larger works, even if they aren't physically very large.

4. Roemmele, Jacqueline A., and Donna Batdorff. *Surviving the "Flesh-Eating Bacteria": Understanding, Preventing, Treating, and Living with the Effects of Necrotizing Fasciitis.* Avery, 2001.

   Put a **colon** between the main title and a subtitle. With larger works, both remain italicized. If the title contains words within quotation marks, those words are also italicized.

5. Bishop, Kyle W. *American Zombie Gothic: The Rise and Fall (and Rise) of* The Walking Dead *in Popular Culture.* McFarland, 2010.

   In this unusual example, however, there is a television series title within the book title that must be *de*-italicized to distinguish it from the rest of the book's title. If a part of the larger work's title would normally be italicized, then you must de-italicize it within the italics of the rest of the title.

SMALLER WORKS (WITHIN A LARGER WORK)

Mark titles with quotation marks when the work is nested within a larger work. For example, for articles within newspapers, journals, or reference books, the article titles go inside quotation marks. You'll also use quotation marks for short stories and essays in an anthology, short poems within a collection, episodes within a television series, songs within an album, pages within a website, and so on.

1. Gladwell, Malcolm. "Being Nice Isn't Really So Awful." *The New Yorker*, vol. 40, no. 89, 9 Dec. 2013.

   A magazine article is a shorter work that's nested inside a larger publication, so it's marked by **quotation marks** rather than italics. Notice that the **period** after this part of the citation slips inside those **quotation marks**.

2. Mahoney, Phillip. "Gray is the New Black: Race, Class, and Zombies." *Generation Zombie: Essays on the Living Dead in Modern Culture*, edited by Stephanie Boluk and Wylie Lenz, McFarland, 2011, pp. 55–72.

   The Mahoney article appears within a larger collection of essays, so its title also appears within quotation marks.

3. Tuchman, Barbara. "Ch. 19: Retreat." *The Guns of August*, Macmillan, 1962, pp. 341–372.

   Chapters or other sections within a book are considered shorter works, even if they are quite long. This one isn't so bad, but some chapters really go on forever.

4. Mayo Clinic Staff. "Gallstones-Definition." *Mayo Clinic*, Mayo Foundation for Medical Education and Research, 25 July 2013, http://www.mayoclinic.org/diseases-conditions/gallstones/basics/definition/con-20020461.

   Web pages are shorter works within websites.

5. Miller, Elise. "The 'Maw of Western Culture': James Baldwin and the Anxieties of Influence." *African American Review*, vol. 38, no. 4, Winter 2004, pp. 625–636.

   When quotation marks appear within the title of a shorter work, the inner quotation marks are **single quotation marks**. With shorter works, you also put a **colon** between the main title and any subtitle.

6. Kenny, Glenn. "A Perfect Day." **Review of *A Perfect Day*, directed by Fernando Leon de Aranoa.** *Rogerebert.com*, Ebert Digital, 15 Jan. 2016, www.rogerebert.com/reviews/a-perfect-day-2016.

   When the work is a review of another work, add **a note** that includes "Review of" and the name of the work being reviewed. Follow that with a **comma** and then the people responsible for the work.

151

C. Container (Publication)

The third and most complex section of an MLA citation is the one that captures publication information about the source. The MLA calls this section a container, but you can also think of it as the publication, which is usually the case.

MLA

Works Cited: Container

MLA

This section will include information about some or all of the following subcategories of information, and always in this order:

1. Title of publication

2. Other contributors

3. Version

4. Number

5. Publisher

6. Publication date

7. Location

Not every source has information for each of the subsections in this list — in fact, most don't. For example, a book by a single author may not have "other contributors" to recognize. A periodical does not typically come in "versions," but in volumes and issues, two variations that fit in the "number" subsection. When a work does not contain information for one of the subsections, move on to the next subsection. Once you're done, place a period at the end of this section to show readers that your publication information is complete.

We'll show you how this works with different types of works.

C1. TITLE OF PUBLICATION

For larger works, the title of the work and the title of the publication are the same thing, so that title goes in section for the title of the work.

1. Boluk, Stephanie, and Wylie Lenz, editors. *Generation Zombie: Essays on the Living Dead in Modern Culture.* McFarland, 2011.

   Because the citation focuses on the book as a whole, there's nothing to put in the title of publication slot. That's okay. Move along.

2. Mahoney, Phillip. "Gray is the New Black: Race, Class, and Zombies." *Generation Zombie: Essays on the Living Dead in Modern Culture,* edited by Stephanie Boluk and Wylie Lenz, McFarland, 2011, pp. 55–72.

However, in this second example, the citation focuses on the Mahoney article within the larger work. Now the article title goes in the title-of-work section, and the title of the larger work goes in this publication section. Add a **comma** after the title of the larger work.

3. Rockmore, Ellen Bresler. "How Texas Teaches History." *The New York Times,* 12 Oct. 2015. www.nytimes.com/2015/10/22/opinion/how-texas-teaches-history.html.

   With articles in periodicals, the title of the publication is typically the name of the journal, magazine, or newspaper.

4. Mayo Clinic Staff. "Gallstones-Definition." *Mayo Clinic,* Mayo Foundation for Medical Education and Research, 25 July 2013, http://www.mayoclinic.org/diseases-conditions/gallstones/basics/definition/con-20020461.

   When the focus of the source is on one page at a website, the name of the website goes into the title-of-publication place.

5. "Agrippina (Agrippina the Younger)." *Encyclopedia of World Crime,* edited by Jay Robert Nash, CrimeBooks, Inc., 1989, pp. 39–40.

   With reference works, the title of publication is the title of the book or website.

6. Silence. "War Drums." *The Deafening Sound of Absolutely Nothing.* Profane Existence, 2016.

   When citing a song, the song title goes in the first title section and the name of the album or collection goes in this slot as the title of the publication.

C2. OTHER CONTRIBUTORS

Other contributors are people who play important roles in creating the publication but are secondary to the named author of the work. These contributors are identified by their role in the publication with terms such as "directed by" or by a title such as "editor," followed by a comma.

You'll find the names of other contributors on title pages or other places where credit is given to collaborators, like the credits of a film or the liner notes of an album. Only bring in the additional contributors whose work is directly applicable to the topic of your writing.

1. Shakespeare, William. *Macbeth.* Edited by David Bevington and David Scott Kastan, Bantam, 2005.

   Name the role of the other contributor(s) first. Then list the contributors by first name and then last name. End with a comma to show that while this slot is over, the publication container continues. In this example, listing the editors helps your reader tell which version of *Macbeth* you used, since editors sometimes change minor words and punctuation in Shakespeare's plays.

2. LaTour, Jason. "Greater Power Part Four." *Spider-Gwen.* <u>Penciled and inked by</u> Robbi Rodriguez**,** <u>colored by</u> Rico Renzi**,** no. 4, Marvel, 2015.

> With works that involve multiple contributors, list each and his or her <u>role</u>, separating each with a **comma**. Combine <u>roles</u> when they are performed by the same person.

C3. VERSION

Works often have multiple versions or editions that are identified by numbers that tell you how many times the publication has been revised — 2nd edition, for example — or names that tell you the nature of the revision — like "unabridged" or "expanded."

When they exist, version numbers or names can usually be found next to the title of the publication.

1. Rottenberg, Annette T., and Donna Haisty Winchell. *The Structure of Argument.* 8th edition**,** Bedford/St. Martin's, 2015.

> Use numbers rather than full words with numbered editions. Do not use superscript endings ("th").

2. *The Bible.* New International Version**,** Zondervan, 1984.

> Write out any named editions in full.

C4. NUMBER

Books that are too long to be published in a single volume are often split into multiple volumes, and each is given its own volume number. In addition, periodicals that are published on an ongoing basis — as is the case with most scholarly journals — are assigned volume, issue, or volume *and* issue numbers to distinguish one publication of the periodical from another.

The number is typically found near the title of the publication. However, it may be found within the publication on a page with more information about the publication, contributors, and so on.

1. Conan Doyle, Arthur. *Sherlock Holmes: The Complete Novels and Stories***.** Vol. 1**,** Bantam Classics, 1986.

> "Vol." is an abbreviation for "volume" and should precede the volume number. Use the numeral rather than the word. Note that the first letter of "Vol." is capitalized only when it appears after a **period** in the citation.

2. Sheffield, Rob. "Getting to Know Colbert." *Rolling Stone,* no. 1295**,** p. 30.

> If there's no volume number, mention the issue number only.

3. Gladwell, Malcolm. "The Bill." *The New Yorker,* vol. 90, no. 43, p. 65.

> If a periodical has both volume number and issue number, mention the volume number first, followed by the issue number. "No." is an abbreviation for "number" and should come before the issue number. Note that "vol." and "no." are lowercase because they each follow a **comma**.

C5. PUBLISHER

The publisher is the company or person who actually produced a book, government report, film, website, or other works. Film and television series generally involve multiple publishers. In that case, cite the publisher that is primarily responsible for the work. Periodicals do not usually have a publisher, in which case you can skip this section.

With works of art, the medium is considered the publisher. Just as a print publisher helps to bring a book into existence, so too do the acrylic paints, clay, or metal play a role in bringing the artistic vision into being. It's a stretch, we know. Just work with us, okay?

With a book, you can find the name of the publisher on the title page or on a page near the front of the book that provides more information about the publication and its copyright. On pamphlets, look on the back or the innermost leaf of the folded paper. On brochures, look at the front or back covers. A website will usually list the publisher at the bottom of the page in the footer or on its version of the "About" page.

1. McCloud, Scott. *The Sculptor.* First Second Books, 2015.

> For books, list the name of the publishing company. In previous versions of MLA, you also listed the city in which the publisher is or was located. That information is now optional and is only included when it avoids confusion.

2. Engber, Daniel. "The Neurologist Who Hacked His Brain—And Almost Lost His Mind." *Wired,* Condé Nast, 26 Jan. 2016. www.wired.com/2016/01/phil-kennedy-mind-control-computer.

> Condé Nast publishes many magazines and websites, including *Wired*. When the publisher of a periodical or online magazine is listed, you can include that information here. If the publisher or publication shares the same name as the website, however, do not include the name.

3. "Frank Lisciandro." *The Writing Life,* produced by Stephen Long, McMinnville Community Media, 21 Mar. 2016.

> With television broadcasts, films, and albums, the publisher is the company or organization that paid for the creation of the work.

4. Siler, Buzz. *Lena (D)*. **Acrylic and oil on canvas,** 2011, Siler Gallery, Portland, OR.

> In a work of art, insert the name the medium itself in the place of the publisher.

C6. PUBLICATION DATE

The publication date is the specific date the work was published. A book is published once and therefore only features the year. A periodical is published regularly throughout the year, so its publication date identifies which part of the year it was published in. A monthly magazine notes the month and year. A daily newspaper lists the day, month, and year.

The location of the publication date varies from publication to publication. In a book, the date should be on the title page or copyright page. The date of articles that appear in periodicals will often appear next to the byline and title of the source. This applies to online articles as well, but if a date is missing, you can also search the bottom of the web page for a publication year to stand in for something more precise.

1. Federoff, Nina, and John Block. "Mosquito vs. Mosquito." *The New York Times*, 6 Apr. 2016, p. A23.

> The most common format is day and month followed by the year because so many works come out on a specific day. Note that the month is abbreviated.

2. Barone, Richard. "The Power of Song: Recording Pete Seeger" *Tape Op*, No. 113, May–June 2016.

> Bimonthly publications will often use a month range followed by a **year**. Only the names of May, June, and July are written out in full. The rest use three-letter abbreviations.

You may use the abbreviation "n.d." for no date, but do not use it lightly. It is rare that a publication date is truly not included in a print source. In web sources, it can be difficult to find, but it almost always exists in the web page's HTML code. Most web browsers will allow you to search the HTML code, but yes, it will take some work. Ask for help if you need it.

The location varies by the type of work. For shorter works within anthologies or periodicals, the location is usually a page number or a range of pages. Film and music locations might be physical discs or their digital equivalent. The location for a work of art is often the place where the piece is on exhibit. For online sources, the location is a web address (URL) or DOI. Because of the possibilities here, your main task is to be as precise as possible.

1. Behar, Evelyn, et al. "Concreteness of Positive, Negative, and Neutral Repetitive Thinking About the Future." *Behavior Therapy*, vol. 43, no. 2, 1998, pp. 300–312.

   ▍ For more than one continuous page, put "pp." before the page range.

2. "OSU Women Try to Keep a Storied Season Going." *The Oregonian*, 2 Apr. 2016, p. A1.

   ▍ If a work appears on only one page, put just the letter "p" and a period before the page numbers. Some page numbers, especially in print newspapers, include **letters** before the number to show in which section the page is located.

3. Erlanger, Steven, Stephen Castle, and Rick Gladstone. "Airing of Hidden Wealth Stirs Inquiries and Rage: Iceland Premier Steps Down as Release of Files Reverberates Around World." *The New York Times*, 6 Apr. 2016, pp. A1+.

   ▍ For a multi-page work that appears on non-consecutive pages, list the first page number and a plus sign.

4. Bartow, Rick. *After the Fall III*. Paint on clay, 1975, Portland Art Museum, Portland, OR.

   ▍ For items that appear in physical locations, name the place where the work is housed and sufficient distinguishing details like city, state, or country.

5. Grosvenor, Emily. "The Dude Abides in Salem." *Desperately Seeking Salem*, 8 Aug. 2010, desperatelyseekingsalem.wordpress.com/2010/08/08/the-dude-abides-in-salem/.

   ▍ For online works, include a **URL** if it will reliably and consistently allow a reader to navigate to the cited page. Avoid using one-time URLs generated for a specific browsing session. They get way too long. Do not include the "http://" part, either, with MLA style.

6. Aagaard, Jesper. "Media Multitasking, Attention, and Distraction: A Critical Discussion." *Phenomenology and the Cognitive Sciences*, vol. 14, no. 4, Dec. 2015, p. 885, doi:10.1007/s11097-014- 9375-x.

   ▍ **DOIs** (digital object identifiers) are more reliable than URLs and should be used when available.

D. Other Information

In addition to the first three mandatory sections of a works cited citation, MLA style also provides a fourth section to include additional information that will usually show readers in more detail where the source is located or clear up possible confusion.

SECOND CONTAINER (PUBLICATION)

This section allows you to provide readers with information about a second publisher when a publication is republished in another book or online or in a library database.

Library databases are a good example of a second publication container. They republish millions of articles that were first published in newspapers, academic journals, and reference works. Streaming services like Spotify and Netflix also provide access to music and film, respectively. Google Books provides access to books online.

The second publication container is usually easy to spot because this is probably where you found the work. In fact, sometimes the harder task is to find out who the first publisher is. If you aren't looking at the actual work itself — you aren't holding a printed book or article in your hands, for example — then what you have is probably something that has been republished for easier access.

1. Kerr, William R., Ramana Nanda, and Matthew Rhodes-Kropf. "Entrepreneurship as Experimentation." *The Journal of Economic Perspectives*, vol. 28, no. 3, 2014, pp. 25–48. *JSTOR*, www.jstor.org/stable/23800574. Accessed 10 Feb. 2016.

   This article was accessed via an academic database. The *URL* works as a second location for the source in this container. Note that the name of the second publisher is italicized.

2. Mark Twain. *Life on the Mississippi*. Harper, 1917. *Google Books*, books.google. com/books?id=h99O07cNtEMC.

   With many books now available online, it's helpful to show readers who has republished them and where they're located.

3. Mould, Bob. "Dreaming, I Am." *Workbook*. Virgin Records America, 1989. **Spotify**. play.spotify.com/track/2SmknAMU59qMW6LwpPw3cL.

   Here, the **name** of streaming music service is the second container, and the URL is the location.

DATE OF ACCESS

Information on a website can change at any time. Date of access documents the precise day and time the person citing the source accessed it.

> Adams, Sarah. "Be Cool to the Pizza Dude." *This I Believe,* hosted by Jay Allison, This I Believe, 29 Dec. 2015, cdn.audiometric.io/9487820912.mp3. Accessed 29 Feb. 2016.

> At the end of the citation, write "Accessed" and then the date of access. Use the same day, month, year format used in the publication section.

This information only relates to sources accessed online. MLA considers this information optional, so defer to your professor as to whether or not you should include it in your citation.

CITY OF PUBLICATION

The city of publication is the name of the place where the publisher is located. It is traditionally located just before the name of the publisher, which is where it goes in the citation as well. This information matters increasingly less to modern scholars and is not required in the newest edition of the *MLA Handbook*. It should only be included when your professor requires it.

1. Ede, Lisa, and Andrea A. Lunsford. *Writing Together: Collaboration in Theory and Practice.* **Boston,** Bedford/St. Martin's, 2012

> If you choose to include it, the city of publication precedes the publisher and is separated from the publisher by a **comma**.

2. Humble, Roy K. *The Humble Argument.* **Dallas, OR,** Problem Child, 2010.

> Only include the state if failing to do so would cause confusion. Here, the state distinguishes the modest town of Dallas in Oregon from the less modest city in Texas.

159

E. Putting It All Together

The table belows shows you how to put the pieces of information about a work into the right order for the citation: You start with the author and just keep working your way down the list. Once you've identified which information goes where, you compile it into an entry on your Works Cited page.

Information	Example 1	Example 2	Example 3
A. Author.		Kerr, William R., et al.	Russell, Mark.
B. Title.	"Facetious."	"Entrepreneurship as Experimentation."	*Prez.*
C. Container (Publication)			
C1. Title of publication,	*Vocabulary.com,*	*The Journal of Economic Perspectives,*	
C2. Other contributors,			Illustrated by Ben Caldwell,
C3. Version,			
C4. Number,		vol. 28, no. 3,	no. 5,
C5. Publisher,			DC,
C6. Publication date,		2014,	Oct. 2014.
C7. Location.	www.vocabulary.com/dictionary/facetious.	pp. 25–48.	
D. Other Information			
Second container, location.		*JSTOR,* www.jstor.org/stable/23800574.	
Date of access.	Accessed 29 Feb. 2016.	Accessed 10 Feb. 2016.	

These are the citations that you then put on your Works Cited page:

"Facetious." *Vocabulary.com*, www.vocabulary.com/dictionary/facetious. Accessed 29 Feb. 2016.

Kerr, William R., et al. "Entrepreneurship as Experimentation." *The Journal of Economic Perspectives*, vol. 28, no. 3, 2014, pp. 25–48. *JSTOR*, www.jstor. org/stable/23800574. Accessed 10 Feb. 2016.

Russell, Mark. *Prez*. Illustrated by Ben Caldwell, no. 5, DC, Oct. 2014.

F. Works Cited Examples

As you see from the past section, MLA style divides works cited citation information into four main sections:

A. Author

B. Title

C. Container (usually a publisher)

D. Other (often including second container)

In each of the examples that follow, we'll show you a complete and formatted sample citation, followed by a numbered breakdown of each section in the citation from the above list.

Even though these are common examples, you still have to adapt them to fit the information about the works you're using. You may have to tinker with the author section or the container section to accurately capture the information about a given work.

But that's a good thing. It means that you can build each citation to match the work instead of having to somehow tailor the information about a work to match a template that doesn't really work.

BOOKS

ONE AUTHOR

Georges, Nicole J. *Calling Dr. Laura*. Houghton Mifflin Harcourt, 2013.

    1. (Author) Georges, Nicole J.
    2. (Title) *Calling Dr. Laura*.
    3. (Container) Houghton Mifflin Harcourt, 2013.
    4. (Other) —

EDITION OTHER THAN THE FIRST

Rottenberg, Annette T., and Donna Haisty Winchell. *The Structure of Argument.* 8th edition, Bedford/St. Martin's, 2015.

> 1. Rottenberg, Annette T., and Donna Haisty Winchell.
> 2. *The Structure of Argument.*
> 3. 8th edition, Bedford/St. Martin's, 2015.
> 4. —

EDITED COLLECTION

Boluk, Stephanie, and Wylie Lenz, editors. *Generation Zombie: Essays on the Living Dead in Modern Culture.* McFarland, 2011.

> 1. Boluk, Stephanie, and Wylie Lenz, editors.
> 2. *Generation Zombie: Essays on the Living Dead in Modern Culture.*
> 3. McFarland, 2011.
> 4. —

ONLINE BOOK

Mark Twain. *Life on the Mississippi.* Harper, 1917. *Google Books*, books.google.com/books?id=h99O07cNtEMC.

> 1. Mark Twain.
> 2. *Life on the Mississippi.*
> 3. Harper, 1917.
> 4. *Google Books*, books.google.com/books?id=h99O07cNtEMC.

SACRED TEXT

The Bible. New International Version, Zondervan, 1984.

> 1. —
> 2. *The Bible.*
> 3. New International Version, Zondervan, 1984.
> 4. —

COMIC BOOK

LaTour, Jason. "Greater Power Part Four." *Spider-Gwen.* Penciled and inked by Robbi Rodriguez, colored by Rico Renzi, no. 4, Marvel, 2015.

> 1. LaTour, Jason.
> 2. "Greater Power Part Four."
> 3. *Spider-Gwen.* Penciled and inked by Robbi Rodriguez, colored by Robbi Rodriguez, colored by Rico Renzi, no. 4, Marvel, 2015.
> 4. —

CHAPTER OF A BOOK

Tuchman, Barbara. "Ch. 19: Retreat." *The Guns of August*, Macmillan, 1962, pp. 341–372.

    1. Tuchman, Barbara.
    2. "Ch. 19: Retreat."
    3. *The Guns of August*, Macmillan, 1962, pp. 341–372.
    4. —

WORK IN AN ANTHOLOGY

Mahoney, Phillip. "Gray is the New Black: Race, Class, and Zombies." *Generation Zombie: Essays on the Living Dead in Modern Culture*, edited by Stephanie Boluk and Wylie Lenz, McFarland, 2011, pp. 55–72.

    1. Mahoney, Phillip.
    2. "Gray is the New Black: Race, Class, and Zombies."
    3. *Generation Zombie: Essays on the Living Dead in Modern Culture*, edited by Stephanie Boluk and Wylie Lenz, McFarland, 2011, pp. 55–72.
    4. —

ARTICLE IN A REFERENCE BOOK (PRINT)

"Agrippina (Agrippina the Younger)." *Encyclopedia of World Crime*, edited by Jay Robert Nash, CrimeBooks, Inc., 1989, pp. 39–40.

    1. —
    2. "Agrippina (Agrippina the Younger)."
    3. *Encyclopedia of World Crime*, edited by Jay Robert Nash, CrimeBooks, Inc., 1989, pp. 39–40.
    4. —

ARTICLE IN A REFERENCE BOOK (LIBRARY DATABASE)

"Iūlia Agrippīna, 'Agrippina the Younger'." *Oxford Dictionary of the Classical World*, edited by John Roberts, Oxford University Press, 2007. *Oxford Reference*. Accessed 30 July 2016.

    1. —
    2. "Iūlia Agrippīna, 'Agrippina the Younger'."
    3. *Oxford Dictionary of the Classical World*, edited by John Roberts, Oxford University Press, 2007.
    4. *Oxford Reference*. Accessed 30 July 2016.

Journal Article (Print)

Racy, A.J. "Domesticating Otherness: The Snake Charmer in American Popular Culture." *Ethnomusicology*, vol. 60, no. 2, Spring/Summer 2016, pp. 197–232.

> 1. Racy, A.J.
> 2. "Domesticating Otherness: The Snake Charmer in American Popular Culture."
> 3. *Ethnomusicology*, vol. 60, no. 2, Spring/Summer 2016, pp. 197–232.
> 4. —

Journal Article (Library Database)

Racy, A. J. "Domesticating Otherness: The Snake Charmer in American Popular Culture." *Ethnomusicology*, vol. 60, no. 2, Spring/Summer 2016, pp. 197–232. *JSTOR*, www.jstor.org/stable/10.5406/ethnomusicology.60.2.0197.

> 1. Racy, A.J.
> 2. "Domesticating Otherness: The Snake Charmer in American Popular Culture."
> 3. *Ethnomusicology*, vol. 60, no. 2, Spring/Summer 2016, pp. 197–232.
> 4. *JSTOR*, www.jstor.org/stable/10.5406/ethnomusicology.60.2.0197.

Magazine Article (Print)

Gladwell, Malcolm. "Being Nice Isn't Really So Awful." *The New Yorker*, vol. 40, no. 89, 9 Dec. 2013.

> 1. Gladwell, Malcolm.
> 2. "Being Nice Isn't Really So Awful."
> 3. *The New Yorker*, vol. 40, no. 89, 9 Dec. 2013.
> 4. —

Magazine Article (Website)

Engber, Daniel. "The Neurologist Who Hacked His Brain—And Almost Lost His Mind." *Wired*, Condé Nast, 26 Jan. 2016, www.wired.com/2016/01/phil-kennedy-mind-control computer.

> 1. Engber, Daniel.
> 2. "The Neurologist Who Hacked His Brain—And Almost Lost His Mind."
> 3. *Wired*, Condé Nast, 26 Jan. 2016, www.wired.com/2016/01/phil-kennedy-mind-control computer.
> 4. —

MAGAZINE ARTICLE (LIBRARY DATABASE)

Koster, John. "Hating the 'Hun' at Home: When America Went to War against the Kaiser, German-Americans Caught Hell." *American History*, vol. 51, no. 3, 2016, pp. 58+. *General OneFile*. Accessed 30 July 2016.

1. Koster, John.
2. "Hating the 'Hun' at Home: When America Went to War against the Kaiser, German-Americans Caught Hell."
3. *American History*, vol. 51, no. 3, 2016, pp. 58+.
4. *General OneFile*. Accessed 30 July 2016.

NEWSPAPER ARTICLE (PRINT)

Erlanger, Steven, Stephen Castle and Rick Gladstone. "Airing of Hidden Wealth Stirs Inquiries and Rage: Iceland Premier Steps Down as Release of Files Reverberates Around World." *The New York Times*, 6 Apr. 2016, pp. A1+.

1. Erlanger, Steven, Stephen Castle and Rick Gladstone.
2. "Airing of Hidden Wealth Stirs Inquiries and Rage: Iceland Premier Steps Down as Release of Files Reverberates Around World."
3. *The New York Times*, 6 Apr. 2016, pp. A1+.
4. —

NEWSPAPER ARTICLE (WEBSITE)

Rockmore, Ellen Bresler. "How Texas Teaches History." *The New York Times*, 12 Oct. 2015, www.nytimes.com/2015/10/22/opinion/how-texas-teaches-history.html.

1. Rockmore, Ellen Bresler.
2. "How Texas Teaches History."
3. *The New York Times*, 12 Oct. 2015, www.nytimes.com/2015/10/22/opinion/how-texas-teaches-history.html.
4. —

NEWSPAPER ARTICLE (LIBRARY DATABASE)

Rector, Kevin. "Hope and Politics Collide at March." *The Baltimore Sun*, first edition, 25 Apr. 2016, pp. A1+. *LexisNexis Academic*. Accessed 30 May 2016.

1. Rector, Kevin.
2. "Hope and Politics Collide at March."
3. *The Baltimore Sun*, first edition, 25 Apr. 2016, pp. A1+.
4. *LexisNexis Academic*. Accessed 30 May 2016.

Reference Article (website)

"Facetious." *Vocabulary.com*, Vocabulary.com, 2016, www.vocabulary.com/dictionary/facetious.

    1. —
    2. "Facetious."
    3. *Vocabulary.com*, Vocabulary.com, 2016, www.vocabulary.com/dictionary/facetious.
    4. —

Reference Article (library database)

"Iūlia Agrippīna, 'Agrippina the Younger'." *Oxford Dictionary of the Classical World*, edited by John Roberts, Oxford University Press, 2007. *Oxford Reference*. Accessed 30 July 2016.

    1. —
    2. "Iūlia Agrippīna, 'Agrippina the Younger'."
    3. *Oxford Dictionary of the Classical World*, edited by John Roberts, Oxford University Press, 2007.
    4. *Oxford Reference*. Accessed 30 July 2016.

ONLINE PUBLICATIONS

Entire Website

Sports Illustrated. Time, 2016, www.si.com.

    1. —
    2. *Sports Illustrated*.
    3. Time, 2016, www.si.com.
    4. —

Web Page

Mayo Clinic Staff. "Gallstones-Definition." *Mayo Clinic*, Mayo Foundation for Medical Education and Research, 25 July 2013, www.mayoclinic.org/diseases-conditions/gallstones/basics/definition/con-20020461.

    1. Mayo Clinic Staff.
    2. "Gallstones-Definition."
    3. *Mayo Clinic*, Mayo Foundation for Medical Education and Research, 25 July 2013, http://www.mayoclinic.org/diseases-conditions/gallstones/basics/definition/con-20020461.
    4. —

SOCIAL MEDIA

@LibrariansTNT. "Cassandrasaurs for Sure Roamed this Earth."
Twitter, 6 Jan. 2016, 8:49 a.m., twitter.com/LibrariansTNT/
status/684778779034517504.

1. @LibrariansTNT.
2. "Cassandrasaurs for Sure Roamed this Earth."
3. *Twitter*, 6 Jan. 2016, 8:49 a.m., twitter.com/LibrariansTNT/status/
684778779034517504.
4. —

BLOG

Grosvenor, Emily. "The Dude Abides in Salem." *Desperately Seeking Salem.*
8 Aug. 2010, desperatelyseekingsalem.wordpress.com/2010/08/08/
the-dude-abides-in-salem/.

1. Grosvenor, Emily.
2. "The Dude Abides in Salem."
3. *Desperately Seeking Salem.* 8 Aug. 2010, desperatelyseekingsalem.wordpress.
com/2010/08/08/the-dude-abides-in-salem/.
4. —

ONLINE VIDEO

ArtsAlive YamhillCo, director. "ArtsAlive: Stephanie Lenox." *YouTube*, 25
Mar. 2015, youtube.com/watch?v=xOQIKeERJTE.

1. ArtsAlive YamhillCo, director.
2. "ArtsAlive: Stephanie Lenox."
3. *YouTube*, 25 Mar. 2015, youtube.com/watch?v=xOQIKeERJTE.
4. —

MEDIA AND PERFORMANCE

FILM

Star Wars: The Force Awakens. Directed by J. J. Abrams, Lucasfilm, 2015.

1. —
2. *Star Wars: The Force Awakens.*
3. Directed by J. J. Abrams. Lucasfilm, 2015.
4. —

Television Show (Broadcast)

"Frank Lisciandro." *The Writing Life*, produced by Stephen Long, McMinnville Community Media, 21 Mar. 2016.

1. —
2. "Frank Lisciandro."
3. *The Writing Life*, produced by Stephen Long, McMinnville Community
Media, 21 Mar. 2016.
4. —

Television Show (Digital)

"World on Fire." *Daredevil*, directed by Farren Blackburn, performances
by Charlie Cox and Vincent D'Onofrio, ABC Studios, 10 Apr. 2015,
Netflix.

1. —
2. "World on Fire."
3. *Daredevil*, directed by Farren Blackburn, performances by Charlie Cox
and Vincent D'Onofrio, ABC Studios, 10 Apr. 2015.
4. *Netflix*.

Online Video

ArtsAlive YamhillCo, director. "ArtsAlive: Stephanie Lenox." *YouTube*, 25
Mar. 2015, youtube.com/watch?v=xOQIKeERJTE.

1. ArtsAlive YamhillCo, director.
2. "ArtsAlive: Stephanie Lenox."
3. *YouTube*, 25 Mar. 2015, youtube.com/watch?v=xOQIKeERJTE.
4. —

Audio (Album)

Mould, Bob. *Workbook*. Virgin Records America, 1989.

1. Mould, Bob.
2. *Workbook*.
3. Virgin Records America, 1989.
4. —

Audio (Digital)

Adams, Sarah. "Be Cool to the Pizza Dude." *This I Believe*, hosted by
Jay Allison, 29 Dec. 2015, cdn.audiometric.io/9487820912.mp3.
Accessed 29 Feb. 2016.

1. Adams, Sarah.
2. "Be Cool to the Pizza Dude."
3. *This I Believe*, hosted by Jay Allison, This I Believe, 29 Dec. 2015, cdn. audiometric.io/9487820912.mp3. Accessed 29 Feb. 2016.
4. —

ADVERTISEMENT (PRINT)

BF Goodrich Co. "Put the Magazine Down and Go." *Automobile Magazine*. The Enthusiast Network, July 2016, p. 5.

1. BF Goodrich Co.
2. "Put the Magazine Down and Go."
3. *Automobile Magazine*. The Enthusiast Network, July 2016, p. 5.
4. —

COMIC STRIP

Barry, Lynda. "Issue." *Ernie Pook's Comeek, City Pages*, 23 Oct. 1985.

1. Barry, Lynda.
2. "Issue."
3. *Ernie Pook's Comeek, City Pages*, 23 Oct. 1985.
4. —

FINE ART

Bartow, Rick. *After the Fall III*. Paint on clay, 1975, Portland Art Museum, Portland, OR.

1. Bartow, Rick.
2. *After the Fall III*.
3. Paint on clay, 1975, Portland Art Museum, Portland, OR.
4. —

PERFORMANCE

Pride and Prejudice. Created by Jane Austen, directed by David Sikking, Arts & Communications Magnet Academy (ACMA) Theatre Company, 14 Mar. 2015, ACMA Visual and Performing Arts Center, Beaverton, OR.

1. —
2. *Pride and Prejudice*.
3. Created by Jane Austen, directed by David Sikking, Arts & Communications Magnet Academy (ACMA) Theatre Company, 14 Mar. 2015, ACMA Visual and Performing Arts Center, Beaverton, OR.
4. —

PAMPHLET, BROCHURE, OR PRESS RELEASE

Travel Guard. *Insure Your Next Trip with Travel Guard.* Travel Guard, 2016.

1. Travel Guard.
2. *Insure Your Next Trip with Travel Guard.*
3. Travel Guard, 2016.
4. —

GOVERNMENT REPORT

U.S. Census Bureau. *Strength in Numbers: Your Guide to 2010 Census Redistricting Data from the U.S. Census Bureau.* U.S. Dept. of Commerce, Economics and Statistics Administration, U.S. Census Bureau, 2010.

1. U.S. Census Bureau.
2. *Strength in Numbers: Your Guide to 2010 Census Redistricting Data from the U.S. Census Bureau.*
3. U.S. Dept. of Commerce, Economics and Statistics Administration, U.S. Census Bureau, 2010.
4. —

UNPUBLISHED DISSERTATION

Kennison, Kristen Renee. *Smoke Derived Taint in Grapes and Wine.* Dissertation, Curtin University, 2011.

1. Kennison, Kristen Renee.
2. *Smoke Derived Taint in Grapes and Wine.*
3. Dissertation, Curtin University, 2011.
4. —

PERSONAL INTERVIEW

Snoek-Brown, Samuel. Interview with Tom Franklin. 21 Mar. 2000.

1. Snoek-Brown, Samuel.
2. Interview with Tom Franklin.
3. 21 Mar. 2000.
4. —

EMAIL

Franklin, Tom. "Re: visit to Texas." Received by Gertrude Mornhenweg, 3 Apr. 2003.

1. Franklin, Tom.
2. "Re: visit to Texas."
3. Received by Gertrude Mornhenweg, 3 Apr. 2003.
4. —

3. Paper Format

MLA style also offers guidance about how to format your paper so that it looks like all the other MLA papers. This helps ensure that readers will stay focused on your ideas.

Here are the general guidelines to keep in mind:

1. Type your paper on a computer and print it out on standard, white 8.5- by 11-inch paper. Set the margins of your document to one inch on all four sides.

2. Use a readable, businesslike font that doesn't draw attention to itself and is easy to read. Times New Roman is a popular choice, and a 12-point size in this font is readable.

3. Double-space everything — no more, no less.

4. Leave only one space after periods or other punctuation marks — unless you're told otherwise by an elderly person who learned how to type on an actual typewriter. It was a different time.

5. Indent the first line of paragraphs one half-inch from the left margin. Use the tab key to do that, too. Pushing the space bar five times to create a half-inch indentation worked on a typewriter, but it doesn't work with computers. These are different times.

6. Create a header in the upper right-hand corner of each page that is one half-inch from the top of the page and even with the right margin. This should include your last name and the page number. Use automatic page numbering for that. Trying to do that manually will cause needless suffering.

7. Never use boldface. Only use italics as required for the titles of larger works and some publications and, with sober moderation, for emphasis within the paper.

We'll show you how this works in the following pages by looking at some examples of actual pages. As we do, we'll add a few more guidelines that apply only in specific situations.

A. First Page

Jack Wiegand **A**

Prof. Roy K. Humble

WR122

29 February 2016

B

Proving the Negative

C   With the arrival of social media, society has seen a marked increase in armchair academia. Like the dilettantes of the Victorian era, today's hobbyist intellectuals spend their free time engaging in the gentleman's sport of debate, study, and showing off their brains, rather than their muscles. Also like the dilettantes of old, they treat it as strictly leisure, while eschewing rigorous academic commitment. While they might be able to regale their friends for hours about the brilliance of Voltaire, they've likely read his Wikipedia page, rather than *Candide*, or *Plato's Dream*. While they may be able to offer a criticism of a documentary about humanism, they would likely struggle to offer a worthwhile analysis of Thomas More's *Utopia*. Not that there's anything wrong with dilettantism. If anything, it does for society much more than reality television or competitive Frisbee.

C   It can, however, create a few issues. In every scholarly field, information tends to change slightly as it moves from the academic sphere to the public sphere. When simplifying ideas to make them accessible to the public, the foundational information — that can, in many cases, take years of study to understand — is necessarily lost. To borrow from *The Science of Discworld*, we tend to "bend the truths just sufficiently to make the basic principles of the operation clear to a layman while not actually being entirely wrong" (Pratchett et al. 14). What the authors go on to describe as "lies to children" may seem wholly benign (15), but they often lead to small misunderstandings, which can accumulate to form vast misunderstandings.

Keep these points in mind when you format your paper:

A. In the upper left-hand corner of the first page of the paper, include your name, the name of your professor, the name of the course, and the date, each on its own line. Note the date format, too.

B. Center the title on the next double-spaced line. Don't add extra space.

C. Indent the first sentence of each paragraph one half-inch.

D. Add a running header at the top of the first and every page.

B. Middle Pages

D

moon, as it moved through its annual cycle, indicated that the moon was a sphere (StarChild Team).

Many people have used this example as an argument against scientific understanding, claiming that if we were wrong about something like that, we could be wrong about anything. In rebuttal, rationalists are fond of saying that while we may not be absolutely right about certain things, we are continuously becoming less wrong. As Richard Feynman put it, in a lecture given at the 1964 Galileo Symposium:

> A scientist is never certain. We all know that. We know that all our statements are approximate statements with different degrees of certainty; that when a statement is made, the question is not whether it is true or false but rather how likely it is to be true or false...We must discuss each question within the uncertainties that are allowed...We absolutely must leave room for doubt or there is no progress and there is no learning. (111-112)

People tend to think of correctness as a binary; one is simply correct or incorrect. To wit, we now know that the Earth is not round, or at least not perfectly so. Isaac Newton observed, correctly, that the Earth is an oblate spheroid rather than a perfect sphere (Choi). While both previously held positions are incorrect, surely it is *less* incorrect to describe the Earth as round rather than flat.

Just as positive evidence can be used to make more reasonable positive statements, so too can negative evidence — or, the *absence* of evidence — be used to make more reasonable negative statements. Unfortunately, this is another case of widespread misunderstanding. The popular belief, known as Rees' Maxim, is that absence of evidence is not evidence of absence. This misunderstanding is not only prevalent in the public sphere, but has also found a foothold among

E. Double-space every line, and don't add any extra space anywhere. Ever.

F. For block quotations, use your word-processor's ruler tool to indent the entire paragraph one inch from the left margin. Leave the right margin alone. Don't try to do this with tabs or spaces. That's a fool's errand.

When you get to the end of your paper, insert a manual page break so that the works cited list will start at the top of its own page.

C. Works Cited Page

A Works Cited

C Cham, Jorge. "PHD Comics: Proving a Negative." *Piled Higher and Deeper*, no. 1194, 3 July 2009. *Comic Rocket*, www.comic-rocket.com/read/piled-higher-and-deeper-phd/1194.

D Choi, Charles Q. "Strange but True: Earth Is Not Round." *Scientific American*, Nature Publishing Group, 12 Apr. 2007, www.scientificamerican.com/article/earth-is-not-round/.

Craig, William Lane. "#115 Is God Imaginary?: Santa Claus, Tooth Fairies, and God." *Reasonable Faith with William Lane Craig*, Reasonable Faith, 29 June 2009, www.reasonablefaith.org/is-god-imaginary.

E "Facetious." *Vocabulary.com*, www.vocabulary.com/dictionary/facetious. Accessed 29 Feb. 2016.

Feynman, Richard P. "What Is and What Should Be the Role of Scientific Culture in Modern Society." *The Pleasure of Finding Things Out: The Best Short Works of Richard P. Feynman*, Perseus, 1999, pp. 111-112.

Jillette, Penn. "There is no God." *This I Believe*, National Public Radio, 21 Nov. 2005, www.npr.org/2005/11/21/5015557/there-is-no-god.

Pratchett, Terry, et al. "Science and Magic." *The Science of Discworld*, Ebury Publishing, 1999, pp. 14-15.

F Rowling, J.K. *Harry Potter and the Deathly Hallows*. Arthur A. Levine Books, 2007.

---. *Harry Potter and the Half-Blood Prince*. Arthur A. Levine Books, 2005.

Sagan, Carl. *The Demon-Haunted World: Science as a Candle in the Dark*. Ballantine, 1997.

StarChild Team. "Who Figured out the Earth Is Round?" *StarChild: A Learning Center for Young Astronomers*, NASA, Feb. 2013, starchild.gsfc.nasa.gov/docs/StarChild/questions/question54.html.

The list of works cited includes all the works that you actually use in your paper. If you read and thought about a work but didn't end up using it, then it doesn't go on this list.

The list of works cited starts at the top of its own separate page. That's why you need to put a manual page break at the end of your paper. If you don't, then every time you add or subtract a line from the body of the paper, it will push the title of this page up or down.

Here's what you keep in mind while formatting this page:

A. The title is "Work Cited" if you just cite one work or "Works Cited" if you cite more than one work. See how that works? Both words are capitalized. Center the title.

B. The running header continues on this page, too.

C. Double-space everything here just like you did on all the other pages. Be vigilant.

D. The first line of each citation should begin at the left margin. Any subsequent lines are indented a half-inch. This is called a **hanging indent**. The only way to do this sensibly is with the ruler tool that comes with your writing software. Even that isn't easy, so search for video tutorials online. It will be worth your while to figure this out.

E. You alphabetize your sources by the first word or words in each citation. If the author isn't known, then you use the title for that work.

F. If you cite more than one source by the same author, you alphabetize by the next word in the citation — first work in the title that is an article like "a" or "the," in other words — and with those other works by the same author, you replace the author's name with three hyphens.

This is another place where taking good notes during the research process will save you time and heartache. You need to include all the information that the MLA style demands. So if you don't already have that information at your fingertips, you need to go back to the work and gather it after the fact, which you may or may not have time to do.

APA Style

The American Psychological Association (APA) is a professional organization that supports research and publication in the behavioral and social sciences, including psychology, sociology, social work and related areas of human services. APA style is a set of agreed-upon guidelines for scholars in these disciplines to follow when writing for classes or for publication. When we follow these guidelines, our readers can easily gather important reference information — like who wrote something, when they wrote it, and on what page — while remaining focused on the ideas in the writing.

Most of the APA disciplines are still relatively new, and the knowledge within them continues to change rapidly. APA style reflects that focus. In the body of papers, APA uses past-tense verbs and cites the author, page number, and — uniquely — the date of publication. That's because *when* an idea is from says a lot about its reliability. Ken Kesey's 1962 novel *One Flew Over the Cuckoo's Nest* depicts a time when scholars believed electroshock therapy, lobotomies, and the institutionalization of the mentally ill were humane, therapeutic treatments. Our ideas have evolved much since then, and a social science source from the mid-twentieth century has a high potential to be as outdated as those ideas.

APA style consists of three main categories — in-text citations, lists of references, and paper formatting. In the body of the paper, you will cite outside sources with APA-style in-text citations. At the end of your paper, you will add an APA-style bibliography called a References page. The paper as a whole uses APA-style formatting to set margins, line spacing, page-numbering, and so on.

Think of APA style as a filter. When your ideas pass through this filter, your paper will conform to APA guidelines and emerge looking like every other APA manuscript. The two things *different* about your paper will be the two most important ingredients — the idea you present and how you explain it to your readers.

1. In-Text Citations

In-text citations show readers that an idea belongs to someone other than the author and usually show where that idea can be found within the original source. They do so by providing readers with the author's last name, the year of the publication, and, if available, the page number where the idea resides.

The two places where you cite your sources in the text are in the introduction of that information and in a trailing **parenthetical citation**. The introduction might consist of an introductory statement or a **signal phrase**, and depending on the size of any direct quotations, some punctuation will also be involved.

It's typical to name the author and year of the work in the introduction and the page number in the parenthetical citation, but you can cite the author, year, and page number in the introduction, or you can cite all in the parenthetical citation. The thing you can't do is cite the information more than once. If you put it in the introduction, don't put it in the parenthetical citation.

A. Author in the Introduction

1. **In "Supporting a Strong Sense of Purpose: Lessons from a Rural Community," Dr. Devora Shamah** (2011) **argues that** "out-of-school activities of all kinds appear to support the development of a sense of purpose" (p. 56).

   The **introduction** tells us who this idea belongs to and when the idea was presented. If you mention the author in the introduction, the publication date goes next to the author's name while "p." and the page number follows in a parenthetical citation at the conclusion of the quotation. Note that the **period** goes *after* the citation and not inside the quotation marks, even if the original quoted material used a period there.

2. **In his review of** *Mouse Guard: Winter 1152* **for** *PopMatters*, <u>Walter Biggins</u> <u>(2009)</u> **claims,** "Because a talking animal wearing human clothes is a ridiculous concept to begin with, most funny-animal comics tend toward exaggeration."

> When there is no page number, as with online articles, you only need to report the <u>author's name</u> and <u>publication date</u>. If you do that in the **intro-duction**, you won't have a parenthetical citation. Note the closing **period** is now tucked inside the closing quotation mark.

3. **Biggins (2009) writes that** "most funny-animal comics tend toward exaggeration."

> When you quote just a part of sentence, and when that direct quotation completes the sentence, there's no punctuation between the **introduction** and the quotation unless it's already there for other reasons.

4. **As Shamah (2011) has shown,** there's a clear relationship between out-of-school activities and a student's sense of purpose <u>(p. 56)</u>.

> The same patterns apply to paraphrased material. If you name the author and publication date in an **introduction**, don't put that information in the <u>parenthetical citation</u>.

B. Author Absent from the Introduction

1. **It's not just one specific or even one type of out-of-school activity that matters:** "Out-of-school activities of all kinds appear to support the development of a sense of purpose" <u>(Shamah, 2011, p. 56)</u>.

> It the author isn't identified in the **introduction**, the last name, publication date, and page number go inside the <u>parenthetical citation</u>. This information, when it is available, goes in either the signal phrase or the parentheses but never both. Note that **commas** separate the different pieces of information.

2. **Most comic artists understand and maximize the conventions of their form:** "Because a talking animal wearing human clothes is a ridiculous concept to begin with, most funny-animal comics tend toward exaggeration" <u>(Biggins, 2009)</u>.

> When there is no page number to cite and no mention of the author in the **introduction**, the author's last name and publication date will be the only information inside the <u>parenthetical citation</u>. Note that **comma**!

3. **At least one expert claims that** there's a clear relationship between out-of-school activities and a student's sense of purpose <u>(Shamah, 2011, p. 56)</u>.

> And it's the same deal with citations of paraphrases or summaries. If you don't name the author in an **introduction**, then put the author's last name, date of publication, and page number in the <u>parenthetical citation</u>.

C. More Than One Work by an Author

If you use more than one work by a single author, the two works remain distinct from each other if the date of publication is different or, if the work is co-authored, if one of the contributing authors is different. If the authors and years are both the same, the standard in-text information will no longer point to a single work on the references list. You must add distinguishing information to the publication date in the in-text citation to properly identify which work you mean.

1. In support of this position, *Shamah* (**2011a**) argues that "out-of-school activities of all kinds appear to support the development of a sense of purpose" (p. 56).

> If you are citing two sources by the same *author* from the same year, add the letter "a" to the **publication date** for the first such entry. Proceed alphabetically to distinguish any remaining sources that overlap in this way.

2. Shamah (**2011a**) claims that there's a clear relationship between out-of-school activities and a student's sense of purpose (p. 56).

> The **date** and letter also appear with paraphrases and summaries.

D. Authors with the Same Last Name

When you use sources written by different authors who happen to have the same last name, include the initials of the author to make it clear which of the sources you are referencing.

1. It's not just one specific or even one type of out-of-school activity that matters: "Out-of-school activities of all kinds appear to support the development of a sense of purpose" (*D*. Shamah, 2011, p. 56).

> Whether it's in the introduction or the parenthetical citation, include the *first initial* with the last name. Of course, that only works if the other author with the same last name has a different first initial.

2. At least one expert claims that there's a clear relationship between out-of-school activities and a student's sense of purpose (*Devora* **Shamah**, 2011, p. 56).

> If the first initial is also shared with a different author, write out the author's entire *first name* and **last name**.

E. Two Authors

For works by two authors, cite both authors and maintain the order listed in the original work.

1. **According to Shamah and MacTavish (2009)**, "The smallness and safety of rural communities promotes the development of place-based knowledge among the youth" (p. 1).

The **introductory signal phrase** maintains the order the authors were listed in the original publication. Note that the <u>author names</u> are separated with the word "and" when listed in the **introduction**.

2. Growing up in a small town affords some important benefits to kids: "The smallness and safety of rural communities promotes the development of place-based knowledge among the youth" (**Shamah & MacTavish,** 2009, p. 1).

When the **author names** appear in the <u>parenthetical citation</u>, they are separated by an **ampersand**.

3. George Orwell, never a healthy man, wrote his masterpiece *Nineteen Eighty-Four* in the last years of his young life while struggling with tuberculosis. Scholars suggest that the dark mood of the book is in part a reflection of the strain he was under, trying to complete the story while grappling with this terrible illness that ultimately led to his death (**Symons, 1992, p. xix; McCrum, 2009**).

When the same idea is conveyed by two different works, separate the **citations** with a **semicolon** within the <u>parenthetical citation</u>. Note that one idea appears on page xix in the introduction to a book, and the other has no page number because it appears in a online article.

F. Three or More Authors

1. **Thomas, Walker, Verplanken,** and **Shaddick** (2016) argue that there is "substantial disagreement amongst people about how most appliances can be categorized" (p.10).

When citing sources authored by three to five people, list all the **names** the first time you refer to them in your paper.

2. **Thomas** <u>et al.</u> (2016) go on to claim their findings support "earlier research demonstrating that householders do not understand domestic energy consumption very well" (pp. 10–11).

After naming all of the authors the first time, shorten any subsequent references in your paper to the **lead author's name** followed "<u>et al.</u>," a Latin phrase meaning "and others."

3. Schilling **et al.** (2016) observe that "very often childhood maltreatment is not the result of one single type of maltreatment" (p. 9).

For a work by six or more authors, list the lead author's name followed by "et. al." at each mention. Forget about listing them the first time. If they wanted to be listed, they should have worked on a smaller team.

4. The problem is often compounded: "Very often childhood maltreatment is not the result of one single type of maltreatment" (<u>Schilling et al., 2016, p. 9</u>).

Do this same "et al." thing when the information goes inside the <u>parenthetical citation</u>, too.

G. Organization or Agency as Author

When the ideas you cite are found within official materials coming from an organization or government agency but are not attributed to a specific author, cite the organization or government agency.

1. According to the **U.S. Department of Housing and Urban Development** (HUD) (2016), there was "a 17 percent decrease in veteran homelessness between January 2015 and January 2016."

   > Place the organization or government agency name in the same place you would place a more traditional author. If the source is commonly known by an acronym, give **the full name** the first time you reference it, followed by the acronym in parentheses.

2. There was "a 47 percent decrease since 2010" (HUD, 2016).

   > Subsequent references in the paper to the same organization or government agency use the acronym only.

H. Unknown Author

If you don't know the author of your source and it isn't an organization or government agency, do some detective work and try to find it out. Seriously. It's not that hard. If the author is really not known, then if the title of the source is short, use that in the citation. If the title is not short, then use a key word or two from the title.

1. The original source material deserves a close examination. Grendel is described as a "brutish demon who lived in darkness" (**Beowulf**, 2008, p. 4).

2. Grendel is described in **Beowulf** (2008) **as** a "brutish demon who lived in darkness" (p. 4).

   > The author of the epic poem *Beowulf* is unknown, so use the **title** in the parenthetical citation where the author would typically go. When the **title** appears in the introduction, it doesn't go inside the parenthetical citation.

3. Ten years ago, the City of Portland set in motion an ambitious plan to end homelessness in this city, but today there are even more homeless men, women, and children living in Portland. (**"Crisis,"** 2015).

4. As reported in **"Crisis"** (2015), there are more homeless men, women, and children living in Portland than there were ten years ago — in spite of the City of Portland's ten-year plan to end homelessness.

   > The author of this online news article is unknown, so we use a **key word** in place of the full title. Because this is a shorter work within a larger publication, the title is marked by quotation marks.

I. Indirect Citation

In her article, Dr. Shamah cites an idea from a book by William Damon. If you want to cite the same idea from Damon that Dr. Shamah cites in her article, what do you do?

You go to the library, of course, and get Damon's book. That's what you should do. If it has *one* idea worth incorporating into your paper, it might have more and better ideas to consider. However, if you don't have time to get that book or your library can't access it, you can use an indirect citation. Give credit in the introduction to the person who came up with the idea, and use parentheses to show the reader exactly which of the sources on your list of references this idea appears within.

1. **Damon claims that** "finding one's place in the world is a developmental process that spans the life course" (as cited in *Shamah,* 2011, p. 45).

   The indirectly cited author appears in the **introduction** while *the author whose work you actually read* appears within the parenthetical citation. Note that you must include the phrase "as cited in" before the author's name in that citation.

2. **One really smart expert claims that** "finding one's place in the world is a developmental process that spans the life course" (Damon, as cited in *Shamah,* 2011, p. 45).

   If neither of the authors is mentioned in the **introduction**, the indirectly cited author and *the author whose work you actually read* both go in the parenthetical citation.

J. Personal Communication

Personal communications like e-mails, letters, memos, phone calls, and personal interviews do not have recoverable data and will not appear in the reference list. Cite them as personal communication within the body of your text instead.

The pecan pie was delicious (**S. Snoek-Brown**, personal communication, May 24, 2011).

   The **author** was telling me about a piece of pie on this day in 2011. Yum. Plus I can't believe I was able to work this into a real college essay.

K. Block Quote

Reserve block quotations for instances where you must quote more than forty words.

1. Roy K. Humble (2010) argues for the use of note cards when organizing a college essay:

> If you're using note cards, you simply unleash their awesome, low-tech power. You lay the note cards on the dinette table and move them around. I know that doesn't sound like much, but trust me — it's awesome and powerful. Note cards allow you to visually arrange the evidence into its natural patterns. (p. 97)

Despite the logic of the argument he presents, many students refuse to try the technique.

> Indent a block quote one half-inch from the left. Block quotations use formatting instead of quotation marks to show the material is a direct quotation. Typically, you should introduce a block quotation with a statement and a **colon**. The parenthetical citation sits just *outside* the **ending punctuation** of the quotation. If the paragraph continues after the block quote, do not indent the sentence that follows the block quote. That shows readers that this enormous quotation of yours is supporting information within a longer paragraph.

2. There are good reasons to use note cards while researching:

> If you're using note cards, you simply unleash their awesome, low-tech power. You lay the note cards on the dinette table and move them around. I know that doesn't sound like much, but trust me — it's awesome and powerful. Note cards allow you to visually arrange the evidence into its natural patterns. (Humble, 2010, 97)

Despite the logic of this argument, however, many students refuse to try the technique.

> If you don't name the author and date in the introduction, then put that in the parenthetical citation. But you know that by now.

2. References

The APA list of references is a complete list of the works that are used — referenced — in your paper. The complete publication information allows your readers to find any work that you used and study it themselves. APA divides that publication information into four elements, typically presented in this order:

A. Author

B. Publication date

C. Title

D. Publication information

A. Author

The author is the person or people or organization responsible for creating the source. This is the first piece of information you must find to build your citation.

With books, the author's name is usually on the spine of the cover. Magazines, newspapers, and journals typically put the author's name near the title of the article. However, the name may also appear at the end of short articles. If the source is a corporate or governmental publication and a specific author is not given, the organization itself is usually the author.

ONE AUTHOR

1. Todd**,** D̲**.** (2012). *Feeding back: Conversations with alternative guitarists from proto-punk to post-rock.* Chicago, IL: Chicago Review Press.

   List the author's last name first, followed by a **comma** and then the author's first initial. End the author section with a **period**.

2. Georges**,** N. K̲**.** (2013). *Calling Dr. Laura.* New York, NY: Houghton Mifflin Harcourt, 2013.

   Include the middle initial or initials if they are listed in the original text.

3. Churchill**,** W**.** (1953). *Triumph and tragedy.* Boston, MA: Houghton Mifflin.

   That's Sir Winston Churchill to you and me, but in a citation, don't include titles like "Sir," "PhD.," "M.S.W.," King," "Saint," or "Dr."

1. Ede, L., **& Lunsford,** A. A. (2012). *Writing together: Collaboration in theory and practice.* Boston, MA: Bedford/St. Martin's.

   Use a **comma** and an **ampersand** between the name of the last author and the next-to-last author. Note that the second author's name is written with the **last name** followed by the first initial and, in this case, a middle initial. Always list the authors in the order they appear in the text, not alphabetically.

2. Murray, R. M., Jones, P. B., Susser, E., van Os, J., **& Cannon, M.** (2002). *The epidemiology of schizophrenia.* Cambridge, UK: Cambridge University Press.

   The same pattern continues up to seven authors, with a **comma** separating each name until the last, which is marked with a **comma** and an **ampersand.**

EIGHT OR MORE AUTHORS

Raggi, A., Corso, B., Minicuci, N., Quintas, R., Sattin, D., De Torres, L., ... Leonardi, M. (2016). Determinants of quality of life in aging populations: Results from a cross-sectional study in Finland, Poland and Spain. *PLoS ONE, 11*(7), e0159293. doi: 10.1371/journal.pone.0159293

With sources with eight or more authors, list the first six names, and then insert an **ellipsis.** End the list with the last author named in the original work. You'll notice that there's no ampersand in this list. Maybe you'll notice. You'll notice if you're paying attention.

ORGANIZATIONAL OR GOVERNMENTAL AUTHOR

Business and professional documents are often considered a work product and property of the company rather than that of the sad, nameless authors who work for that organization. In that case, list the organization as the author.

U.S. Census Bureau. (2010). *Strength in numbers: Your guide to 2010 census redistricting data from the U.S. Census Bureau.* Washington, DC: U.S. Dept. of Commerce, Economics and Statistics Administration, Author.

For an organizational or government author, abbreviate commonly understood terms like "U.S." instead of writing out "United States." More complex or unfamiliar acronyms should be written out.

SCREEN NAME

Many online authors write under a screen name. You don't have to go searching for the author's secret (true) identity. You can use the screen name.

> chewingofthecud. (2014, March 13). What currents or movements are currently happening in literature? [Forum post]. Retrieved from https://www.reddit.com/r/literature/comments/20by05/what_currents_or_movements_are_currently/

> Simply list the screen name in the author's place in the citation. You can also see in this example the importance of choosing a good screen name.

NO AUTHOR

If no author is listed for the text, skip the author's place and begin the citation with the title. Do not use the word "Anonymous" in place of the author.

> Facetious. (2016). In *Vocabulary.com*. Retrieved from https://www.vocabulary.com/dictionary/facetious

> Don't use a date of publication for the first word of a citation. Move the title over to the author's place and then proceed as normal.

NON-TRADITIONAL AUTHORS

Occasionally, the person or organization most important to your discussion of a source contributed something other than the writing of the words. Some terms you are likely to use in your documentation are "performer," "director," "producer," and "reporter." However, abbreviate "editor(s)" to "Ed." or "Eds." and "translator(s)" to "Trans."

1. Abrams, J. J. (Director). (2015). *Star wars: The force awakens* [Motion picture]. United States: Lucasfilm.

> Capitalize the contributor's role, which appears inside **parentheses** and is followed by a **period**.

2. Low, A. K. (Producer), & O'Brien, B. (Writer & Reporter). (1985). *The Hoboken sound* [Documentary movie]. United States: Metromedia Telecenter. Retrieved from https://www.youtube.com/watch?v=clNuALHa_6E

> Place the role next to the contributor's name. If the contributor performed more than one key role, separate the roles as you would when listing multiple authors, using an **ampersand** in place of the "and."

3. Boluk, S., & Lenz, W. (Eds.). (2011). *Generation zombie: Essays on the living dead in modern culture.* Jefferson, NC: McFarland.

> When the principles responsible for a source are the editors, put the abbreviated role "Eds." within **parentheses**, followed by a **period**.

B. Publication Date

The publication date is the specific date the work was published. A book is published once and therefore only features the year. A periodical is published regularly throughout the year, so its publication date identifies which part of the year it was published in. A monthly magazine notes the month and year. A daily newspaper lists the day, month, and year.

The location of the publication date varies from publication to publication. In a book, the date will be on the title page or copyright page. Articles that appear in periodicals will often appear next to the byline and title of the source. This applies to online articles as well, but if a date is missing, you can also search the bottom of the web page for a publication year to stand in for something more precise.

1. Humble, R. K. **(2010).** *The humble argument.* Dallas, OR: Problem Child Press.

> For books, movies, and other works published on a non-periodic basis, put the year inside a set of **parentheses** followed by a **period**.

2. Federoff, N. & Block, J. (2016**,** <u>April 6</u>). Mosquito vs. mosquito [Editorial]. *The New York Times,* p. A23.

> Daily publications will name the year followed by **a comma** and the <u>month</u> and <u>day</u>. Months are not abbreviated in APA.

3. Barone, R. (2016**,** <u>May/June</u>). The power of song: Recording Pete Seeger. *Tape Op,* 113, 36–44.

> Bimonthly publications will often use year followed by **a comma** and a <u>month range</u> separated by a slash.

You may use the abbreviation "n.d." for no date, but do not use it lightly. It is rare that a publication date is truly not included in a print source. In web sources, it can be difficult to find, but it almost always exists in the web page's HTML code. Most web browsers will allow you to search the HTML code, but it may take some work. Ask for help.

C. Title

The next key element in an APA citation is the title of the work. In reference lists, APA style requires you to capitalize the first word of the title, the first word of the subtitle, and all proper nouns for the titles of books and articles while all other words are left in lowercase. APA also requires you to format the title to distinguish between larger and smaller works.

Occasionally, you'll need to cite non-routine information in the title. In such case, put the information within brackets and a short description of the source. Common examples are as follows:

[Letter to the editor]
[Abstract]
[Audio podcast]
[Brochure]
[Motion picture]
[MP3 file]

These are not to be confused with what APA considers "gray literature." **Gray literature** refers to sources like dissertations and technical reports that are not published formally but nevertheless contain valuable information for scholars. For these, follow the title with a description inside parentheses.

Look for the title of the source near the author's name, usually at the beginning of the work.

LARGER WORKS

APA uses formatting to quickly indicate whether the title of the source is a larger, self-contained work or a smaller work within a larger one. In APA, you italicize titles of sources that are the name of the larger work itself. You'll see this often with books, anthologies and other collections, book-length poems, movie and album names, and the names of websites.

1. Georges, N. J. (2013). *Calling Dr. Laura.* New York, NY: Houghton Mifflin Harcourt, 2013.

   This is a full-length book, so the **title** is italicized. All the words are capitalized in this title because the words are either proper nouns or the first word of the title. Put a **period** at the end of this section.

2. Roemmele, J. A., & Batdorff, D. (2001). ***Surviving the "flesh-eating bacteria":*** *Understanding, preventing, treating, and living with the effects of necrotizing fasciitis.* New York, NY: Avery.

> Put a **colon** between the **main title** and a <u>subtitle</u>. With larger works, both remain italicized. If the title contains words within quotation marks, those words are also italicized. Also, notice that only the first word of the title and subtitle are capitalized because this time, the title includes no proper nouns.

3. Bishop, K. W. (2010). *American zombie gothic: The rise and fall (and rise) of* <u>The Walking Dead</u> *in popular culture.* Jefferson, NC: McFarland.

> In this unusual example, however, there is a <u>television series title</u> within the book title that must be *de*-italicized to distinguish it from the rest of the book's title. If a part of the larger work's title would normally be italicized, then you must de-italicize it within the italics of the rest of the title.

4. Bartow, R. (1975). *After the fall III* [Paint on clay]. Portland, OR: Portland Art Museum.

> APA considers works of art to be larger works, even if they aren't physically very large, so those titles are also italicized. Non-routine sources will have a <u>short description</u> within brackets that describes the work. A **period** follows the description but not the title.

5. Kennison, K. R. (2011). *Smoke derived taint in grapes and wine* (<u>Doctoral dissertation</u>). Retrieved from http://espace.library.curtin.edu.au/R?func=d-bin-jump-full&local_base=gen01-era02&object_id=185451

> Non-routine works published informally, such as a dissertation or thesis, come with a <u>short description</u> within parentheses. A **period** follows the description.

SMALLER WORKS WITHIN A LARGER WORK

Smaller works are usually nested within a larger work. For these, APA leaves the title of the smaller work unitalicized and does not mark it with quotation marks. The first word in a title or subtitle is capitalized but all other words other than proper nouns are not capitalized. APA considers smaller works things like short stories and essays in an anthology, short poems within a collection, episodes within a television series, songs within an album, articles within a website, and so on.

1. Gladwell, M. (2013, December 10). Being nice isn't really so awful. *The New Yorker, 40*(89). Retrieved from http://www.newyorker.com

> The title is left unitalicized because it appears within a larger work, in this case an online magazine.

2. Mahoney, P. (2011). Gray is the new black: <u>Race, class, and zombies.</u> In S. Boluk, & W. Lenz (Eds.), *Generation zombie: Essays on the living dead in modern culture* (pp. 55–72). Jefferson, NC: McFarland.

> This citation refers to an article within an edited book, so the **title** is not italicized. Notice how the first letter of the <u>subtitle</u> is capitalized.

3. Tuchman, B. (1962). **Ch. 19: Retreat.** *The guns of August.* (pp. 341–372). London, England: Macmillan.

> Chapters or other sections within a book are considered shorter works, even if they are quite long, so the title is not italicized.

4. Mayo Clinic. (2013, July 25). **Gallstones-Definition.** *Mayo clinic.* Retrieved from http://www.mayoclinic.org/diseases-conditions/gallstones/basics/definition/con-20020461

> **Web pages** are shorter works within websites. There are no brackets explaining this as a website because, let's face it, information from websites is as routine at it gets.

5. ArtsAlive YamhillCo. (2015, March 25). **ArtsAlive Stephanie Lenox** [<u>Video file</u>]. Retrieved from https://www.youtube.com/ watch?v=xOQIKeERJTE.

> This is a smaller work, so the title isn't italicized. While information from websites is routine, multimedia on the web is still considered non-routine. Therefore the title includes a <u>short description</u> within **brackets** that describes the work and a **period** that follows the description.

6. Grosvenor, E. (2010, August 7). The dude abides in Salem. [Blog post]. Retrieved from https://desperatelyseekingsalem.wordpress.com/2010/08/08/the-dude-abides-in-salem/

> Yes, we know that blogs are routine, but APA has other ideas. Sometimes it seems to use these <u>short descriptions</u> to look down its collective nose at some sources.

7. Kenny, G. (2016, January 15). A perfect day [Review of the film *A perfect day*, by F. L. de Aranoa]. *rogerebert.com.* Retrieved from http://www.rogerebert.com/reviews/a-perfect-day-2016

> When the work is a review of another work, add a note that includes "Review of," the type and title of the work, and the principle author responsible, all within **brackets** and followed by a **period**. A **comma** separates the title of the reviewed work from its author.

APA

D. Publication

The fourth and most complex element of an APA citation is the one that captures publication information about the source. This section will include information about some or all of the following subcategories of information:

1. Other contributors

2. Title of publication

3. Version

4. Number

5. Publisher

6. Publisher location

Not every source will use each of the subcategories described in this section. For example, a periodical does not typically come in "versions," but in volumes and issues, two variations covered by "number." In such cases, when your source does not contain one of the subcategories, move on to the next one on the list.

D1. OTHER CONTRIBUTORS

Other contributors are people who play integral roles in creating the publication but are secondary to the named author of the source. These contributors must be identified by their role in the publication with terms such as "Trans." (translator), "Ed.," (editor), and so on.

You'll find the names of other contributors on title pages or other places where credit is given to collaborators, like the credits of a film or the liner notes of an album. Only bring in the additional contributors whose work is directly applicable to the topic of your writing.

1. Bolano, R. (2008). *The savage detectives.* (N. Wimmer, Trans.). New York, NY: Picador.

> When the main work has an additional contributor, the contributor name goes inside **parentheses**, followed by a **comma** and the role. Note that the first initial of the contributor precedes the last name.

2. Mahoney, P. (2011). Gray is the new black: Race, class, and zombies. In S. Boluk & W. Lenz (Eds.), *Generation zombie: Essays on the living dead in modern culture* (pp. 55-72). Jefferson, NC: McFarland.

When the work being cited is included within a larger work, start with the preposition "In" and then list the contributors' **names**. Use the first initial and then the last name. After that, put the <u>role</u> of the contributors within a set of **parentheses**, followed by a **comma**.

D2. TITLE OF PUBLICATION

The title of publication is used when a shorter work is published within a larger work, such as a news article inside a newspaper. The name of the shorter work goes in the regular title section of the citation. The name of the larger work goes after that as the title of publication.

1. Boluk, S., & Lenz, W. (Eds.). (2011). *Generation zombie: Essays on the living dead in modern culture.* Jefferson, NC: McFarland.

   When the work cited is a larger work like this book, the title goes into the main title section. So there's nothing to put here for title of publication. That's okay. Move along.

2. Mahoney, P. (2011). Gray is the new black: Race, class, and zombies. In S. Boluk, & W. Lenz (Eds.), *Generation zombie: Essays on the living dead in modern culture* (pp. 55–72). Jefferson, NC: McFarland.

   In this example, the citation focuses on an article within the larger work. The name of the anthology goes here as the title of publication.

3. Rockmore, E.B. (2015, October 15). How Texas teaches history. *The New York Times.* Retrieved from http://www.nytimes.com

   With articles in periodicals, the title of publication is typically the name of the journal, magazine, or newspaper.

4. Mayo Clinic. (2013, July 25). Gallstones-Definition. *Mayo Clinic.* Retrieved from http://www.mayoclinic.org/diseases-conditions/gallstones/basics/definition/con-20020461

   When the focus of the source is on one page at a website, the title of publication is the name of the website.

5. Agrippina (Agrippina the younger). (1989). In *Encyclopedia of world crime* (Vol. 1, pp. 39-40). Wilmette, IL: CrimeBooks, Inc.

   With an article in a reference work, the title of publication is the title of the main reference work, preceded by the preposition "In."

6. Silence (2016). War drums. On *The deafening sound of absolutely nothing* [<u>MP3 file</u>]. Huntington, WV: Profane Existence.

   When citing a song, the song title is in the main title section, and the name of the album is the title of publication, preceded by the preposition "On." A <u>description</u> of the non-routine source is in **brackets**.

D3. VERSION

Works often have multiple versions or editions identified by numbers that tell you how many times the publication has been revised — 2nd edition, for example — or names that tell you the nature of the revision — like "unabridged" or "expanded."

When they exist, version numbers or names can usually be found next to the title of the publication.

> Rottenberg, A.T., & Winchell, D. H. (2015). *The structure of argument* **(**8th ed.**).** Boston, MA: Bedford/St. Martin's.

> Use numbers rather than spelling out editions distinguished by an ordinal number. Don't use superscript for the number either. Put the version within **parentheses** and follow that with a **period**.

D4. NUMBER

Books that are too long to be published in a single publication are often split into multiple publications, and each is given its own volume number. In addition, periodicals that are published on an ongoing basis — as is the case with most scholarly journals — are assigned volume, issue, or volume *and* issue numbers to distinguish one publication of the periodical from another.

The number is typically found near the title of the publication. However, it may be found within the publication on a page with more information about the publication, contributors, and so on.

1. Ruiz, G., & Sánchez, N. (2014). Wolfgang Köhler's *The Mentality of Apes* and the animal psychology of his time. *The Spanish Journal of Psychology, 17,* E69.

> When a journal is paginated by volume only, the italicized volume number will follow the publication title, followed by a **comma**.

2. Gladwell, M. (2013, December 10). Being nice isn't really so awful. *The New Yorker, 40*(89). Retrieved from http://www.newyorker.com

> If a journal has both volume number and issue number, mention the italicized volume number first, followed by the issue number within parentheses, leaing no space between the two.

3. Sheffield, R. (2015). Getting to know Colbert. *Rolling Stone,* 1295, 30.

> If there is no volume number, mention the issue number only.

4. Agrippina (Agrippina the younger). (1989). In *Encyclopedia of world crime* (Vol. 1, pp. 39-40). Wilmette, IL: CrimeBooks, Inc.

> While you don't write "Vol." when referring to a periodical, you do use the abbreviation when citing one volume in a multi-volume book.

D5. PUBLISHER

The publisher is the company or person who actually produced a book, government publication, film, or website. Film and television series generally involve multiple publishers. In such cases, cite the publisher primarily responsible for the work. Periodicals often do not have a publisher, in which case you can skip this section. In addition, APA does not record publishers of websites.

With a book, you can find the name of the publisher on the title page or on a page near the front of the book that provides more information about the publication and its copyright. On pamphlets, look on the back or the innermost leaf of the folded paper. On brochures, look at the front or back covers.

1. McCloud, S. (2015). *The sculptor*. New York**,** NY**:** First Second Books, 2015.

   For books printed in the United States, separate the city and state abbreviation with a **comma**. Then, add a **colon** and list the name of the publishing company.

2. Murray, R. M., Jones, P. B., Susser, E., van Os, J., & Cannon, M. (2002). *The epidemiology of schizophrenia*. Cambridge**,** UK**:** Cambridge University Press.

   With books published out of the country, separate the city and country with a **comma,** followed by **colon** and the name of the publishing company.

3. Frank Lisciandro. [Television series episode]. (2016). In *The writing life*. McMinnville, OR: McMinnville Community Media, MCM-TV.

   With television broadcasts, films, and albums, the publisher is the company or organization that paid for the creation of the work.

4. Travel Guard. (2016). *Insure your next trip with Travel Guard* [Brochure]. Stevens Point, WI: Author.

   For self-published works, such as this brochure, write the word "Author" to show that the author and the publishing company are the same.

D6. LOCATION

The location varies by the type of work. For shorter works within anthologies or periodicals, the location is usually a page number or a range of pages. The location for a work of art is often the place where the piece is on exhibit. For online sources, the location is a **URL** or **DOI**. Because of the possibilities here, your main task is to be precise as possible.

1. Behar, E., McGowan, S., McLaughlin, K., Borkovec, T., Goldwin, M., & Bjorkquist, O. (1998). Concreteness of positive, negative, and neutral repetitive thinking about the future. *Behavior Therapy, 43*(2), 300–312**.**

   Use an **en-dash** to separate a range of pages. Put a **period** after the last page.

2. OSU women try to keep a storied season going. (2016, April 2). *The Oregonian*, p. A1.

> Page numbers in a newspaper source are preceded by a "p." for information on one page or "pp." for information on multiple pages. The page numbers often include a letter that refers to one section of the newspaper.

3. Erlanger, S., Castle, S., & Gladstone, R. (2016, April 6). Airing of hidden wealth stirs inquiries and rage: Iceland premier steps down as release of files reverberates around world. *The New York Times*, pp. A1**,** A6.

> For a multi-page work that appears on non-consecutive pages, list each page separately, separated by a **comma**.

4. Grosvenor, E. (2010, August 7). The dude abides in Salem [Blog post]. Retrieved from https://desperatelyseekingsalem.wordpress.com/2010/08/08/the-dude-abides-in-salem/

> For online works, write "Retrieved from" and the URL. Only use a URL if it will reliably and consistently allow a reader to navigate to the cited page and only give enough information to get to the desired source. Avoid using one-time URLs generated for a specific browsing session.

5. Aagaard, J. (2015, December.) Media multitasking, attention, and distraction: A critical discussion. *Phenomenology and the Cognitive Sciences, 14*(4), 885. doi:10.1007/s11097-014- 9375-x

> A digital object identifier (**DOI**) is more reliable than a URL, and if that's available, that's what you should use. You do not need to use "Retrieved from" when you use a DOI, which is more elegant.

6. Racy, A.J. (2016, Spring/Summer). Domesticating otherness: The snake charmer in American popular culture. *Ethnomusicology, 60*(2), 197–232. Retrieved from www.jstor.org/stable/10.5406/ethnomusicology.60.2.0197

> In general, don't include database information unless the work can only be found in an electronic database. In such case, give the URL for the online archive and add "Retrieved from."

7. Bartow, R. (1975). *After the fall III* [Paint on clay]. Portland, OR: Portland Art Museum.

> For items that appear in physical locations, name the place the work is housed with sufficient distinguishing detail like city, state, or country.

E. Reference List Examples

As you see from the past section, APA style divides reference list information into four main sections:

A. Author

B. Publication date

C. Title

D. Publication information

In the examples that follow, we'll show you how to format citations for your references list and then the information that goes into each main section.

Even though these are common examples, you still have to adopt them to fit the information about the works you're using. You may have to tinker with the author section or the publication section to accurately capture the information about a given work.

But that's a good thing. It means that you can build each citation to match the works instead of having to somehow tailor the information about a work to fit a template that doesn't really fit.

BOOKS

ONE AUTHOR (PRINT)

Georges, N. J. (2013). *Calling Dr. Laura*. New York, NY: Houghton Mifflin Harcourt.

> 1. (Author) Georges, N. J.
> 2. (Publication date) (2013).
> 3. (Title) *Calling Dr. Laura*.
> 4. (Publication information) New York, NY: Houghton Mifflin Harcourt.

EDITION OTHER THAN THE FIRST

Rottenberg, A.T., & Winchell, D. H. (2015). *The structure of argument* (8th ed.). Boston, MA: Bedford/St. Martin's.

> 1. Rottenberg, A.T., & Winchell, D. H.
> 2. (2015).
> 3. *The structure of argument* (8th ed.).
> 4. Boston, MA: Bedford/St. Martin's.

APA

EDITED COLLECTION

Boluk, S., & Lenz, W. (Eds.). (2011). *Generation zombie: Essays on the living dead in modern culture.* Jefferson, NC: McFarland.

1. Boluk, S., & Lenz, W. (Eds.).
2. (2011).
3. *Generation zombie: Essays on the living dead in modern culture.*
4. Jefferson, NC: McFarland.

ONLINE BOOK

Twain, Mark. (1917). *Life on the Mississippi.* New York, NY: Harper & Brothers Publishers. Retrieved from books.google.com

1. Twain, Mark.
2. (1917).
3. *Life on the Mississippi.*
4. New York, NY: Harper & Brothers Publishers. Retrieved from books. google.com

SACRED TEXT

Use in-text citations only. Do not cite in the references list.

PARTS OF BOOKS

CHAPTER OF A BOOK

Tuchman, B. (1962). Ch. 19: Retreat. *The guns of August.* (pp. 341–372). London, England: Macmillan.

1. Tuchman, B.
2. (1962).
3. Ch. 19: Retreat.
4. *The guns of August.* (pp. 341–372). London, England: Macmillan.

WORK IN AN ANTHOLOGY

Mahoney, P. (2011). Gray is the new black: Race, class, and zombies. In S. Boluk, & W. Lenz (Eds.), *Generation zombie: Essays on the living dead in modern culture* (pp. 55–72). Jefferson, NC: McFarland.

1. Mahoney, P.
2. (2011).
3. Gray is the new black: Race, class, and zombies.
4. In S. Boluk, & W. Lenz (Eds.), *Generation zombie: Essays on the living dead in modern culture* (pp. 55–72). Jefferson, NC: McFarland.

Article in a Reference Book

Agrippina (Agrippina the younger). (1989). In *Encyclopedia of world crime* (Vol. 1, pp. 39–40). Wilmette, IL: CrimeBooks, Inc.

> 1. —
> 2. (1989).
> 3. Agrippina (Agrippina the younger).
> 4. In *Encyclopedia of world crime* (Vol. 1, pp. 39–40). Wilmette, IL: Crime-Books, Inc.

ARTICLES

Journal Article (Print)

Racy, A.J. (2016, Spring/Summer). Domesticating otherness: The snake charmer in American popular culture. *Ethnomusicology, 60*(2), 197–232.

> 1. Racy, A.J.
> 2. (2016, Spring/Summer).
> 3. Domesticating otherness: The snake charmer in American popular culture.
> 4. *Ethnomusicology, 60*(2), 197–232.

Journal Article (Library Database)

Racy, A.J. (2016, Spring/Summer). Domesticating otherness: The snake charmer in American popular culture. *Ethnomusicology, 60*(2), 197–232. Retrieved from www.jstor.org/stable/10.5406/ethnomusicology.60.2.0197

> 1. Racy, A.J.
> 2. (2016, Spring/Summer).
> 3. Domesticating otherness: The snake charmer in American popular culture.
> 4. *Ethnomusicology,* 60(2), 197–232. Retrieved from www.jstor.org/stable/10.5406/ethnomusicology.60.2.0197

Magazine Article (Print)

Barone, R. (2016, May/June). The power of song: Recording Pete Seeger. *Tape Op,* 113, 36–44.

> 1. Barone, R.
> 2. (2016, May/June).
> 3. The power of song: Recording Pete Seeger.
> 4. *Tape Op,* 113, 36–44.

APA
References Examples

MAGAZINE ARTICLE (WEBSITE)

Engber, D. (2016, January 26). The neurologist who hacked his brain—
and almost lost his mind. *Wired*. Retrieved from http://www.wired.
com/2016/01/phil-kennedy-mind-control-computer/

1. Engber, D.
2. (2016, January 26).
3. The neurologist who hacked his brain—and almost lost his mind.
4. *Wired*. Retrieved from http://www.wired.com/2016/01/phil-kennedy-
   mind-control-computer/

NEWSPAPER ARTICLE (PRINT)

Erlanger, S., Castle, S. & Gladstone, R. (2016, April 6). Airing of hidden
wealth stirs inquiries and rage: Iceland premier steps down as release
of files reverberates around world. *The New York Times*, pp. A1, A6.

1. Erlanger, S., Castle, S. & Gladstone, R.
2. (2016, April 6).
3. Airing of hidden wealth stirs inquiries and rage: Iceland premier steps
   down as release of files reverberates around world.
4. *The New York Times*, pp. A1, A6.

NEWSPAPER ARTICLE (WEBSITE)

Rockmore, E.B. (2015, October 15). How Texas teaches history. *The New
York Times*. Retrieved from http://www.nytimes.com

1. Rockmore, E.B.
2. (2015, October 15).
3. How Texas teaches history.
4. *The New York Times*. Retrieved from http://www.nytimes.com

REFERENCE ARTICLE (PRINT)

Agrippina (Agrippina the younger). (1989). In *Encyclopedia of world crime*
(Vol. 1, pp. 39-40). Wilmette, IL: CrimeBooks, Inc.

1. —
2. (1989).
3. Agrippina (Agrippina the younger).
4. In *Encyclopedia of World Crime* (Vol. 1, pp. 39–40). Wilmette, IL: Crime-
   Books, Inc.

Facetious. (2016). In *Vocabulary.com*. Retrieved from https://www.vocabu-
 lary.com/dictionary/facetious

  1. —
  2. (2016).
  3. Facetious.
  4. In *Vocabulary.com*. Retrieved from https://www.vocabulary.com/dictio-
   nary/facetious

Reference Article (Library Database)

Iūlia Agrippīna (Agrippina the younger). (2007). In Roberts, J.
 (Ed.), *Oxford dictionary of the classical world*, Oxford, England:
 Oxford University Press. Retrieved from http://www.oxfordref-
 erence.com/view/10.1093/acref/9780192801463.001.0001/acref-
 9780192801463-e-1165

  1. —
  2. (2007).
  3. Iūlia Agrippīna (Agrippina the younger).
  4. In Roberts, J. (Ed.), *Oxford dictionary of the classical world*, Oxford, England:
   Oxford University Press. Retrieved from http://www.oxfordreference.com/
   view/10.1093/acref/9780192801463.001.0001/acref-9780192801463-e-1165

ONLINE PUBLICATIONS

Entire Website

APA rules state that you should *not* include an entire website in the list of
references. Instead, the URL should be included in the text of the paper in
parentheses.

Web Page

Mayo Clinic. (2013, July 25). Gallstones-Definition. *Mayo Clinic*.
 Retrieved from http://www.mayoclinic.org/diseases-conditions/gall-
 stones/basics/definition/con-20020461

  1. Mayo Clinic.
  2. (2013, July 25).
  3. Gallstones-Definition.
  4. *Mayo Clinic*. Retrieved from http://www.mayoclinic.org/diseases-con-
   ditions/gallstones/basics/definition/con-20020461

Social Media

LibrariansTNT. (2016, January 6). Cassandrasaurs for sure roamed
this earth. Retrieved from https://twitter.com/LibrariansTNT/
status/684778779034517504.

1. LibrariansTNT.
2. (2016, January 6).
3. Cassandrasaurs for sure roamed this earth.
4. Retrieved from https://twitter.com/LibrariansTNT/status/684778779034517504.

Blog

Grosvenor, E. (2010, August 7). The dude abides in Salem [Blog
post]. Retrieved from https://desperatelyseekingsalem.wordpress.
com/2010/08/08/the-dude-abides-in-salem/

1. Grosvenor, E.
2. (2010, August 7).
3. The dude abides in Salem [Blog post].
4. Retrieved from https://desperatelyseekingsalem.wordpress.com/2010/08/08/
   the-dude-abides-in-salem/

Online Video

ArtsAlive YamhillCo. (2015, March 25). ArtsAlive Stephanie Lenox
[Video file]. Retrieved from https://www.youtube.com/ watch?v=xO-
QIKeERJTE.

1. ArtsAlive YamhillCo.
2. (2015, March 25).
3. ArtsAlive Stephanie Lenox [Video file].
4. Retrieved from https://www.youtube.com/ watch?v=xOQIKeERJTE.

MEDIA AND PERFORMANCE

Film

Abrams, J. J. (Director). (2015). *Star wars: The force awakens* [Motion
picture]. United States: Lucasfilm.

1. Abrams, J. J. (Director).
2. (2015).
3. *Star wars: The force awakens* [Motion picture].
4. United States: Lucasfilm.

Television Show (Broadcast)

Frank Lisciandro [Television series episode]. (2016). In *The writing life*.
McMinnville, OR: McMinnville Community Media, MCM-TV.

APA

References Examples

1. —
2. (2016).
3. Frank Lisciandro [Television series episode].
4. In *The writing life*. McMinnville, OR: McMinnville Community Media, MCM-TV.

TELEVISION SHOW (DIGITAL)

Cox, C., & D'Onofrio, V. (Performers). (2015). World on fire [Television series episode]. In F. Blackburn (Director), *Daredevil*. Burbank, CA: ABC Studios.

1. Cox, C., & D'Onofrio, V. (Performers).
2. (2015).
3. World on fire [Television series episode].
4. In F. Blackburn (Director), *Daredevil*. Burbank, CA: ABC Studios.

ONLINE VIDEO

ArtsAlive YamhillCo. (2015, March 25). ArtsAlive Stephanie Lenox [Video file]. Retrieved from https://www.youtube.com/ watch?v=xO-QIKeERJTE.

1. ArtsAlive YamhillCo.
2. (2015, March 25).
3. ArtsAlive Stephanie Lenox [Video file].
4. Retrieved from https://www.youtube.com/ watch?v=xOQIKeERJTE.

AUDIO (ALBUM)

Mould, Bob. (1989). *Workbook*. Beverly Hills, CA: Virgin Records America.

1. Mould, Bob.
2. (1989).
3. *Workbook*.
4. Beverly Hills, CA: Virgin Records America.

AUDIO (DIGITAL)

Adams, S. (2016, December 29). Be cool to the pizza dude. *This I believe* [Audio podcast]. Retrieved from http://cdn.audiometric. io/9487820912.mp3

1. Adams, S.
2. (2016, December 29).
3. Be cool to the pizza dude.
4. *This I believe* [Audio podcast]. Retrieved from http://cdn.audiometric. io/9487820912.mp3

Advertisement

BF Goodrich Co. (2016, July). Put the magazine down and go [Advertisement]. *Automobile Magazine, 31*(4). (p. 5). Ann Arbor, MI: The Enthusiast Network.

1. BF Goodrich Co.
2. (2016, July).
3. Put the magazine down and go [Advertisement].
4. *Automobile Magazine, 31*(4). (p. 5). Ann Arbor, MI: The Enthusiast Network.

Fine Art

Bartow, R. (1975). *After the fall III* [Paint on clay]. Portland, OR: Portland Art Museum.

1. Bartow, R.
2. (1975).
3. *After the fall III* [Paint on clay].
4. Portland, OR: Portland Art Museum.

Performance

Sikking, D. (Director). (2015, March 5-14). *Pride and prejudice*, by J. Austen [Theatre performance]. ACMA Theater Company, Arts & Communications Magnet Academy Theater, Beaverton, OR.

1. Sikking, D. (Director).
2. (2015, March 5-14).
3. *Pride and prejudice*, by J. Austen [Theatre performance].
4. ACMA Theater Company, Arts & Communications Magnet Academy Theater, Beaverton, OR.

OTHER

Pamphlet, Brochure, or Press Release

Travel Guard. (2016). *Insure your next trip with Travel Guard*. Stevens Point, WI: Author.

1. Travel Guard.
2. (2016).
3. *Insure your next trip with Travel Guard*.
4. Stevens Point, WI: Author

U.S. Census Bureau. (2010). *Strength in numbers: Your guide to 2010 census redistricting data from the U.S. Census Bureau.* Washington, DC: U.S. Dept. of Commerce, Economics and Statistics Administration, Author.

1. U.S. Census Bureau.
2. (2010).
3. *Strength in numbers: Your guide to 2010 census redistricting data from the U.S. Census Bureau.*
4. Washington, DC: U.S. Dept. of Commerce, Economics and Statistics Administration, Author.

DISSERTATION

Kennison, K. R. (2011). *Smoke derived taint in grapes and wine* (Doctoral dissertation). Retrieved from http://espace.library.curtin.edu.au/R?func=dbin-jump-full&local_base=gen01-era02&object_id=185451

1. Kennison, K. R.
2. (2011).
3. *Smoke derived taint in grapes and wine* (Doctoral dissertation).
4. Retrieved from http://espace.library.curtin.edu.au/R?func=dbin-jump-full&local_base=gen01-era02&object_id=18545

PERSONAL INTERVIEW

APA does not require a citation in your references. Simply indicate the personal interview within the text of your essay. See the section in this chapter on personal communications and in-text citations for more about this.

EMAIL

APA directs you to cite emails within your text, so there's no need for a reference entry. See the section in this chapter on personal communications and in-text citations for more about this.

3. Paper Format

APA style also offers guidance about how to format your paper so that it looks like all the other APA papers. This helps ensure that readers will stay focused on your ideas. Here are the general guidelines to keep in mind:

1. Type your paper on a computer and print it out on standard, white 8.5- by 11-inch paper. Set the margins of your document to one inch on all four sides.

2. Use a readable, businesslike font that doesn't draw attention to itself and is easy to read. Times New Roman is a popular choice, and a 12-point size in this font is readable.

3. Double-space everything — no more, no less.

4. Leave two spaces after periods.

5. Indent the first line of paragraphs one half-inch from the left margin. Use the tab key to do that, too. Pushing the space bar five times to create a half-inch indentation worked on a typewriter, but it doesn't work with computers. These are different times.

6. Create a header in the upper right-hand corner of each page that is one half-inch from the top of the page and even with the right margin. This should include your last name and the page number. Use automatic page numbering for that. Trying to do that manually will cause needless suffering.

7. Never use boldface. Only use italics as required for the titles of larger works and some publications and, with grave restraint, for emphasis within the paper.

In addition to these general guidelines, APA style also provides guidelines for how to format different pages within a paper. In the following pages, we'll show you how that works with formatted examples.

APA style requires a title page, so here are points to keep in mind for that page:

A. In the upper left hand corner, one half-inch from the top of the page, put "Running head," followed by a colon and then the title of your paper in all capital letters. Do not include a subtitle here.

A. Title Page

A Running head: PROVING THE NEGATIVE

1 B

Proving the Negative

C

Jack Wiegand

Chemeketa Community College

APA
Paper Format

B. In the upper right hand corner of the page, one half-inch from the top of the paper, put the page number without any other words. This runs throughout the entire paper, so use automatic numbering in the header section of your document for that.

C. In the upper half of the title page, put the title of your paper, and beneath that your name, and beneath that the name of the school you attend. If your paper contains a subtitle, put a colon after the title and put the subtitle on its own line beneath that. Center all of these lines on the page.

207

B. Abstract

D PROVING THE NEGATIVE   2

E Abstract

F Folk logic holds that you can't prove a negative. The purpose of this paper is to explain why this

sentiment is universally rejected among logicians. The author explains that negative categorical

propositions come in two forms and describes methods by which each can be proven true. Type

O propositions take the form $(\exists x)(Sx \cdot {\sim}Px)$, or "Some S are not P." A Type O statement such as

"not all dogs have four legs" can be proven by observing a dog with any number of legs besides

four. Type E propositions take the form $(x)(Sx \Rightarrow {\sim}Px)$, or "No S is P." The majority of these

statements can only be proven by way of inference, as observation of every x is not possible.

However, exceptions exist. For example, a statement such as "no bachelors are married" can be

proven by illustrating that the phrase "married bachelor" is internally inconsistent. This paper

also points out that the statement "You can't prove a negative" is, itself, a Type E proposition,

and that if you could prove it, it wouldn't be true. This paper further argues that the lack of

absolute proof does not preclude reasonable certainty and that sufficient absence of evidence

should be regarded as evidence of absence.

APA

APA
Paper Format

The second page contains an abstract, which is a short summary of your paper's contents. The abstract should be 250 words or fewer.

D. The title of your paper in all caps appears in the upper left hand corner but without the "Running head" from the title page.

E. The title is "Abstract." Center the title.

F. Note that you do not indent the abstract paragraph.

Now it's time to start presenting the actual paper. On the first page of

C. First Page

H Proving the Negative

With the arrival of social media, society has seen a marked increase in armchair academia. Like the dilettantes of the Victorian era, today's hobbyist intellectuals spend their free time engaging in the gentleman's sport of debate, study, and showing off their brains, rather than their muscles. Also like the dilettantes of old, they treat it as strictly leisure, while eschewing rigorous academic commitment. While they might be able to regale their friends for hours about the brilliance of Voltaire, they've likely read his Wikipedia page, rather than *Candide,* or *Plato's Dream.* While they may be able to offer a criticism of a documentary about humanism, they would likely struggle to offer a worthwhile analysis of Thomas More's *Utopia.* Not that there's anything wrong with dilettantism. If anything, it does for society much more than reality television or competitive Frisbee.

I   It can, however, create a few issues. In every scholarly field, information tends to change slightly as it moves from the academic sphere to the public sphere. When simplifying ideas to make them accessible to the public, the foundational information — that can, in many cases, take years of study to understand — is necessarily lost. To borrow from *The Science of Discworld,* we tend to "bend the truths just sufficiently to make the basic principles of the operation clear to a layman while not actually being entirely wrong" (Pratchett, Stewart, and Cohen, 2003, p. 14). What the authors go on to describe as "lies to children" may seem wholly benign (p. 15), but they often lead to small misunderstandings, which can accumulate to form vast misunderstandings.

In philosophy, we might call these bits of misinformation folk logic. These are most easily described as bad ideas that agree with common sense. While most people tend to hold common sense in high regard, it is a very inefficient means of understanding the universe, as it

APA

APA
Paper Format

your essay or research paper, do this:

G. Put the title of your paper in all caps in the upper left hand corner and the page number in the right hand corner. This running header will continue through the rest of the paper, so we'll shut up about it.

H. Center the title on the next double-spaced line. Don't add extra spaces before or after.

I. Indent the first sentence of each paragraph exactly one half-inch. Use tabs to do that. Spaces are not precise enough.

D. Middle Pages

moon, as it moved through its annual cycle, indicated that the moon was a sphere (StarChild Team, 2013).

Many people have used this example as an argument against scientific understanding, **J** claiming that if we were wrong about something like that, we could be wrong about anything. In rebuttal, rationalists are fond of saying that while we may not be absolutely right about certain things, we are continuously becoming less wrong. As Richard Feyman (1999) put it in a lecture given at the 1964 Galileo Symposium:

> **K** A scientist is never certain. We all know that. We know that all our statements are approximate statements with different degrees of certainty; that when a statement is made, the question is not whether it is true or false but rather how likely it is to be true or false...We must discuss each question within the uncertainties that are allowed...We absolutely must leave room for doubt or there is no progress and there is no learning. (pp. 111-112)

People tend to think of correctness as a binary; one is simply correct or incorrect. To wit, we now know that the Earth is not round, or at least not perfectly so. Isaac Newton observed, correctly, that the Earth is an oblate spheroid rather than a perfect sphere (Choi, 2007). While both previously held positions are incorrect, surely it is *less* incorrect to describe the Earth as round rather than flat.

Just as positive evidence can be used to make more reasonable positive statements, so too can negative evidence — or, the *absence* of evidence — be used to make more reasonable negative statements. Unfortunately, this is another case of widespread misunderstanding. The popular belief, known as Rees' Maxim, is that absence of evidence is not evidence of absence. This misunderstanding is not only prevalent in the public sphere, but has also found a foothold

APA
Paper Format

In the middle pages of the paper, there are few more things to remember:

J. Continue to double-space every line, no more and no less. Check your word processing software's paragraph formatting to make sure it doesn't add extra spacing at the end of each paragraph.

K. For block quotations, use your word-processor's ruler tool to indent the entire paragraph one half-inch from the left margin. Leave the right margin alone. Don't try to do this with tabs or spaces. To do so will only cause painful and permanent regret.

E. References

L References

Cham, J. (2009, July 3). PHD comics: Proving a negative. *Piled Higher and Deeper*. Retrieved

M   from http://www.comic-rocket.com/read/piled-higher-and-deeper-phd/1194

Choi, C. Q. (2007, April 12). Strange but true: Earth is not round. *Scientific American*. Retrieved

        from http://www.scientificamerican.com   N

Craig, W. L. (2009, June 29). Is God imaginary?: Santa Claus, tooth fairies, and God.

        Reasonable Faith with William Lane Craig. Retrieved February 29, 2016 from

        http://www.reasonablefaith.org/is-god-imaginary

O Facetious. (2016). In *Vocabulary.com*. Retrieved from

        https://www.vocabulary.com/dictionary/facetious

Feynman, R. P. (1999). What is and what should be the role of scientific culture in modern

        society. In J. Robbins, *The Pleasure of Finding Things Out: The Best Short Works of*

        Richard P. Feynman (pp. 111-112). Cambridge, MA: Perseus.

Hales, S. (2005). Thinking tools: You *can* prove a negative. *Think*, *4*(10), 109-112.

Pratchett, T., Stewart, I., & Cohen, J. (1999). *The science of Discworld*. London, England: Ebury

        Publishing.

Rowling, J.K. (2005). *Harry Potter and the half-blood prince*. New York, NY: Arthur A. Levine

P   Books.

Rowling, J.K. (2007). *Harry Potter and the deathly hallows*. New York, NY: Arthur A. Levine

        Books.

StarChild Team. (2013, February). Who figured out the Earth is round? *StarChild: A Learning*

        Center for Young Astronomers. Retrieved February 29, 2016 from

        http://starchild.gsfc.nasa.gov/docs/StarChild/questions/question54.html

APA

APA
Paper Format

When you get to the end of your paper, insert a manual page break so that the references list will start at the top of its own page. The list includes all the works that you actually use in your paper.

Below, and continuing on the next page, is what to keep in mind :

L. The title is "Reference" if you just cite one work or "References" if you cite more than one work. Capitalize and center the title.

M. The first line of each citation begins at the left margin. Subsequent lines are indented a half-inch. This is called a **hanging indent**. The most sensible way to do this is with the ruler tool that comes with your writing software. Even that isn't easy to figure out on your own, so search for video tutorials online. Once you get the hang of it, though, it's no big deal.

N. Double-space everything here just like you did on all the other pages. Be steadfast. Do *not* add a little extra space after each entry.

O. Alphabetize your sources by the first word or words in each citation. If the author isn't known, then you use the title for that work.

P. If you cite more than one source by the same author, you alphabetize by the next part of the citation. If the next part of the citation is a second author, use the second author. If the next part of the citation is the year, use the year.

That doesn't seem so hard.

Chicago Style

The Chicago style of citation emerged out of the needs of the University of Chicago Press, beginning in 1891. To aid in the printing of professors' academic work, the editorial staff at the Press developed a style sheet. That sheet developed into a published book, and the *Chicago Manual of Style* has gone through sixteen editions in the years since. Today, the Chicago style is used by many disciplines in the humanities, including history, as a set of agreed-upon guidelines for scholars in these disciplines to follow when writing for classes or for publication. When we follow these guidelines, our readers can quickly understand and evaluate our sources while remaining focused on the ideas in the writing.

Chicago style is particularly well suited for historical research because the citations for historical writing are often quite long. Historical citations need to identify individual primary documents as well as the name of the collection in which they are located and the name and location of the historical archive. It's common in historical research to have multiple sources written by the same author, too, such as letters or diaries in a large collection. We can cite these using the longer citation format for footnotes, allowing future researchers to more readily retrace the author's steps through historical archives to locate the source.

Chicago style consists of three main categories — footnotes, bibliography, and paper formatting. In the body of the paper, you cite outside sources with Chicago-style footnotes. At the end of the paper, you will add a Chicago-style bibliography. The paper as a whole uses Chicago-style formatting to set margins, line spacing, page-numbering, and so on.

Think of Chicago style as a filter. When your ideas pass through this filter, your paper will conform to Chicago guidelines and emerge looking like every other Chicago manuscript. The two things different about your paper will be the two most important ingredients — the idea you present and how you explain it to your readers.

1. Footnotes

Chicago style allows authors to document citations within the text through one of two methods — footnotes or endnotes. Both systems have advantages and disadvantages, but this chapter focuses on footnotes due to their usefulness to the college writer. Footnotes allow readers to see the complete citation quickly with a downward glance of the eyes that doesn't interrupt the visual flow of the words in the text itself. Footnotes also allow readers to quickly understand whether you're using primary or secondary sources, whether you're using popular or academic sources, and whether your sources are up-to-date and relevant. This allows the reader to assess the quality of your research based on the choice of sources you make.

A footnote comes in two parts. In the body of the paper, you identify outside materials with a **superscript** number. Put the number at the end of the sentence or the clause that refers to a source. The numbers goes after any punctuation mark except for the dash, which it precedes. A corresponding, numbered note appears at the bottom — or foot — of the page where the idea appears. Start your footnotes with the number one, and then continue from there. If your paper only uses a few footnotes, you can use symbols instead. The order for the symbols you use should be *, †, ‡, and §. Any more than that, and you should really just use numbers.

1. Shamah argues that it's not just one specific or even one type of out-of-school activity that matters: "Out-of-school activities of all kinds appear to support the development of a sense of purpose."[1]

   The <u>footnote number</u> appears in superscript after the final punctuation — in this case, a **closing quotation mark**.

2. At least one expert claims that there's a clear relationship between out-of-school activities and a student's sense of purpose[4] — an idea that's been the subject of an increasing amount of attention by scholars.

> The idea being referenced appears before the dash, so the <u>footnote number</u> appears before the **dash** as well.

3. There's been an increasing amount of attention by scholars (at least one expert claims that there's a clear relationship between out-of-school activities and a student's sense of purpose[8]) but more still needs to be learned.

> A <u>footnote number</u> can appear inside of the **closing parenthesis** when the footnote refers to material inside the parentheses rather than to the sentence the parentheses appears within.

At the bottom of the page containing the footnote, include reference material about the work you just noted. How you document that source material will vary depending upon how many times you've cited the work, what you cited directly before this citation, and sometimes where you found the source material.

A. Initial Note

The first time you cite a source with a footnote, include the full citation information. Footnotes will include the author's name, the title of the work, and the publication information. The entire note will be single spaced, and the first line will be indented half an inch.

1. **David** <u>Todd</u>**,** *Feeding Back: Conversations with Alternative Guitarists from Proto-Punk to Post-Rock* **(**Chicago: Chicago Review Press, 2012**),** 100**.**

> With books and works appearing in books, list the **first name**, followed by the <u>last name</u>, followed by a **comma**. Next, list the *title of the book*. The publication information goes inside a set of **parentheses**. Follow the **closing parenthesis** with a **comma** and the page number where the material referenced by your footnote appears. Close the note with a **period**.

2. Nicole **J.** Georges, *Calling Dr. Laura* (New York: Houghton Mifflin Harcourt, 2013), <u>5–6</u>.

> If the author lists a **middle name** or **middle initial**, include it in the initial note. If the material you reference appears within a <u>page range</u>, separate the pages in that range with an **en dash** (usually option-hyphen or alt-hyphen).

3. Devora Shamah**,** "<u>Supporting a Strong Sense of Purpose: Lessons from a Rural Community</u>**,**" *New Direction for Youth Development* 132 (2011): 56.

> When the <u>title of the work</u> is different from the *publication*, separate the two with a **comma**, not parentheses.

4. Lisa Ede**, and** Andrea A. Lunsford**,** *Writing Together: Collaboration in Theory and Practice* (Boston: Bedford/St. Martin's, 2012), 46.

> When citing two or three authors, separate each entry with a **comma**. Use the **conjunction** "and" before the last author named.

5. Robin M. Murray et al.**,** *The Epidemiology of Schizophrenia* (Cambridge: Cambridge University Press, 2002), 14.

> When more than three authors share the authorship of a text, list the first author listed in the source. Follow the name with "et al.," a Latin phrase that means "and others." Place a **comma** after the period in "al." but not between "et al." and the author's name.

6. Julian Symons, preface to *Nineteen Eighty-four*, by George Orwell (London: David Campbell Publishers, 1992), xix**;** Robert McCrum, "The Masterpiece that Killed George Orwell," *Guardian*, May 9, 2009, accessed February 29, 2016, https://www.theguardian.com/books/2009/may/10/1984-george-orwell.

> When the same idea is conveyed by two different works, separate the two notes with a **semicolon**. Use only one footnote number to mark the idea in the text.

B. Subsequent Notes

After providing the full reference material in the initial note, use a shortened version for any later notes that refer to the same source. Just like the initial note, the subsequent notes are single-spaced and indented one half-inch.

7. **Shamah,** "Supporting**,**" 57**.**

> Only last names are needed in subsequent notes. Shorten the title to a key word or words unless it's already four words or fewer. Separate the author, title, and page number with **commas**. End the note with a **period**.

8. **D**. Shamah, "Supporting," 57.

8. **Devora** Shamah, "Supporting," 57.

> If **an initial** or **full name** is required to prevent confusion with another author already cited, add it to the note.

9. **Ede** and **Lunsford**, *Writing Together*, 46.

> When citing a work with two or three authors, give the **last names of each**. Be sure to maintain the order the names appear in the publication. That's how we know which one is the primary author.

10. **Murray** et al.**,** *The Epidemiology of Schizophrenia*, 14.

> If citing a work with more than three authors, list the **first author** followed by et al. and a **comma.**

C. Citing the Same Source Consecutively

If you cite the same source consecutively, replace the duplicate information with "Ibid.," an abbreviation of a Latin term that means "in the same place."

> 1. Shamah, "**Supporting,**" 56**.**
>
> 2. Ibid**.,** 57**.**

> Here, "Ibid." stands in for the <u>author</u> and **title** because they are the same as in the previous citation. Make sure to include the **period** that concludes the abbreviation and a **comma** that precedes the page number. The note ends with a final **period**.

> 3. Shamah, "**Supporting,**" *56.*
>
> 4. Ibid.

> In this example, the fourth citation also refers to page 56 from Shamah, so "Ibid." stands in for <u>author</u>, **title**, and *page number*.

D. Indirect Citation

Within her article, Dr. Shamah cites an idea from a book by William Damon. If you want to cite the same idea from Damon that Dr. Shamah cites in her article, what do you do? You go to the library, of course, and get Damon's book. That's what you do. If it has *one* idea worth incorporating into your paper, it might have more and better ideas for you to consider.

However, if you don't have time to get that book or your library can't access it, you can use an indirect citation. Within the footnote, cite the work where the information first appeared. Then cite the information for the work where you found the material. At the end of the paper, your bibliography reference will also contain a single entry with information about both works.

> 1. <u>William Damon</u>, *The Path to Purpose: Helping Our Children Find Their Calling in Life.* (New York: Free Press), 17**,** quoted in **Devora Shamah, "Supporting a Strong Sense of Purpose: Lessons from a Rural Community,"** *New Direction for Youth Development* **132 (2011): 56**.

> Cite <u>the work where the material was first published</u> followed by a **comma** and the phrase "quoted in." Then, provide information for **the work you actually found and read**.

> 2. <u>William Damon</u>, *The Path to Purpose: Helping Our Children Find Their Calling in Life.* (New York: Free Press), 17, quoted in **Shamah, "Supporting," 56**.

> This cites the same <u>indirect source</u>, but it only provides information required for subsequent citations for **the work you actually found** because this isn't the first time you've cited it. You've cited it a lot, actually.

E. Block Quotations

Use block quotations for those rare occasions when you must quote five or more lines or two or more paragraphs of prose, or two or more lines of poetry.

Roy K. Humble argues for the use of note cards:

> If you're using note cards, you simply unleash their awesome, low-tech power. You lay the note cards on the dinette table and move them around. I know that doesn't sound like much, but trust me — it's awesome and powerful. Note cards allow you to visually arrange the evidence into its natural patterns.[17]

Despite the logic of the argument he presents, many students refuse to try the technique.

> Block quotations use formatting instead of quotation marks to show that this is a direct quotation. Typically, you should introduce a block quotation with a statement and a **colon**. Indent a block quotation one half-inch from the left margin, and double-space it like the rest of the paper. The footnote number sits just outside the ending punctuation of the quotation. If the paragraph continues after the block quotation, do not indent the sentence that follows the block quotation. That shows readers that this enormous quotation of yours is supporting information within a longer paragraph.

2. Bibliography

A Chicago-style bibliography includes every source examined in the course of research, regardless of whether or not every source is mentioned in the essay text itself. In this way, it is distinct from the MLA-style work(s) cited page or the APA-style reference(s) page.

The complete publication information allows your readers to find any work that you used and study it themselves. Chicago divides that publication information into three elements, typically presented in this order:

A. Author

B. Title

C. Publication information

A. Author

The author is the person or people or organization responsible for creating the source. This is the first piece of information you must find to build your citation.

With books, the author's name is usually on the spine. Magazines, newspapers, and journals typically put the author's name near the title of the article. However, the name may also appear at the end of short articles. If the source is a corporate or governmental publication and a specific author is not given, the organization itself is usually the author.

ONE AUTHOR

1. **Todd,** David. *Feeding Back: Conversations with Alternative Guitarists from Proto-Punk to Post-Rock*. Chicago: Chicago Review Press, 2012.

   > List the author's **last name** first, followed by a **comma** and then the author's first name. End the author section with a **period**.

2. Williams, John Sibley. *Controlled Hallucinations*. Hayesville, NC: FutureCycle Press, 2013. Kindle edition.

   > Include the middle name or middle initial if it's listed in the original text. Don't provide the full name if the author (C. S. Lewis or J. D. Salinger, for example) prefers initials.

3. Churchill, Winston. *Triumph and Tragedy*. Boston: Houghton Mifflin, 1953.

   > That's Sir Winston Churchill to you and me, but in a citation, don't include titles like "Sir," "PhD.," "M.S.W.," "King," "Saint," or "Dr."

TWO TO TEN AUTHORS

1. Ede, Lisa, **and** Andrea A. Lunsford. *Writing Together: Collaboration in Theory and Practice*. Boston: Bedford/St. Martin's, 2012.

   > Use a *comma* and the **conjunction** "and" between the authors' names. Note that the second author's name is written with the first name followed by the last name. Always list the authors in the order they appear in the text, not alphabetically.

2. Murray, Robin M., Peter B. Jones, Ezra Susser, Jim van Os, and Mary Cannon. *The Epidemiology of Schizophrenia*. Cambridge, UK: Cambridge University Press, 2012.

   > The same pattern continues up to ten authors, with a **comma** separating each name until the last, which is marked with a **comma** and the conjunction "and." List them all.

ELEVEN OR MORE AUTHORS

Anastassopoulos, V., M. Arik, S. Aune, K. Barth, A. Belov, H. Bräuninger, G. Cantatore, et al. "Search for Chameleons with CAST." *Physics Letters B* 749, no. 7 (October 2015): 72–180. doi:10.1016/j.physletb.2015.07.049.

> With sources with eleven or more authors, if you can believe that such a thing exists, list the first seven names, separating each with a **comma**. After the seventh, put "et al" for "and others" and a **period**. Do you wonder why we're suddenly using initials to list the first names of all these chameleon scientists? See the next example.

AUTHORS OF SCIENTIFIC SOURCES

Roy, N., and N. Banerjee. "Dynamical Systems Study of Chameleon Scalar Field." *Annals of Physics* 356 (2015): 452–466. doi:10.1016/j.aop.2015.03.013.

> With scientific sources, Chicago style abbreviates author first names just as APA style does. With Chicago, however, the first author is named with the last name followed by initials but all other authors are listed with the initials before the last name. **Commas** also separate the names of all the authors from one another.

ORGANIZATIONAL OR GOVERNMENTAL AUTHOR

Business and professional documents are often considered a work product and property of the company rather than that of the nameless, faceless authors who work for that organization. In that case, list the organization as the author.

U.S. Census Bureau. *Strength in Numbers: Your Guide to 2010 Census Redistricting Data from the U.S. Census Bureau.* Washington, DC: U.S. Dept. of Commerce, Economics and Statistics Administration, U.S. Census Bureau, 2010.

> Abbreviate commonly understood terms like "U.S." instead of writing out "United States." More complex or particular acronyms should be written out.

SCREEN NAME

Many online authors write under a screen name. You don't have to go searching for the author's secret (true) identity. You can use the screen name.

1. chewingofthecud. "What Currents or Movements are Currently Happening in Literature?" Reddit. March 13, 2014. Accessed February 29, 2016. https://www.reddit.com/r/literature/comments/20by05/what_currents_or_movements_are_currently/.

> Simply list the screen name in the author's place.

CHI

Bibliography: Author

2. [Fittz, Christopher]. "The Unbridled Joy of Adrian Beltre." *Lone Star Ball* (blog), April 16, 2016. Accessed April 17, 2016. http://www.lonestarball. com/2016/4/16/11443156/the-unbridled-joy-of-adrian-beltre.

> If the author's real name is known but not named as the author of the work, you can include that real name in the author's place in the citation but you must use **brackets** around the name. In this case, Christopher Fittz is the known author of a blog article posted under the screen name ghostofErikThompson.

NO AUTHOR

If no author is listed for the text, skip the author's place and begin the citation with the information for the next element — the title of the work. Avoid the word "Anonymous" in place of the author unless grouping several anonymous works together in a bibliography.

Go Ask Alice. New York: Simon and Schuster, 1971.

> If there is no author listed for the text, skip the author's place and begin the citation with the information for the next element — the *title*.

OTHER CONTRIBUTORS

Occasionally the person or organization most important to your discussion of a source contributed something other than the writing of the words. When you list the person or organization's role as a **noun**, it is abbreviated in the bibliography. For example, "editors" becomes "eds.," and "translator" becomes "trans." When you use the term as a verb, as in "edited by" or "translated by," the role is not abbreviated.

Bevington, David, and David Scott Kastan**,** eds. *Macbeth*. By William Shakespeare. New York: Bantam, 2005.

> If a paper about Shakespeare's play *Macbeth* emphasizes the edited collection in which the play appears rather than the play itself, list the editors in the author's place. Follow the contributors' names with a **comma** and their role.

B. Title

The second key element in a Chicago citation is the title. Chicago style requires you to capitalize the first word and all nouns, verbs, adjectives, and adverbs in the title. MLA also requires you to format the title to distinguish between larger or smaller works.

Look for the title of the source near the author's name, usually at the beginning of the work.

LARGER WORKS

Chicago uses formatting to quickly indicate whether the title of the work is a larger, self-contained work or a smaller work within a larger one. Larger works includes books, anthologies, magazines, newspapers, websites, book-length poems, movies, and so on. Italicize the titles of these larger works.

1. Georges, Nicole J. *Calling Dr. Laura.* New York: Houghton Mifflin Harcourt, 2013.

   > *Calling Dr. Laura* is the title of an entire book and should be italicized. Put a **period** at the end of this section.

2. Roemmele, Jacqueline A., and Donna Batdorff. ***Surviving the "Flesh-Eating Bacteria":*** *Understanding, Preventing, Treating, and Living with the Effects of Necrotizing Fasciitis.* New York: Avery, 2001.

   > Put a **colon** between the **main title** and a <u>subtitle</u>. With larger works, both remain italicized. If the title contains words within quotation marks, those words are also italicized.

3. Rayburn, Kevin. *The 1920s.* October 12, 2008. Accessed February 29, 2016. http://www.louisville.edu/~kprayb01/1920s.html.

   > Chicago only italicizes website titles when they are analogous to printed books or periodicals. If the site provides a comprehensive or steady stream of content, it's safe to italicize the website name.

4. Bartow, R. *After the fall III,* <u>1975</u>. Paint on clay, 7 5/8 in. × 5 7/8 in. × 1/4 in. Portland Art Museum, Portland, OR.

   > Chicago style considers most works of art to be larger works, even if they aren't physically large, so those titles are also italicized. Put a comma after the **title** and then <u>the year it was produced</u>.

5. Bishop, Kyle W. *American Zombie Gothic: The Rise and Fall (and Rise) of* <u>The Walking Dead</u> *in Popular Culture.* Jefferson, NC: McFarland, 2010.

   > If a part of the larger work's title would normally be italicized, as with <u>the title of a television show</u>, de-italicize it within the italics of the rest of the title.

SMALLER WORKS WITHIN A LARGER WORK

When the work is nested within a larger work — such as articles within newspapers, journals, or reference books — it's considered a shorter work, and the article titles go inside quotation marks. You'll also use quotation marks for short stories and essays in an anthology, short poems within a collection, episodes within a television series, songs within an album, articles within a website, and so on.

1. Gladwell, Malcolm. "The Bill." *New Yorker*, January 12, 2015, 65.

   A magazine article is a shorter work that's nested inside a larger publication, so it's marked by **quotation marks** rather than italics. Notice that the **period** after this part of the citation slips inside those **quotation marks**.

2. Mahoney, Phillip. "Gray is the New Black: Race, Class, and Zombies." In *Generation Zombie: Essays on the Living Dead in Modern Culture*, edited by Stephanie Boluk and Wylie Lenz, 55–72. Jefferson, NC: McFarland, 2011.

   The Mahoney article appears within a larger collection of essays, so its title also appears within **quotation marks.**

3. Tuchman, Barbara. "Retreat." Chap. 19 in *The Guns of August*. New York: Macmillan, 1962.

   Chapters or other sections within a book are considered shorter works, even if they're quite long.

4. Mayo Clinic Staff. "Gallstones-Definition." Mayo Clinic. Mayo Foundation for Medical Education and Research. July 25, 2013. Accessed February 29, 2016. http://www.mayoclinic.org/diseases-conditions/gallstones/basics/definition/con-20020461.

   Web pages are shorter works within websites.

5. Miller, Elise. "The 'Maw of Western Culture': James Baldwin and the Anxieties of Influence." *African American Review* 38, no. 4 (Winter 2004): 625–636.

   When quotation marks appear within the title of a shorter work, the inner quotation marks are **single quotation marks**. With shorter works, you also put a **colon** between the main title and a subtitle.

6. Kenny, Glenn. "A Perfect Day," review of *A Perfect Day*, directed by Fernando Leon de Aranoa. *Rogerebert.com*. January 15, 2016. Accessed February 29, 2016. http://www.rogerebert.com/reviews/a-perfect-day-2016.

   The **title of an individual article** reviewing another work should be in **double quotation marks** even if the title of the work being reviewed is italicized. In this case, the review is a small work appearing on a website, and the film of the same title is the larger work.

C. Publication Information

The third and most complex section of a Chicago citation is the one that captures publication information about the source. This section will include information about some or all of the following subcategories of information:

1. Title of publication

2. Other contributors

3. Version

4. Number

5. Publisher

6. Publication date

7. Publisher location

Not every source will use each of the subcategories described in this section. For example, a book by a single author may not have "other contributors" to recognize. A periodical does not typically come in "versions," but in volumes and issues, two variations covered by "number." When your source does not contain one of the subcategories, move on to the next one on the list. Once you are done, place a period at the end of this section to show readers that your publication information is complete.

C1. TITLE OF PUBLICATION

For a larger work, the title of the work and the title of the publication are the same thing, so that title goes after the author in the title section (as seen in "Larger Works" two pages ago).

1. Boluk, Stephanie, and Wylie Lenz, eds. *Generation Zombie: Essays on the Living Dead in Modern Culture.* Jefferson, NC: McFarland, 2011.

   > Because the citation focuses on the book as a whole, there's nothing to list as the title of the publication. That's okay. Move along.

2. Mahoney, Phillip. "Gray is the New Black: Race, Class, and Zombies." In *Generation Zombie: Essays on the Living Dead in Modern Culture,* edited by Stephanie Boluk and Wylie Lenz, 55–72. Jefferson, NC: McFarland, 2011.

   > However, this citation focuses on the shorter Mahoney article within the larger collection. The title of the zombie anthology therefore appears in the title-of-publication section of this citation.

3. Rockmore, Ellen Bresler. "How Texas Teaches History." *New York Times,* October 12, 2015. Accessed February 29, 2016. http://www.nytimes.com/2015/10/22/opinion/how-texas-teaches-history.html.

> With articles in periodicals, the title of the publication is typically the name of the journal, magazine, or newspaper. Chicago style removes "The" from the start of the titles, which is fine.

4. Mayo Clinic Staff. "Gallstones-Definition." **Mayo Clinic.** Mayo Foundation for Medical Education and Research. July 25, 2013. Accessed February 29, 2016. http://www.mayoclinic.org/diseases-conditions/gallstones/basics/definition/con-20020461.

> When the focus of the source is on one page at a website, the name of the website goes into the title-of-publication slot.

5. Silence. "War Drums." *The Deafening Sound of Absolutely Nothing.* Profane Existence EXIST 161, 2016, vinyl LP.

> When citing a song, the title of the song goes in the title section as a shorter work, and the name of the album or collection goes in this slot.

C2. OTHER CONTRIBUTORS

Other contributors are people who play integral roles in creating the publication but are secondary to the named author of the work. Contributors can be identified by their role in the work, such as "performer," "director," "editor(s)," "translator," "writer," and "producer." Use phrases like "edited by," "translated by," or "directed by" with these contributors.

You'll find the names of other contributors on title pages or other places where credit is given to collaborators, like the credits of a film or the liner notes of an album.

1. Shakespeare, William. *Macbeth.* **Edited by** David Bevington and David Scott Kastan. New York: Bantam, 2005.

> Name the **role** first. Then, list the contributors by first and then last name.

2. Bolano, Roberto. *The Savage Detectives.* **Translated by** Natasha Wimmer. New York: Picador, 2008.

> The same goes for any **role.**

3. Mahoney, Phillip. "Gray is the New Black: Race, Class, and Zombies." In *Generation Zombie: Essays on the Living Dead in Modern Culture,* **edited by** Stephanie Boluk and Wylie Lenz, 55-72. Jefferson, NC: McFarland, 2011.

> When the work cited is within a larger work, a **comma** separates the title of the publication and the other contributors, so the **role** is written lowercase.

C3. VERSION

Works often have multiple versions or editions identified by numbers that tell you how many times the publication has been revised — 2nd edition, for example — or names that tell you the nature of the revision — like "unabridged" or "expanded."

When they exist, version numbers or names can usually be found next to the title of the publication within the original source.

> Rottenberg, Annette T., and Donna Haisty Winchell. *The Structure of Argument*, 8th ed. Boston: Bedford/St. Martin's, 2015.

> Use numbers rather than spelling out editions distinguished by an ordinal number.

C4. NUMBER

Books that are too long to be published in a single publication are often split into multiple publications, and each is given its own volume number. In addition, periodicals that are published on an ongoing basis — as is the case with most scholarly journals — are assigned volume, issue, or volume *and* issue numbers to distinguish one publication of the periodical from another.

Like versions, the number is typically found near the title of the publication. However, it may be found within the publication on a page with more information about the publication, contributors, and so on.

> 1. Conan Doyle, Arthur. *Sherlock Holmes: The Complete Novels and Stories*, vol. <u>1</u>. New York: Bantam Classics, 1986.

> "Vol." is an abbreviation for "volume" and should precede the volume number in large works. Use a <u>number</u> rather than spelling out the word.

> 2. Racy, A.J. "Domesticating Otherness: The Snake Charmer in American Popular Culture." *Ethnomusicology* **60**, no. <u>2</u> (2016): 197–232.

> For academic journals and other small works, there is no "vol." before the **volume number**, but there is an abbreviated "no." for "number" before the <u>issue number</u>. You'll notice, hopefully, that there is no punctuation before the volume or after the issue.

> 3. Sheffield, Rob. "Getting to Know Colbert." *Rolling Stone*, October 8, 2015, 30.

> Magazines don't feature issue or volume or issue numbers in Chicago style, even if the original sources have them.

The publisher is the company or person who actually produced a book, government publication, film, or website. Film and television series generally involve multiple publishers. In such cases, cite the publisher primarily responsible for the work. Periodicals often do not have a publisher, in which case you can skip this section.

With a book, you can find the name of the publisher on the title page or on a page near the front of the book that provides more information about the publication and its copyright. On pamphlets, look on the back or the innermost leaf of the folded paper. On brochures, look at the front or back covers. A website will usually list the publisher at the bottom of the page in the footer or on its version of the "About" page.

1. McCloud, Scott. *The Sculptor*. New York: **First Second Books**, 2015.

   Name the city where the publisher is located, then place a **colon** and then the **name** of the publishing company.

2. Bishop, Kyle W. *American Zombie Gothic: The Rise and Fall (and Rise) of* The Walking Dead *in Popular Culture*. Jefferson, NC: McFarland, 2010.

   When the city of publication is not immediately recognizable, add a **comma** and the state, using the two-character postal code.

3. Murray, R. M., P. B. Jones, E. Susser, J. van Os, and M. Cannon. *The Epidemiology of Schizophrenia*. Cambridge: Cambridge University Press, 2002.

   When you have two cities known for publishing, the less well-known city is distinguished with a state abbreviation. That means you, Cambridge, MA.

4. Mayo Clinic Staff. "Gallstones-Definition." Mayo Clinic. **Mayo Foundation for Medical Education and Research**. July 25, 2013. Accessed February 29, 2016. http://www.mayoclinic.org/diseases-conditions/gallstones/basics/definition/con-20020461.

   Websites are often published by a sponsoring organization. List them if they are not the same as the name of the website and if the website is not considered analogous to a larger work like a periodical or a book.

5. Engber, Daniel. "The Neurologist Who Hacked His Brain—And Almost Lost His Mind." *Wired*, February 8, 2016. Accessed February 29, 2016. http://www.wired.com/2016/01/phil-kennedy-mind-control-computer/.

   Wired is published by Condé Nast, but because Chicago considers it an online magazine, don't list the publisher. In general, if you italicize the website, you don't need to list a publisher. If you don't italicize the website name, then you do list the publisher. Unless it's the same name as the site. Got that?

6. Lisciandro, Frank. Interview by Steve Long. *The Writing Life*. McMinnville Community Media, March 21, 2016.

  ▌ For broadcast works, name the network.

7. Silence. "War Drums." *The Deafening Sound of Absolutely Nothing*. Profane Existence <u>EXIST 161</u>, 2016, vinyl LP.

  ▌ For albums, name the publishing company and the <u>catalog number</u> with no intervening punctuation.

C6. PUBLICATION DATE

The publication date is the specific date the work was published. A book is published once and therefore only features the year. A periodical is published regularly throughout the year, so its publication date identifies which part of the year it was published in. A monthly magazine notes the month and year. A daily newspaper lists the day, month, and year.

The location of the publication date varies from publication to publication. In a book, the date will be on the title page or copyright page. Articles that appear in periodicals will often appear next to the byline and title of the source. This applies to online articles as well, but if a date is missing, you can also search the bottom of the web page for a publication year to stand in for something more precise.

1. Humble, Roy K. *The Humble Argument*. Dallas, OR: Problem Child Press**,** 2010.

  ▌ With books, movies, and other works published on a non-periodic basis, put a **comma** after the name of the publisher and then the year.

2. Federoff, Nina, and John Block. "Mosquito vs. Mosquito." *New York Times*, April 6**,** <u>2016</u>, p. A23.

  ▌ With works like magazines, journals, and newspapers that are published periodically, the most common format is month and day followed by a **comma** and the <u>year</u> since so many works come out on a specific day. Months are not abbreviated in Chicago style.

3. Barone, Richard. "The Power of Song: Recording Pete Seeger." *Tape Op*. May–June <u>2016</u>, 36–44.

  ▌ Bimonthly publications will often use a month range followed by a <u>year</u>.

You may use the abbreviation "n.d." for no date, but do not use it lightly. It is rare that a publication date is truly not included in a print source. In web sources, it can be difficult to find, but it almost always exists in the web page's HTML code, which isn't *that* hard to examine.

The location varies by the type of publication. For stand-alone books, the location is usually the city where the publisher is located. For shorter works within anthologies or periodicals, the location is usually a page number or a range of pages. In online sources, the location is a URL or DOI. Film and music locations might be physical discs or their digital equivalent. The location for a work of art is often the place where the piece is on exhibit or housed in a collection. With the abundance of variety among mediums, the general rule is that you should document the location as accurately and precisely as possible.

1. Behar, Evelyn, Sarah McGowan, Katie McLaughlin, T.D. Borkovec, Michelle Goldwin, and Olivia Bjorkquist. "Concreteness of Positive, Negative, and Neutral Repetitive Thinking About the Future." *Behavior Therapy* 43, no. 2 (1998): pp. <u>300–312</u>.

> For more than one continuous page, put "pp." before the <u>page range</u> if you think it will cause confusion about what the number refers to. Chicago does not strictly require "p." or "pp." before a page number. Use an **en dash** to separate the pages in a <u>page range</u>.

2. "OSU Women Try to Keep a Storied Season Going." *Oregonian*, April 2, 2016, <u>A</u>1.

> Some page numbers (especially print newspapers) include <u>letters</u> that identify the section of the newspaper in which those pages are located.

3. Erlanger, Steven, Stephen Castle, and Rick Gladstone. "Airing of Hidden Wealth Stirs Inquiries and Rage: Iceland Premier Steps Down as Release of Files Reverberates Around World." *New York Times*, April 6, 2016, early edition**,** <u>sec. A</u>.

> That being said, Chicago style does not consider the page number an essential element for newspaper articles, so it can be omitted if you feel like it. When you know the edition of the newspaper, you can include that information here with the <u>section</u>, separated by a **comma**.

4. Grosvenor, Emily. "The Dude Abides in Salem." *Desperately Seeking Salem* (blog). August 8, 2010. Accessed <u>February 29, 2016</u>**.** https://desperate-lyseekingsalem.wordpress.com/2010/08/08/the-dude-abides-in-salem/**.**

> For online works, include a URL if it will reliably and consistently allow a reader to navigate to the cited page. Avoid using one-time URLs generated during a specific browsing session. Note that Chicago style requires a **period** at the end of the URL, unlike other documentation styles. Also note that you must include "Accessed" and the <u>date</u> you reviewed the site before the URL. Follow the accessed date with a **period**.

5. Aagaard, Jesper. "Media Multitasking, Attention, and Distraction: A Critical Discussion." *Phenomenology and the Cognitive Sciences* 14, no. 4 (December 2015): <u>885</u>. Accessed February 29, 2016. doi:10.1007/s11097-014-9375-x.

> **DOIs** (digital object identifiers) are more stable online locations than URLs, so use them when they are available. Add when you accessed the work, too. The DOI location is in addition to the page location conveyed by the <u>page number</u>.

6. Kerr, William R., Ramana Nanda, and Matthew Rhodes-Kropf. "Entrepreneurship as Experimentation." *The Journal of Economic Perspectives* 28, no. 3 (2014): <u>25–48</u>. www.jstor.org/stable/23800574.

> For sources found through a database, add a stable URL or DOI if the database provides one. You don't need a date of access unless the original source doesn't have a publication date. If there are <u>page numbers</u>, include those first as part of the location.

7. Koster, John. "Hating the 'Hun' at Home: When America Went to War against the Kaiser, German-Americans Caught Hell." *American History* 51, no. 3 (2016): **58**. Accessed February 29, 2016. <u>General OneFile</u> (A453285833).

> When the database doesn't provide a stable URL or DOI, list the <u>name</u> of the database and, in parentheses, any identification number included with the source. And, as you might expect, add any **page numbers** first. Add the accessed date, too.

8. Mould, Bob. *Workbook*. Virgin Records America OVED 340, 1989, vinyl LP.

> For physical objects, describe the type of work that it is.

D. Bibliography Examples

As you see from the past section, Chicago style divides bibliographic information into three main sections:

A. Author

B. Title

C. Publication information

In the examples that follow, we'll break down citations into these three categories of information and then show you how to format both the initial footnote and the bibliography citation.

Even though these are common examples, you still have to adopt them to fit the information about the works you're using. You may have to tinker with the author section or the publication information section to accurately capture the information about a given work. But that's a good thing. It means that you can build each citation to match the works instead of having to somehow tailor the information about a work to fit a template that doesn't really fit.

BOOKS

ONE AUTHOR (PRINT)

Todd, David. *Feeding Back: Conversations with Alternative Guitarists from Proto-Punk to Post-Rock.* Chicago: Chicago Review Press, 2012.

1. (Author) Todd, David.
2. (Title) *Feeding Back: Conversations with Alternative Guitarists from Proto-Punk to Post-Rock.*
3. (Publication information) Chicago: Chicago Review Press, 2012.

Initial Footnote

1. David Todd, *Feeding Back: Conversations with Alternative Guitarists from Proto-Punk to Post-Rock* (Chicago: Chicago Review Press, 2012.), 14.

EDITED COLLECTION

Boluk, Stephanie, and Wylie Lenz, eds. *Generation Zombie: Essays on the Living Dead in Modern Culture.* Jefferson, NC: McFarland, 2011.

1. Boluk, Stephanie, and Wylie Lenz, eds.
2. *Generation Zombie: Essays on the Living Dead in Modern Culture.*
3. Jefferson, NC: McFarland, 2011.

Initial Footnote

    1. Stephanie Boluk and Wylie Lenz, eds., *Generation Zombie: Essays on the Living Dead in Modern Culture* (Jefferson, NC: McFarland, 2011), 19.

EBOOK

Williams, John Sibley. *Controlled Hallucinations*. Hayesville, NC: Future-Cycle Press, 2013. Kindle edition.

    1. Williams, John Sibley.
    2. *Controlled Hallucinations.*
    3. Hayesville, NC: FutureCycle Press, 2013. Kindle edition.

Initial Footnote

    1. John Sibley Williams, *Controlled Hallucinations* (Hayesville, NC: FutureCycle Press, 2013), Kindle edition, pt. 3.

ONLINE BOOK

Twain, Mark. *Life on the Mississippi*. New York: Harper, 1917. Google Books, books.google.com/books?id=h99O07cNtEMC.

    1. Twain, Mark.
    2. *Life on the Mississippi.*
    3. New York: Harper, 1917. Google Books, books.google.com/books?id=h99O07cNtEMC.

Initial Footnote

    1. Mark Twain, *Life on the Mississippi*, New York: Harper, 1917, Google Books, books.google.com/books?id=h99O07cNtEMC, 153.

SACRED TEXT

For sacred texts, only use footnotes. Do not cite in the bibliography.

Initial Footnote

    1. 1 Thess. 5:16-17.

Chapter of a Book

Tuchman, Barbara. "Retreat." Chap. 19 in *The Guns of August*. New York: Macmillan, 1962.

> 1. Tuchman, Barbara.
> 2. "Retreat."
> 3. Chap. 19 in *The Guns of August*. New York: Macmillan, 1962.

Initial Footnote

> 4. Barbara Tuchman, "Retreat," chap. 19 in *The Guns of August* (New York: Macmillan, 1962), 341-72.

Work in an Anthology

Mahoney, Phillip. "Gray is the New Black: Race, Class, and Zombies." In *Generation Zombie: Essays on the Living Dead in Modern Culture*, edited by Stephanie Boluk and Wylie Lenz, 55–72. Jefferson, NC: McFarland, 2011.

> 1. Mahoney, Phillip.
> 2. "Gray is the New Black: Race, Class, and Zombies."
> 3. In *Generation Zombie: Essays on the Living Dead in Modern Culture*, edited by Stephanie Boluk and Wylie Lenz, 55–72. Jefferson, NC: McFarland, 2011.

Initial Footnote

> 1. Phillip Mahoney, "Gray is the New Black: Race, Class, and Zombies," in *Generation Zombie: Essays on the Living Dead in Modern Culture*, eds. Stephanie Boluk and Wylie Lenz (Jefferson, NC: McFarland, 2011), 55–72.

Article in a Reference Book

For reference articles, only use footnotes. Do not cite in the bibliography.

Initial Footnote

> 1. *The Encyclopedia of World Crime*, 1st ed. (Wilmette, IL: Crime-Books, Inc., 1989), s.v. "Agrippina (Agrippina the Younger)."

JOURNAL ARTICLE (PRINT)

Racy, A.J. "Domesticating Otherness: The Snake Charmer in American Popular Culture." *Ethnomusicology* 60, no. 2 (2016): 197–232.

> 1. Racy, A.J.
> 2. "Domesticating Otherness: The Snake Charmer in American Popular Culture."
> 3. *Ethnomusicology* 60, no. 2 (2016): 197–232.

Initial Footnote

> 1. A.J. Racy, "Domesticating Otherness: The Snake Charmer in American Popular Culture," *Ethnomusicology* 60, no. 2 (2016): 232.

JOURNAL ARTICLE (WITH DOI)

Aagaard, Jesper. "Media Multitasking, Attention, and Distraction: A Critical Discussion." *Phenomenology and the Cognitive Sciences* 14, no. 4 (December 2015): 885. Accessed February 29, 2016. doi:10.1007/s11097-014- 9375-x.

> 1. Aagaard, Jesper.
> 2. "Media Multitasking, Attention, and Distraction: A Critical Discussion."
> 3. *Phenomenology and the Cognitive Sciences* 14, no. 4 (December 2015): 885. Accessed February 29, 2016. doi:10.1007/s11097-014- 9375-x.

Initial Footnote

> 1. Jesper Aagaard, "Media Multitasking, Attention, and Distraction: A Critical Discussion," *Phenomenology and the Cognitive Sciences* 14, no. 4 , December 2015: 885, accessed February 29, 2016, doi:10.1007/s11097-014- 9375-x.

JOURNAL ARTICLE (DATABASE WITH A STABLE URL)

Kerr, William R., Ramana Nanda, and Matthew Rhodes-Kropf. "Entrepreneurship as Experimentation." *The Journal of Economic Perspectives* 28, no. 3 (2014): 25–48. www.jstor.org/stable/23800574.

> 1. Kerr, William R., Ramana Nanda, and Matthew Rhodes-Kropf.
> 2. "Entrepreneurship as Experimentation."
> 3. *The Journal of Economic Perspectives* 28, no. 3 (2014): 25–48. www.jstor.org/stable/23800574.

Initial Footnote

> 1. William R. Kerr, Ramana Nanda, and Matthew Rhodes-Kropf, "Entrepreneurship as Experimentation," *The Journal of Economic Perspectives* 28, no. 3, 2014: 40, www.jstor.org/stable/23800574.

CHI

Bibliography: Examples

Journal Article (Database with No Stable URL)

Koster, John. "Hating the 'Hun' at Home: When America Went to War against the Kaiser, German-Americans Caught Hell." *American History* 51, no. 3 (2016): 58. Accessed February 29, 2016. General OneFile (A453285833).

1. Koster, John.
2. "Hating the 'Hun' at Home: When America Went to War against the Kaiser, German-Americans Caught Hell."
3. *American History* 51, no. 3 (2016): 58. Accessed February 29, 2016. General OneFile (A453285833).

Initial Footnote

John, Koster, "Hating the 'Hun' at Home: When America Went to War against the Kaiser, German-Americans Caught Hell," *American History* 51, no. 3, 2016: 58, accessed February 29, 2016, General OneFile (A453285833).

Journal Article (Online)

Behar, Evelyn, Sarah McGowan, Katie McLaughlin, T.D. Borkovec, Michelle Goldwin, and Olivia Bjorkquist. "Concreteness of Positive, Negative, and Neutral Repetitive Thinking About the Future." *Behavior Therapy* 43, no. 2 (1998): 300–312. Accessed February 29, 2016. www.sciencedirect.com/science/article/pii/S0005789411001109.

1. Behar, Evelyn, Sarah McGowan, Katie McLaughlin, T.D. Borkovec, Michelle Goldwin, and Olivia Bjorkquist.
2. "Concreteness of Positive, Negative, and Neutral Repetitive Thinking About the Future."
3. *Behavior Therapy* 43, no. 2 (1998): 300–312. Accessed February 29, 2016. www.sciencedirect.com/science/article/pii/S0005789411001109.

Initial Footnote

1. Evelyn Behar, Sarah McGowan, Katie McLaughlin, T.D. Borkovec, Michelle Goldwin, and Olivia Bjorkquist, "Concreteness of Positive, Negative, and Neutral Repetitive Thinking About the Future," *Behavior Therapy* 43, no. 2 (1998): 312, accessed February 29, 2016, www.sciencedirect.com/science/article/pii/S0005789411001109.

Magazine Article (Print)

Barone, Richard. "The Power of Song: Recording Pete Seeger." *Tape Op*,
May–June 2016, 42.

> 1. Barone, Richard.
> 2. "The Power of Song: Recording Pete Seeger."
> 3. *Tape Op*. May–June 2016, 42.

Initial Footnote

1. Richard Barone, "The Power of Song: Recording Pete Seeger," *Tape Op*, May–June 2016, 36–44.

Magazine Article (Online)

Engber, Daniel. "The Neurologist Who Hacked His Brain—And Almost
Lost His Mind." *Wired*, February 8, 2016. Accessed February 29,
2016. http://www.wired.com/2016/01/phil-kennedy-mind-con-
trol-computer/.

> 1. Engber, Daniel.
> 2. "The Neurologist Who Hacked His Brain—And Almost Lost His Mind."
> 3. *Wired*, February 8, 2016. Accessed February 29, 2016. http://www.wired.
> com/2016/01/phil-kennedy-mind-control-computer/.

Initial Footnote

1. Daniel Engber, "The Neurologist Who Hacked His Brain—And Almost Lost His Mind," *Wired*, February 8, 2016, accessed February 29, 2016, http://www.wired.com/2016/01/phil-kennedy-mind-control-computer/.

Newspaper Article (Print)

Erlanger, Steven, Stephen Castle, and Rick Gladstone. "Airing of Hidden
Wealth Stirs Inquiries and Rage: Iceland Premier Steps Down as
Release of Files Reverberates Around World." *New York Times*, April 6,
2016, early edition, sec. A.

> 1. Erlanger, Steven, Stephen Castle, and Rick Gladstone.
> 2. "Airing of Hidden Wealth Stirs Inquiries and Rage: Iceland Premier Steps
> Down as Release of Files Reverberates Around World."
> 3. *New York Times*, April 6, 2016, early edition, sec. A.

Initial Footnote

1. Steven Erlanger, Stephen Castle, and Rick Gladstone, "Airing of Hidden Wealth Stirs Inquiries and Rage: Iceland Premier Steps Down as Release of Files Reverberates Around World," *New York Times*, April 6, 2016, early edition, sec. A.

Newspaper Article (Online)

Rockmore, Ellen Bresler. "How Texas Teaches History." *New York Times*, October 12, 2015. Accessed February 29, 2016. http://www.nytimes.com/2015/10/22/opinion/how-texas-teaches-history.html.

> 1. Rockmore, Ellen Bresler.
> 2. "How Texas Teaches History."
> 3. *New York Times*, October 12, 2015. Accessed February 29, 2016. http://www.nytimes.com/2015/10/22/opinion/how-texas-teaches-history.html.

Initial Footnote

> 1. Ellen Bresler Rockmore, "How Texas Teaches History," *New York Times*, October 12, 2015, accessed February 29, 2016, http://www.nytimes.com/2015/10/22/opinion/how-texas-teaches-history.html.

Reference Article

Only use footnotes. Do not cite in bibliography.

Initial Footnote (Print)

> 1. *The Encyclopedia of World Crime*, 1st ed. (Wilmette, IL: CrimeBooks, Inc., 1989), s.v. "Agrippina (Agrippina the Younger)."

Initial Footnote (Digital)

> 2. *Vocabulary.com*, s.v. "facetious," accessed February 10, 2016, https://www.vocabulary.com/dictionary/facetious.

WEBSITE PUBLICATIONS

Entire Website

Chicago style recommends citing specific pages or articles on a website rather than the site as a whole.

Page from a Website

Mayo Clinic Staff. "Gallstones-Definition." Mayo Clinic. Mayo Foundation for Medical Education and Research. July 25, 2013. Accessed February 29, 2016. http://www.mayoclinic.org/diseases-conditions/gallstones/basics/definition/con-20020461.

> 1. Mayo Clinic Staff.
> 2. "Gallstones-Definition."
> 3. Mayo Clinic. Mayo Foundation for Medical Education and Research. July 25, 2013. Accessed February 29, 2016. http://www.mayoclinic.org/diseases-conditions/gallstones/basics/definition/con-20020461.

1. Mayo Clinic Staff, "Gallstones-Definition," Mayo Clinic, Mayo Foundation for Medical Education and Research, July 25, 2013, accessed February 29, 2016, http://www.mayoclinic.org/diseases-conditions/gall-stones/basics/definition/con-20020461.

SOCIAL MEDIA

The Librarians. "Cassandrasaurs for Sure Roamed this Earth." Twitter. January 6, 2016. Accessed February 29, 2016. https://twitter.com/LibrariansTNT/status/684778779034517504.

> 1. The Librarians.
> 2. "Cassandrasaurs for Sure Roamed this Earth."
> 3. Twitter. January 6, 2016. Accessed February 29, 2016. https://twitter.com/LibrariansTNT/status/684778779034517504.

Initial Footnote (Digital)

1. The Librarians, "Cassandrasaurs for Sure Roamed this Earth," Twitter, January 6, 2016, accessed February 29, 2016, https://twitter.com/LibrariansTNT/status/684778779034517504.

BLOG

Grosvenor, Emily. "The Dude Abides in Salem." *Desperately Seeking Salem* (blog). August 8, 2010. Accessed February 29, 2016. https://desperate-lyseekingsalem.wordpress.com/2010/08/08/the-dude-abides-in-salem/.

> 1. Grosvenor, Emily.
> 2. "The Dude Abides in Salem."
> 3. *Desperately Seeking Salem* (blog). August 8, 2010. Accessed February 29, 2016. https://desperatelyseekingsalem.wordpress.com/2010/08/08/the-dude-abides-in-salem/.

Initial Footnote

1. Emily Grosvenor, "The Dude Abides in Salem," *Desperately Seeking Salem* (blog), August 8, 2010, accessed February 29, 2016, https://desper-atelyseekingsalem.wordpress.com/2010/08/08/the-dude-abides-in-salem/.

*F*ILM

Kasdan, Lawrence, J. J. Abrams, and Michael Arndt. *Star Wars: The Force Awakens*. Directed by J. J. Abrams. 2015. San Francisco: Lucasfilm, 2016. DVD.

> 1. Kasdan, Lawrence, J. J. Abrams, and Michael Arndt.
> 2. *Star Wars: The Force Awakens*.
> 3. Directed by J. J. Abrams. 2015. San Francisco: Lucasfilm, 2016. DVD.

Initial Footnote

> 1. Lawrence Kasdan, J. J. Abrams, and Michael Arndt. *Star Wars: The Force Awakens*, directed by J. J. Abrams, 2015 (San Francisco: Lucasfilm, 2016.) DVD.

*T*ELEVISION *S*HOW *(B*ROADCAST*)*

Lisciandro, Frank. Interview by Steve Long. *The Writing Life*. McMinnville Community Media, March 21, 2016.

> 1. Lisciandro, Frank. Interview by Steve Long.
> 2. *The Writing Life*.
> 3. McMinnville Community Media, March 21, 2016.

Initial Footnote

> 1. Frank Lisciandro, interview by Steve Long, *The Writing Life*, McMinnville Community Media, March 21, 2016.

*T*ELEVISION *S*HOW *(D*IGITAL*)*

Kalteux, Luke. "World on Fire." *Daredevil*. Directed by Farren Blackburn. Performed by Charlie Cox and Vincent D'Onofrio. Burbank, CA: ABC Studios, April 10, 2015.

> 1. Kalteux, Luke.
> 2. "World on Fire."
> 3. *Daredevil*. Directed by Farren Blackburn. Performed by Charlie Cox and Vincent D'Onofrio. Burbank, CA: ABC Studios, April 10, 2015.

Initial Footnote (Digital)

> 1. Luke Kalteux, "World on Fire," *Daredevil*, directed by Farren Blackburn, performed by Charlie Cox and Vincent D'Onofrio (Burbank, CA: ABC Studios, April 10, 2015), Netflix.

CHI
Bibliography: Examples

"ArtsAlive Stephanie Lenox." YouTube video, 14:49. Posted by ArtsAlive
    YamhillCo. March 25, 2015. https://www.youtube.com/watch?v=xO-
    QIKeERJTE.

        1. —
        2. "ArtsAlive Stephanie Lenox."
        3. YouTube video, 14:49. Posted by ArtsAlive YamhillCo. March 25, 2015.
           https://www.youtube.com/watch?v=xOQIKeERJTE.

Initial Footnote

    1. "ArtsAlive Stephanie Lenox," YouTube video, 14:49, posted
by ArtsAlive YamhillCo, March 25, 2015, https://www.youtube.com/
watch?v=xOQIKeERJTE.

CHI

AUDIO (ALBUM)

Mould, Bob. *Workbook*. Virgin Records America OVED 340, 1989, vinyl
    LP.

        1. Mould, Bob.
        2. *Workbook*.
        3. Virgin Records America OVED 340, 1989, vinyl LP.

Initial Footnote

    1. Bob Mould, *Workbook*, Virgin Records America OVED 340, 1989,
vinyl LP.

AUDIO (DIGITAL)

Adams, Sarah. "Be Cool to the Pizza Dude." *This I Believe*. NPR. Podcast
    audio. December 29, 2015. Accessed February 29, 2016. http://cdn.
    audiometric.io/9487820912.mp3.

        1. Adams, Sarah.
        2. "Be Cool to the Pizza Dude."
        3. *This I Believe*. NPR. Podcast audio. December 29, 2015. Accessed February
           29, 2016. http://cdn.audiometric.io/9487820912.mp3.

Initial Footnote

    1. Sarah Adams, "Be Cool to the Pizza Dude," *This I Believe*, NPR,
podcast audio, December 29, 2015, accessed February 29, 2016, http://
cdn.audiometric.io/9487820912.mp3.

CHI
Bibliography: Examples

ADVERTISEMENT (PRINT)

BF Goodrich Co. "Put the Magazine Down and Go." Advertisement.
  Automobile Magazine, July 2016, 5.

> 1. BF Goodrich Co.
> 2. "Put the Magazine Down and Go." Advertisement.
> 3. *Automobile Magazine,* July 2016, 5.

Initial Footnote

  1. BF Goodrich Co., "Put the Magazine Down and Go," advertisement, *Automobile Magazine,* July 2016, 5.

PERFORMANCE

Pride and Prejudice. By Jane Austen. Directed by David Sikking. ACMA
  Theater Company. Arts & Communications Magnet Academy Theater,
  Beaverton, OR. March 5-14, 2015.

> 1.
> 2. *Pride and Prejudice.* By Jane Austen.
> 3. Directed by David Sikking. ACMA Theater Company. Arts & Communications Magnet Academy Theater, Beaverton, OR. March 5-14, 2015.

Initial Footnote

  1. *Pride and Prejudice*, by Jane Austen, directed by David Sikking, ACMA Theater Company, Arts & Communications Magnet Academy Theater, Beaverton, OR, March 5-14, 2015.

OTHER

PAMPHLET, BROCHURE, OR PRESS RELEASE

Travel Guard. *Insure Your Next Trip with Travel Guard.* Stevens Point, WI:
  Travel Guard, 2016.

> 1. Travel Guard.
> 2. *Insure Your Next Trip with Travel Guard.*
> 3. Stevens Point, WI: Travel Guard, 2016.

Initial Footnote

  1. Travel Guard, *Insure Your Next Trip with Travel Guard* (Stevens Point, WI: Travel Guard, 2016), 1.

GOVERNMENT REPORT

U.S. Census Bureau. *Strength in Numbers: Your Guide to 2010 Census Redistricting Data from the U.S. Census Bureau*. Washington, D.C.: U.S. Dept. of Commerce, Economics and Statistics Administration, U.S. Census Bureau, 2010.

> 1. U.S. Census Bureau.
> 2. *Strength in Numbers: Your Guide to 2010 Census Redistricting Data from the U.S. Census Bureau.*
> 3. Washington, D.C.: U.S. Dept. of Commerce, Economics and Statistics Administration, U.S. Census Bureau, 2010.

Initial Footnote

> 1. U.S. Census Bureau, *Strength in Numbers: Your Guide to 2010 Census Redistricting Data from the U.S. Census Bureau*, (Washington, DC: U.S. Dept. of Commerce, Economics and Statistics Administration, U.S. Census Bureau, 2010), 2.

UNPUBLISHED DISSERTATION

Kennison, Kristen Renee. "Smoke Derived Taint in Grapes and Wine." PhD diss., Curtin University, Bentley, Australia, 2011. eSpace (185451).

> 1. Kennison, Kristen Renee.
> 2. *Smoke Derived Taint in Grapes and Wine.*
> 3. PhD diss., Curtin University, Bentley, Australia, 2011. eSpace (185451).

Initial Footnote

> 1. Kristen Renee Kennison, "Smoke Derived Taint in Grapes and Wine" (PhD diss, Curtin University, Bentley, Australia, 2011), eSpace (185451), 3.

PERSONAL INTERVIEW, LETTER, OR EMAIL

Only use footnotes. Do not cite in bibliography.

Initial Footnote (Personal Interview)

> 1. Tom Franklin, interview by Sam Snoek-Brown, March 21, 2000.

Initial Footnote (Unpublished Letter)

> 2. Walter Biggins, letter to Daniel Couch, March 23, 2015.

Initial Footnote (Email)

> 3. Tom Franklin, e-mail message to Gertrude Mornenweg, April 3, 2003.

3. Paper Format

Chicago style also offers guidance about how to format your paper so that it looks like all the other Chicago papers. This helps ensure that readers will stay focused on your ideas. Here are the general guidelines to keep in mind:

1. Type your paper on a computer and print it out on standard, white 8.5- by 11-inch paper. Set the margins of your document to 1 inch on all four sides.

2. Use a readable, businesslike font that doesn't draw attention to itself and is easy to read. Times New Roman is a popular choice, and a 12-point size in this font is pleasant and readable.

3. Double-space the text of your paper.

4. Leave only one space after periods or other punctuation marks — unless you're told otherwise by an elderly person who has fond memories of the days when typewriters ruled the land.

5. Indent the first line of paragraphs one half-inch from the left margin. Use the tab key to do that, too. Pushing the space bar five times to create a half-inch indentation doesn't work with computers.

6. Create a header in the upper right-hand corner of each page that is one half-inch from the top of the page and even with the right margin for the page number. Use automatic page numbering for that. Trying to do that manually will cause you anguish.

7. Never use boldface. Only use italics as required for the titles of larger works and some publications and, with caution, for emphasis within the paper.

We'll show you how this works in the following pages by looking at some examples of actual pages. As we do, we'll add a few more guidelines that apply only in specific situations.

A. Title Page

A Proving the Negative

B & C   Jack Wiegand
Writing 122
Prof. Roy K. Humble
February 29, 2016

Chicago style requires a title page, so keep these points in mind:

A. Place your title one-third of the way down the page. If your paper contains a subtitle, put it on a separate line directly after the title.

B. Place your name, the course, your instructor's name, and the date about two-thirds of the way down the page.

C. Center and single-space all the lines on this page.

On the first page, you don't put a title (you just had a whole page for

B. First Page

E   With the arrival of social media, society has seen a marked increase in armchair academia. Like the dilettantes of the Victorian era, today's hobbyist intellectuals spend their free time engaging in the gentleman's sport of debate, study, and showing off their brains, rather than their muscles. Also like the dilettantes of old, they treat it as strictly leisure, while eschewing F rigorous academic commitment. While they might be able to regale their friends for hours about the brilliance of Voltaire, they've likely read his Wikipedia page, rather than *Candide,* or *Plato's Dream.* While they may be able to offer a criticism of a documentary about humanism, they would likely struggle to offer a worthwhile analysis of Thomas More's *Utopia.* Not that there's anything wrong with dilettantism. If anything, it does for society much more than reality television or competitive Frisbee.

E   It can, however, create a few issues. In every scholarly field, information tends to change slightly as it moves from the academic sphere to the public sphere. When simplifying ideas to make them accessible to the public, the foundational information — that can, in many cases, take years of study to understand — is necessarily lost. To borrow from *The Science of Discworld,* we tend to "bend the truths just sufficiently to make the basic principles of the operation clear to a layman while not actually being entirely wrong."[1] What the authors go on to describe as "lies to children"[2] may seem wholly benign, but they often lead to small misunderstandings, which can accumulate to form vast misunderstandings.

E   In philosophy, we might call these bits of misinformation folk logic. These are most easily described as bad ideas that agree with common sense. While most people tend to hold common sense in high regard, it is a very inefficient means of understanding the universe, as it requires that any new information conform to old information.

G   1 Terry Pratchett, Ian Stewart, and Jack Cohen, "Science and Magic," in *The Science of Discworld* (London: Ebury Publishing, 1999), 14–15.
2 Ibid.

that, right?), but there are other things to do:

D. Place the page number in the upper- or lower-right-hand corner of the page. The first page of text should be page two.

E. Indent the first sentence of each paragraph one half-inch.

F. Double-space every line of text.

G. Footnotes should appear on the same page as their corresponding number within the paper. Unlike the rest of your text, they are single-spaced.

C. Middle Pages

things, we are continuously becoming less wrong. As Richard Feynman put it, in a lecture given at the 1964 Galileo Symposium:

> A scientist is never certain. We all know that. We know that all our statements are approximate statements with different degrees of certainty; that when a statement is made, the question is not whether it is true or false but rather how likely it is to be true or false...We must discuss each question within the uncertainties that are allowed...We absolutely must leave room for doubt or there is no progress and there is no learning.[10]

People tend to think of correctness as a binary; one is simply correct or incorrect. To wit, we now know that the Earth is not round, or at least not perfectly so. Isaac Newton observed, correctly, that the Earth is an oblate spheroid, rather than a perfect sphere.[11] While both previously-held positions are incorrect, surely it is *less* incorrect to describe the Earth as round rather than flat.

Just as positive evidence can be used to make more reasonable positive statements, so too can negative evidence — or, the *absence* of evidence — be used to make more reasonable negative statements. Unfortunately, this is another case of widespread misunderstanding. The popular belief, known as Rees' Maxim, is that absence of evidence is not evidence of absence. This misunderstanding is not only prevalent in the public sphere, but has also found a foothold among academics, including science educator and cosmologist Carl Sagan, and Christian apologist William Lane Craig.[12]

---

10 Feynman, "Role of Scientific Culture," 111–112.
11 Choi, "Strange but True: Earth Is Not Round."
12 Carl Sagan, *The Demon-Haunted World: Science as a Candle in the Dark* (New York: Ballantine, 1997); William Lane Craig, "#115 Is God Imaginary?: Santa Claus, Tooth Fairies, and God," Reasonable Faith with William Lane Craig, June 29, 2009, accessed January 10, 2016, http://www.reasonablefaith.org/is-god-imaginary.

The middle pages continue on with double spacing for the text and single spacing for the footnotes.

H. For block quotations, use your word processor's ruler tool to indent the entire paragraph one half-inch from the left margin.

I. Footnotes 10 and 11 are shortened because the author referred to the sources earlier in the paper. Footnote 12 cites the same idea found in two sources.

When you get to the end of your paper, insert a manual page break so

D. Bibliography Page

J Bibliography

Cham, Jorge. "PHD Comics: Proving a Negative." Comic Rocket. July 3, 2009. Accessed
L   January 10, 2016. http://www.comic-rocket.com/read/piled-higher-and-deeper-phd/1194.

Choi, Charles Q. "Strange but True: Earth Is Not Round." *Scientific American*, April 12, 2007. M
        Accessed January 10, 2016. http://www.scientificamerican.com/article/earth-is-not-
        round/.

Craig, William Lane. "#115 Is God Imaginary?: Santa Claus, Tooth Fairies, and God"
        Reasonable Faith with William Lane Craig. June 29, 2009. Accessed January 10, 2016.
        http://www.reasonablefaith.org/is-god-imaginary.

Feynman, Richard P. "What Is and What Should Be the Role of Scientific Culture in Modern
        Society," In *The Pleasure of Finding Things Out: The Best Short Works of Richard P.*
O   *Feynman*, 111-112. New York: Perseus, 1999. N

Hales, Steven. "Thinking Tools: You *Can* Prove a Negative." *Think* 4, no. 10, 2005: 109-112.

Jillette, Penn. "There is no God." *This I Believe*. National Public Radio. November 21, 2005.
        Accessed January 10, 2016. http://www.npr.org/2005/11/21/5015557/there-is-no-god.

Pratchett, Terry, Ian Stewart, and Jack Cohen. "Science and Magic." In *The Science of
        Discworld*, 14-15. London: Ebury Publishing, 1999.

Rowling, J.K. *Harry Potter and the Deathly Hallows*. New York: Arthur A. Levine Books, 2007.

P -------. *Harry Potter and the Half-Blood Prince*. Arthur A. Levine Books, 2005.

Sagan, Carl. *The Demon-Haunted World: Science as a Candle in the Dark*. New York:
        Ballantine, 1997.

StarChild Team. "Who Figured out the Earth Is Round?" *StarChild: A Learning Center for
        Young Astronomers*. NASA. February 2013. Accessed January 10, 2016.
        http://starchild.gsfc.nasa.gov/docs/StarChild/questions/question54.html.

Truthem. "Ayn Rand - Faith vs Reason." YouTube video, 1:04. Posted [10 July 2008].
        https://www.youtube.com/watch?v=dErp5_ICjjU.

that the bibliography will start at the top of its own page. The list includes all the works that you examined in the writing of your paper. If you read and thought about a work but didn't end up using it, put it on this list.

Here's what you keep in mind while formatting this page:

J. The title is "Bibliography," regardless of how many sources appear on the list. Center the title.

K. The page numbering continues on this page, too.

L. The first line of each citation should begin at the far left margin. Any subsequent lines are indented a half-inch. This is called a **hanging indent**. The most sensible way to do this is with the ruler tool that comes with your writing software. It's not hard once you get the hang of it.

M. Single-space each reference.

N. Add an extra line of space *after* each reference to create space that makes the references more distinct visually.

O. Alphabetize your sources by the first word or words in each citation. If the author isn't known, then you use the title for that work.

P. If you cite more than one source by the same author, alphabetize by the next word in the citation — from the first word of title that isn't an article like "a" or "the," in other words — and with those other works by the same author, you replace the author's name with em dashes.

This is another place where taking good notes during the research process will save you time and heartache. You need to include all the information that the Chicago style demands. So if you don't already have that information at your fingertips, you need to go back to the work and gather it after the fact, which you may or may not have time to do.

Glossary

A

Abbreviation: A shortened version of a word.

Acronym: Initials that stand for a group of words.

Adjective: A word that describes a noun.

Adjective, possessive: An adjective that shows ownership.

Adverb: A word that describes a verb, adjective, or adverb.

Anecdote: A short story used to illustrate a point.

Antecedent: The word to which a pronoun refers.

Appositive: A noun that renames the noun beside it in the sentence.

Article: A type of adjective that precedes a noun to qualify it as specific or general.

Attribution: Credit given to a source for an idea, a fact, or other information.

B

Bias: A preconceived attitude toward a person, group of people, or idea that obscures objectivity.

C

Citation, end-of-text: The listing of a source or sources used in a paper that contains the information necessary for the reader to locate the origin of the source(s).

Citation, in-text: A method of attributing quoted, paraphrased, and summarized ideas to their sources within a paragraph.

Citation, parenthetical: The portion of an in-text citation that appears within parentheses at the end of a word or phrase.

Clause: A group of words containing a subject and a verb that express an idea.

Clause, dependent: A group of words that depend on a main clause to express their full meaning. Dependent clauses, which cannot stand alone as a sentence, often begin with a subordinating conjunction like *after, although*, or *as if*.

Clause, independent: A group of words that express a complete thought. Independent clauses contain a subject and a verb that can stand alone as a sentence.

Clause, introductory: A dependent clause that opens a sentence and is almost always followed by a comma.

Clause, nonrestrictive: A dependent clause that is not essential to the main idea of the sentence and is often set off from the rest of the sentence with commas.

Clause, relative: A dependent clause that starts with a relative pronoun. A relative clause can be either restrictive or nonrestrictive and refers to something that precedes it in the sentence.

Clause, restrictive: A dependent clause that is essential to the main idea of the sentence and unlike nonrestrictive clauses is not usually set off with commas.

Cliché: An overused phrase or metaphor.

Comma splice: Two independent clauses joined with a comma to create a run-on sentence.

Complement: A noun phrase that completes the meaning of a subject or object of a sentence by describing it with necessary information.

Conjunction: A word that joins parts of a sentence.

Conjunction, coordinating: One of seven specific conjunctions — *and, but, or, yet, for, nor, so* — that join parts of a sentence.

Conjunction, subordinating: A conjunction that introduces a dependent clause and indicates the relationship between the clause and the rest of the sentence.

Connotation: The psychological or ideological values that color a word through cultural, historical, or personal associations.

Contraction: Two words combined into one with an apostrophe standing in for the missing letter(s).

D

Determiner: A word that precedes and modifies a noun. Articles, possessive pronouns, and demonstrative pronouns are all types of determiners.

DOI (Digital Object Identifier): An alphanumeric designation used in source citation of electronic publications, often assigned to online or digital documents as a permanent, stable identifier.

F

Formal language: Precise, professional writing with a level of diction and a tone appropriate for academic and business contexts.

Fragment: An incomplete sentence. **See also:** Clause, dependent.

G

Gerund: A noun derived from a verb by adding *–ing* to the end.

Gray literature: A broad category of literature that is not produced to be published and may have only limited distribution within an academic, professional, or governmental field.

H

Hanging indent: The indentation of the second and all subsequent lines of text while the first line remains in line with the margin.

I

Idiom: A common figurative expression.

Infinitive: A noun or adverb phrase formed by *to* plus the root form of a verb and indicating no specific tense.

Interjection: A verbal interruption in a sentence separated by a comma from the main action of the sentence.

J

Jargon: Wording that is usually familiar only to a specific group of people such as within a profession, field, or hobby.

M

Metaphor: A non-literal comparison that suggests by association some quality of a person, thing or action.

N

Noun: A word that represents people, places, things or ideas.

O

Object: The part of a sentence that receives or explains the action of the verb.

P

Paragraph: A grouping of sentences that together express a single, focused idea.

Patchwriting: The swapping out of words in a sentence while maintaining the general structure and meaning from the original source.

Phrase: A group of words that act as a unit in a sentence for a common purpose.

Predicate: The verb or verb phrase that expresses the action of the sentence.

Preposition: Words used with an object in a phrase to express some quality of time, space, or reason.

Prepositional phrase: A preposition followed by a determiner and any adjectives coupled with a noun or pronoun.

Pronoun: A word that stands in for or refers back to a previously expressed noun.

Pronoun, demonstrative: A pronoun that can refer back to or identify a noun. A demonstrative pronoun may also be used as a determiner to modify a noun.

Pronoun, relative: A pronoun such as *this, that, these,* or *those* that relates groups of words to nouns or pronouns. A relative pronoun often introduces relative clauses.

Punctuation: Marks — such as commas, periods, apostrophes, quotation marks, and hyphens — that separate words and sentences and add meaning to writing according to the rules for each type of mark.

R

Run-on sentence: Two or more independent clauses joined in a single sentence without the punctuation necessary to separate them.

S

Sentence: A complete statement, question or command consisting of, at a minimum, a subject and verb. **See also:** Clause, independent.

Sentence, complex: A sentence in which at least one independent clause is coupled with one or more dependent clauses.

Sentence, compound: A sentence in which at least two independent clauses are joined with the appropriate punctuation.

Signal phrase: A phrase that introduces evidence or other information by attributing it to the source in the body of the sentence.

Slanted language: Words that skew the reader toward a particular point of view.

Subject: The part of a sentence that joins with a verb to form a clause. The subject performs the action of the verb.

Suffix: An ending placed on a word, usually a verb form, that changes its tense or meaning.

Superscript: Typographical category for a number or other symbol that is small in size and placed slightly higher on the line than other type in a document. Superscript is often used to indicate a footnote or endnote.

T

Thesis: A reasonable idea you have about a topic that serves as the central argument of a piece of writing.

Topic Sentence: The main idea of a paragraph expressed in a sentence within that paragraph.

U

URL (Uniform Resource Locator): The web address used to locate web resources and other online material.

V

Verb: A word that expresses action or state of being.

Verb, helping: Also known as auxiliary verbs, these are words used in combination with the main verb to show time, duration, or mood.

Verb, irregular: Verbs that do not follow a standard pattern of conjugation.

Verb, linking: A verb that connects a subject and a complement. Usually a form of "to be" but can include any of the five sense verbs or verbs that show a particular state of being.

Voice, active: A sentence where the subject of the sentence performs the action of the sentence.

Voice, passive: A sentence where the object of the sentence is placed in the subject's place and appears to perform the action of the sentence.

Expanded Table of Contents

Chapter 4: Word Choice

PART TWO: RESEARCH BASICS

Chapter 5: Research

Chapter 6: MLA Style

Chapter 7: APA Style